AF477664

Merchants, Traders, Entrepreneurs

*Also by Claude Markovits:*

INDIAN BUSINESS AND NATIONALIST POLITICS

THE GLOBAL WORLD OF INDIAN MERCHANTS

THE UN-GANDHIAN GANDHI

A HISTORY OF MODERN INDIA 1480–1950 *(editor)*

# Merchants, Traders, Entrepreneurs

## Indian Business in the Colonial Era

Claude Markovits

South Asian edition first published 2008 by
PERMANENT BLACK
'Himalayana', Mall Road, Ranikhet Cantt
Ranikhet  263645
perblack@gmail.com

First published 2008 by
PALGRAVE MACMILLAN

Palgrave Macmillan in the UK is an imprint of Macmillan Publishers Limited, registered in England, company number 785998, of Houndmills, Basingstoke, Hampshire RG21 6XS.

Palgrave Macmillan in the US is a division of St Martin's Press LLC, 175 Fifth Avenue, New York, NY 10010.

Palgrave Macmillan is the global academic imprint of the above companies and has companies and representatives throughout the world.

Palgrave® and Macmillan® are registered trademark in the United States, the United Kingdom, Europe and other countries.

ISBN-13: 978–0–230–20598–7 hardback
ISBN-10: 0–230–20598–4 hardback





A catalogue record for this book is available from the British Library.

Library of Congress Cataloging-in-publication Data

Markovits Claude.
Merchants, traders, entrepreneurs: Indian business in the Colonial Era
        p.m.
    Includes bibliographical references and index.
    ISBN 0–230–20598–4 (alk. paper)
        1. Business and politics–India–History–20th century.
        2. Businesspeople–India–Social conditions–20th century. 3. India
    Commerce–20th century. 4. India–Foreign economic relations. I.Title
    HC435.M3263 2008
381.0954–dc22                                                    2008025123
10   9   8   7   6   5   4   3   2   1
17   16   15   14   13   12   11   10   09   08

Printed and bound in Great Britain by
CPI Antony Rowe, Chippenham and Eastbourne

To the memory of
ALICE THORNER

# CONTENTS

# PREFACE

THE MERCHANT WORLD REPRESENTS A RELATIVELY NEG-
lected area in South Asian history. Merchants were, however,
important actors in the economic, political, social, and even
cultural life of India, and they deserve more attention than they have
been given. This book aims at bridging a gap by bringing together a
number of articles written between 1981 and 2003 which deal with
the Indian mercantile world in colonial India, and its relationship
with politics and the broader society. The book is divided into three
parts. Part I, under the heading 'Business and Politics', looks at the
relationship between the business world and the world of politics
in the late colonial era, with special emphasis on the links between
business interests and political nationalism. Part II, entitled 'Entrepreneurship and Society', looks at the position of merchants and big
businessmen in relation to society and the economy. It focuses on
particular groups, such as Muslim businessmen, particular locations
(Bombay), and specific firms (Tatas). Part III, 'Merchant Networks',
introduces a new dimension, that of circulation, and looks at the way
in which specific trading networks with a regional base extended the
range of their operations, during the colonial period, across the entire
subcontinent as well as across different regions of the wider world.

My original interest in the topic of Indian capitalism, in the early
1970s, owed a lot to the influence of a book by Charles Bettelheim, a
French Marxist economist who had been seconded to P.C. Mahala-
nobis at the Indian Planning Commission: *l'Inde Indépendante,* an

analysis of India's political economy in which the capitalist bourgeoisie figured in an important place. That is where I first heard about the Tatas and the Birlas, and, when I started doing research in Indian history at Cambridge, I immediately connected what I was reading about India's independence struggle with what I had learned from Bettelheim about Indian capitalists, and found that there was a gap in the scholarly literature, as, with the exception of A.R. Desai's very general treatment of the question in his *Social Background of Indian Nationalism*, no study had been done of the relationship between Indian capital and Indian nationalism. Little did I know then that one of D.A. Low's students, A.D.D. Gordon, was engaged in a study of the relationship between Congress and business in Bombay, which came out in the form of a book in 1978. My supervisor at Cambridge, Anil Seal, was encouraging when I sounded him out on the possibility of choosing such a topic for a Ph.D.

Research on this subject, however, proved, to be a rather tricky proposition, as I started realizing how little was actually known about the history of the Indian business world, and how difficult it was to get access to private archives of business families. The existence of the important collection of private papers left to the Nehru Memorial Library by the heirs of prominent Bombay businessman Sir Purshot-tamdas Thakurdas, to which my attention was drawn by the then Deputy Director of the Library, Shri V.C. Joshi, proved to be a god-send. Added to the use of official archives in Delhi and London, it allowed me to acquire a decent grasp of the documentation then available which helped the writing of a Cambridge Ph.D. which served as a base for a book published in 1985. The first two chapters in the present book embody aspects of this work. Chapter 1, reprinted from the volume of a conference held in 1984 at the University of California at Los Angeles, under the stewardship of Richard Sisson and Stanley Wolpert, puts forward a general interpretation of the relationship be-tween the Congress Party and the Indian business class during the period from 1885 to 1947, while Chapter 2 , reprinted from a special issue of *Modern Asian Studies*, focuses more specifically on the period of the Congress provincial governments, 1937–9, which was a defining moment in the relationship. Chapter 3 represents an extension of the research into the immediate post-war years to look at the relationship between business and Partition, and was first presented at a conference organized in 1989 at the Indian Institute of Management, Ahmedabad, subsequently published in a volume edited by Dwijendra Tripathi.

The four chapters in Part II represent separate forays into different aspects of business history in which I developed an interest while researching the book and elaborated upon at a later stage. Chapter 4 was published in French as part of an issue in the collection *Purusartha* on Islam and society in South Asia edited by Marc Gaborieau and put together some data and reflections about the place of Muslims in the business world of India, a little-researched topic. Chapter 5, a broad comparison between Bombay and Calcutta as business centres in the colonial period, was presented at the conference organized in Bombay in December 1992 by Sujata Patel and the late Alice Thorner, and published in the first of the two conference volumes, *Bombay: Metaphor for Modern India*. Chapter 6, a short piece on the history of the firm of Tatas, was first presented at a conference organized in 1992 at the School of African and Oriental Studies by Peter Robb and the late Burton Stein and subsequently published in one of the two conference volumes, edited by Sanjay Subrahmanyam and Burton Stein. Chapter 7, dealing in a broad fashion with the position of businessmen within the Indian middle classes, was presented at a conference held in 2001 at Neemrana Fort Palace, organized by Imtiaz Ahmad and Helmut Reifeld.

The two chapters in Part III represent a novel orientation in my work towards the study of Indian merchant networks both within India and in the world at large. The history of circulation had been chosen as the theme of a research group which worked at the Centre d'Etudes de l'Inde et de l'Asie du Sud in 1994–8, in which I was actively involved. Chapter 8 looks at merchant circulations in colonial India and was specially written as an article for the volume on *Society and Circulation* which I co-edited with Jacques Pouchepadass and Sanjay Subrahmanyam, which was the outcome of the labours of the research group. Chapter 9, a broad attempt at a synthesis on the history of Indian merchant networks outside India, was actually written in 1994 and published only in 1999 in *Modern Asian Studies*. In that article I try out some of the ideas which I developed more fully in my book, *The Global World of Indian Merchants* (2000).

I have added as an epilogue a lecture which I gave in January 2006 at the Centre of Indian and South Asian Studies of the University of California at Los Angeles, 'Returning the Merchant to South Asian History?', which is a foray into recent historiographical developments. I am grateful to Sanjay Subrahmanyam, a friend of many years, for having given me the opportunity to air some of my ideas in front of a Californian audience.

The book is dedicated to the memory of Alice Thorner, who, apart from encouraging me in my efforts, was always particularly kind to my wife and my family. I shall never forget the many lovely hours spent in 9 rue Guy de la Brosse.

Paris, July 2007                                    CLAUDE MARKOVITS

1

# CONGRESS POLICY TOWARDS BUSINESS IN THE PRE-INDEPENDENCE ERA*

THE RELATIONSHIP BETWEEN THE CONGRESS PARTY AND the Indian business class is a relatively neglected area of inquiry, especially for the pre-Independence period. The few existing studies centre around the political attitude of the Indian business class and its response to the rise of political nationalism, but none focuses on Congress attitudes and policies towards business interests.[1] The paucity of sources available regarding Congress policy-making is a serious limiting factor; thus much of what is presented here must be considered tentative and is more a reconstruction of broad trends than a detailed analysis of processes. The first section of this analysis entails a general overview of trends in Congress policy between 1885 and 1937; those following involve a more detailed examination of the last decade before Independence, which witnessed the emergence of a clear pattern in the hitherto fluctuating relationship between the Congress and the Indian business class.

*From R. Sisson and S. Wolpert (eds), *Congress and Indian Nationalism: The Pre-Independence Phase* (Berkeley: University of California Press, 1988), pp. 250–68.

## Congress and the Business Class, 1885–1937

When the Congress was founded the modern Indian business class was still in its infancy. British businessmen occupied a clearly dominant position in most of the rising sectors of the Indian colonial economy (foreign trade, plantation agriculture, finance, transport, and the jute industry). Of all the 'modern' activities, only in the cotton textile industry had Indian capitalists secured a clear lead over Europeans. Leaving aside the small millowning elite of Bombay and Ahmedabad, most Indian businessmen were still engaged in 'traditional' fields such as trading, moneylending, and 'indigenous' banking. Many worked as intermediaries for the large British commercial firms. On the whole, the indigenous business community was a socially and organizationally fragmented sector of Indian society, which prevented it from playing a significant political role, except at the local level. In terms of educational development, it lagged behind the new urban elite, and members of the rising Western-educated middle classes often tended to look down on the merchants as a backward and obscurantist group. It is not surprising that leaders of the early Congress paid little attention to the specific problems of their compatriots in the business professions.

A review of Congress resolutions of 1885–1905 unequivocally shows that in the early Congress sessions only minimal attention was given to economic issues. At the 1888 Allahabad session, however, a resolution was adopted calling for the creation of a commission to inquire into the industrial condition of the country;[2] demands for removal of the cotton excise duty were advanced at Madras in 1894 and at Ahmedabad in 1902, while the Lucknow session in 1899 condemned the introduction of the gold standard.[3] Discussion of economic issues was left mainly to industrial conferences, which met regularly after 1890 during Congress sessions; however, those conferences were not organically linked to the Congress and were peripheral to its major interests. Businessmen, in turn, were marginal to Congress politics, although some merchant-princes of Bombay played a role in the beginnings of Congress activities. By the 1890s, however, they had tended to withdraw from the political life of the city.[4] The attitude of most businessmen seems to have been cautiously apolitical, and Congress politicians do not appear to have made a determined attempt at gaining business support.

With the Swadeshi movement of 1904–7, direct links were established between political and economic demands and between national freedom and indigenous enterprise. Economic nationalism became an essential feature of nationalist programmes with economic issues starting to figure much more prominently in the resolutions passed at Congress sessions. This still did not result, however, in the forging of close links between the Congress and Indian businessmen. As A.P. Kannangara has shown, businessmen, especially the millowners of western India, responded cautiously to the rise of mass economic nationalism.[5] With the division and growing paralysis of the Congress from 1907 to 1917, no coherent approach emerged towards the problems of Indian business, and it was left to Gandhi to establish a permanent link between Indian capitalists and the nationalist movement.

The First World War had an intense impact on the Indian business class which, thanks to the capital accumulated in various speculative activities, was able to strengthen its position in the Indian economy, partly at the expense of British businessmen. As they enlarged the scope of their activities, Indian businessmen became more ambitious and, in the euphoria of the immediate post-war boom, made great plans for the future industrial development of India which seemed to evoke a sympathetic response from the government. Government policy did not meet their expectations, however: the Fiscal Commission rejected a strong protectionist policy and settled instead for 'discriminative' protection, and direct aid to industry did not develop on the scale needed. The resultant frustration made Indian businessmen more receptive to the Congress's nationalist message, especially as it was advocated by Gandhi. His personality undoubtedly played a major role in bringing together for the first time the Congress and a large section of the Indian capitalists. His own Gujarati *bania* origins, connections he had built in South Africa with Gujarati merchants and his crucial role as mediator in a labour conflict in Ahmedabad, gave him a special position in the eyes of merchants, particularly his Gujarati countrymen. Friendships developed later with stalwarts of the Marwari business community such as Jamnalal Bajaj and G.D. Birla helped to widen Gandhi's appeal in the business world. His 'saintly' style of politics appealed to pious Hindu and Jain merchants, even if some of his unorthodox views shocked them.

Gandhi's greatest achievement was to raise a large amount of money from the business class through the Tilak Swaraj Fund, which for the first time gave the Congress a sound financial base and allowed it to successfully carry out its transformation into a mass party.[6] The Congress connection with Indian business thus came to depend heavily on Gandhi's personal intervention. It was not an institutionalized relationship between a closely knit social group and a political party, but rather a complex nexus of highly individualized relationships between a few prominent men of business (Kasturbhai Lalbhai and Ambalal Sarabhai in Ahmedabad, Jamnalal Bajaj in Bombay, G.D. Birla in Calcutta) and one political leader. The whole of the business class was obviously not involved in this type of a relationship. At a lower level in the business hierarchy, the Gandhian connection operated in a less personalized and more corporatist fashion: small merchants and traders, especially among the Gujaratis and to a lesser extent the Marwaris, recognized Gandhi as their political leader, and their support for him was channelled through their various associations.

As a result of this highly specific pattern of relationships, the Congress found it difficult to maintain close links to the business class during the periods when Gandhi was out of active politics. During the 1923–8 period, therefore, the relations between the Swaraj Party and Indian businessmen, after a promising start, eventually sank to a low ebb, and in 1928 Motilal Nehru expressed his exasperation at the attitude of businessmen.[7] He and other Congress leaders did not develop skills comparable to Gandhi's in dealing with them. It was again Gandhi's intervention that was responsible for the unprecedented display of support given by businessmen to the Congress during the first phase of the Civil Disobedience movement in 1930–1.[8]

The eventual failure of the movement, however, leading to its abandonment in 1934, brought a profound change in the nature of the relationships between Indian business and Congress. As Gandhi once more withdrew from the forefront of the political struggle to reemerge only in 1940–2, other Congress leaders, particularly Vallabh-bhai Patel, assumed the task of strengthening the links of Congress with businessmen. Lacking the Mahatma's charisma and 'personal touch', they found themselves in a very different position in relation to the Congress business supporters, that of 'broker' rather than that of 'guru'. They managed, however, to consolidate the relationship between the Congress and Indian business, because new trends, both economic and political, favoured a gradual institutionalization of this relationship. At the economic level, the major factor was the spectacular growth of Indian business groups during the 1930s and 1940s, which by 1947 made them as powerful as British groups. Politically, the most far-reaching development was the gradual transformation of the Congress Party from a broad national liberation movement into a party capable of assuming power from the British. An important moment in this transformation was the party's first assumption of power, at the provincial level, in 1937–9. Although the experiment was cut short by the war, the experience gained during those two years played a crucial role in shaping Congress views of the problem of governing India. A new round of provincial governance in 1946–7, followed by the formation of the interim cabinet prior to the transfer of power, served as final apprenticeship.

There is thus good reason to give special attention to the period 1937–47. During this decade the Congress had to maintain the widest possible appeal as a national liberation movement to achieve independence for the country, while at the same time it began to confront concrete problems of governance, which engaged it with pressures from competing groups seeking to further their own interests. The accommodation of specific interests without losing sight of the broader necessities of the national struggle was no easy task.

## Major Constraints on Congress Policy Towards Business Interests

In dealing with the business class, the Congress could not avoid making cost-benefit calculations. What advantages could it derive from a close alliance with businessmen, and what cost would it have to pay in terms of risking the alienation of other groups in Indian society? From the point of view of the Congress, the most obvious advantage to be gained from a close relationship with businessmen was the assurance of a regular and dependable service of financial contributions to the party. By the end of the 1930s, however, Indian businessmen were far from being as wealthy as they are now. At that time the wealth of the Indian princes and zamindars far surpassed that of all but a few capitalists, but given their privileged links with the British, they could not be expected to extend support to the nationalist cause. Business-men, even if they were not always very wealthy, were thus the most readily available source of funds, although not the only one; wealthy urban professionals, generally nationalist-minded, were also an im-portant source, as were well-to-do peasants in some regions.

However, the richest businessmen were not necessarily the most nationalist-minded (the Tatas, the most important business family in India, for instance, never gave money to the Congress), and more generally the extreme heterogeneity of the business community, with its fractiousness, generating internal tensions, made it difficult to treat it as a whole. Within the Indian business sector a growing polarization was noticeable, between a small elite, composed of a few large capitalist groups with diversified interests, and other sections of the community that were not doing as well. Smaller businessmen often resented the rise of the big groups. These intra-business tensions were particularly in evidence in Bombay, where, as A.D.D. Gordon has shown,[9] there was a long-standing fight over the control of the cotton market between the 'industrialists' and the 'marketeers', and in Calcutta, where the Bengalis deplored Marwari dominance in the most profitable markets. These tensions did not facilitate the task of the Congress strategists. They could not use an existing vertical structure of mobilization: on the contrary, if they relied too much on big business, the most pro-mising sector in purely financial terms, they risked alienating small businessmen, who—in view of their numbers and social influence—were a crucial segment of the population in Indian cities and towns. A delicate balance had to be constantly maintained between these antagonistic components of the business class.

The same principles applied to the regional aspect of the business connection. Some regional business communities had a more extended network than others and therefore seemed to offer more interesting prospects for a nationalist party. This was particularly true of the Marwaris, who were spread all over northern and central India. It is thus not surprising to find that, while in the 1920s as a result of Gandhi's special role, the Congress business connection was mainly Gujarati, in the 1930s and 1940s it became more Marwari. Too heavy a reliance on the Marwaris, a staunchly orthodox Hindu community, however, involved the risk of alienating Muslim businessmen. More generally, the growing strength of its Marwari business connection was one of the factors that made the Congress more of a Hindu party, endangering its secular appeal.

One of the most delicate problems confronting the Congress was how to maintain some kind of balance between capitalists and the working class. From the mid-1930s onward, the problem of labour became a major constraint influencing the Congress-business relationship. The new importance acquired by labour issues resulted from a sudden spurt in the growth of the labour movement combined with a growing tendency for labour relations to fall within the sphere of the state. While the labour movement had already emerged on the Indian scene during the 1920s and made significant strides, the problems of labour had remained largely divorced from those of nationalist struggle. This was partly a function of the 'sectarian' line pursued by the Communists, whose influence in the labour movement was at the time dominant, especially in Bombay, and partly because of the general lack of interest by Congressmen in industrial workers. The result had been near-total isolation of working-class struggles from nationalist agitations, well illustrated by the fact that the Civil Disobedience movement was launched just after the great textile strikes in Bombay had been defeated. Labour–nationalist relations began to change in the mid-1930s, however, when the labour movement began to recover from the losses, as a result of repression and depression, suffered from 1929 to 1934, and entered a new phase of growth. Working-class leaders, partly under the influence of the change in communist policy towards 'popular fronts,' now tried to link workers' struggles to the broader struggle for national freedom. The new socialist wing within the Congress tended, moreover, to view the working class as an essential component of its 'anti-imperialist' front. Congress socialists now became active in the trade union movement. The All India Trade Union Congress (AITUC) in particular sought to establish a permanent relationship with Congress. The Congress moderate leaders had strong misgivings regarding trade unions which followed a line of class struggle, however, and did not hide their preference for the kind of trade unionism embodied by the Ahmedabad Mazdoor Mahajan, a Gandhian union dominant in Ahmedabad's textile industry. Labour policy thus became one of the major areas of conflict in the confrontation between the moderate leadership and the Left wing in the Congress. While previously labour issues had been of peripheral concern for the Congress, they now came to assume major importance.

The state itself was also now becoming involved in the problems of labour.[10] Increasing state intervention in labour issues was resented by Indian capitalists, who preferred to keep relations with their workers within the sphere of 'private' affairs. Paternalism was the dominant ideology of Indian industrialists who viewed themselves as the fathers, benevolent as well as severe, of their employees, a view to which Gandhi subscribed with one qualification: he placed special emphasis on the obligations that this situation created for the employers. The whole Gandhian theory of 'trusteeship' and more generally Gandhi's distrust of the state as an instrument of regulation of social relations militated against a direct involvement of the Congress in the question of employer–worker relations. Once the Congress became involved in governance from 1937 onwards, however, it found it difficult to reverse the existing trend. It was drawn, so to speak, against its will into intervening in the relations between employers and workers.

Although Congress leaders were drawn from elite sections of Indian society, the rank-and-file members generally came from the middle and lower-middle rungs of society, mainly from different sections of the peasantry and from the urban middle or lower-middle classes, including the class of small traders. Industrial and agricultural workers were largely absent from party rolls. Leaders and the rank-and-file members did not always hold identical views on basic economic and social issues. The vague populism that constituted the dominant ideology within the Congress was open to diverging interpretations. Recent research has shed some light on 'popular' interpretations of Gandhism and has shown how it could be reinterpreted along millenarian and socially radical lines.[11] Scattered evidence such as that of underground Congress bulletins published in Bombay during the Civil Disobedience movement tends to suggest that anti-capitalist feelings were quite widespread among rank-and-file Congress members.[12]

The relative success, after 1934, of the Socialists with their anti-capitalist commitment strongly suggests that part of the Congress base was quite receptive to anti-capitalist themes. The nature of this anti-capitalism is not easy to grasp. It was certainly not very systematic and seems to have been closely derived from anti-imperialism: capitalism was associated with the exploitation of India by foreigners, and Indian capitalists were often viewed as junior partners of the British exploiters rather than as an independent group. There was thus a strong undercurrent of hostility towards big capital, British as well as Indian. Small businessmen, of course, were not victims of the same strictures and were often regarded with sympathy. It should not be overlooked, however, that in the traditional *varna* hierarchy, the merchants were ranked the lowest of the twice-born and with the growing tendency by clean *shudra* (largely peasant) castes to claim *kshatriya* status, the latter, which were well represented within Congress, could look down on the merchants. Anti-capitalism could thus easily blend with traditional perceptions of social hierarchy to produce a negative image of the businessman. On the whole there is no doubt that the Congress rank and file showed little enthusiasm for the prospect of a close alliance with Indian business, particularly the large capitalists.

The political-ideological environment of the 1930s and early 1940s, characterized by the currency of Leftist ideas, was not conducive to a close alliance between the Congress and business, although a rapprochement occurred gradually, and on the eve of Independence the Congress leadership had established a close relationship with Indian big business. The reason why Congress leadership pushed forward the policy of conciliation of business interests against heavy odds, such as a constant opposition from the increasingly powerful Congress Left and the risk of becoming unpopular, will now be examined in greater detail. I shall first deal with the new trend in Congress ideas regarding economics and second, with the impact of governmental experience.

### The Changing Face of Economic Nationalism: New Ideas on Indian Economics and Their Impact on Congress–Business Relations

Congressmen's ideas on Indian economics were a heritage of that early generation of nationalist thinkers represented by Dadabhai Naoroji, R.C. Dutt, and M.G. Ranade. The core of nationalist economic doctrine was a neo-mercantilist theory of imperialist exploitation based on the concept of 'drain of wealth'.[13] In this formulation the scarcity of capital caused by this drain was seen as the major obstacle to the economic development of India. Economic regeneration of the country required the emergence of a strong and enterprising indigenous capitalist class, and existing Indian capitalists were found wanting. Early nationalists seem to have largely adhered to the prevailing British stereotype of Indian capitalists as greedy, conservative banias preferring to invest in trade rather than in industrial ventures. The actual achievements of pioneering Indian capitalists, such as the birth of a modern cotton textile industry and the creation of chemical and metallurgical industries, tended to be belittled by the nationalists, since in their eyes they fell short of the requirements of Indian economic development. To stimulate national enterprise, great hopes were placed on such voluntaristic devices as the Swadeshi movement together with state intervention. This intervention was to acquire three main forms: (1) customs protection (an essential element in any neomercantilist policy in the Listian tradition), (2) the encouragement of technical education, and (3) direct financial aid to new industries. The growing economic successes of Japan, which attracted increasing attention from

Indian nationalists, seemed to confirm the soundness of that type of policy package. However, capitalist response to that economic programme remained limited before the First World War. Liberal ideas were still very influential in business circles, particularly in Bombay, and Indian businessmen were still too timid to dare to openly criticize the colonial government—which, on its side, in spite of Chatterton's attempts in Madras to push forward a policy of state aid to industry—remained firmly committed to laissez-faire.[14] It is only when the colonial government, following the war, showed signs of becoming wedded to a more interventionist policy that Indian businessmen started to show a greater interest in the ideas of economic nationalism.

In the 1920s, however, there were new developments. The birth of a working-class movement, which succeeded in stirring the conscience of the middle classes, together with Gandhi's open indictment of Western industrialism, combined to produce a shift in Congressmen's ideas about capitalist industrialization. Gandhian hopes for a regeneration of the country centred around the village, and although it is difficult to determine how deeply these ideas penetrated, they undoubtedly had an impact, which was visible in the literature of the period.[15] The 'dark satanic mill' could no longer hold the key to the future of India. Indian capitalists were now perceived in a new light: their existence was a positive fact, inasmuch as it limited the drain, by keeping in the country some of the profits for capital investment. They had to reform themselves by acting as 'trustees' rather than merely as 'owners' of their enterprises, and had to pay more attention to charities, *khaddar*, social reform activities, and nationalist struggles. Provided they conformed to the code of conduct prescribed by Gandhi, they were acceptable, even honourable, and their workers were advised to treat them as paternal benefactors rather than as greedy exploiters. Modern industrialization was not to be the essential aim of nationalist economic policy, however. Capitalists do not seem to have resented the new role assigned to them. They were more interested in Gandhi's anticlass struggle sermons than worried by his anti-industrial rhetoric.[16]

In the 1930s there occurred a reversal of ideological trends regarding industrialization. The world depression made evident the fragility of a raw-materials-producing economy heavily dependent on foreign markets for the sale of many essential commodities. Industrialization behind the wall of protective tariffs seemed to offer the prospect of escaping cyclical instability. In the wake of the depression, independent countries such as Brazil, Argentina, and Australia had taken measures to support their industries, and their relative successes were an inspiration to some Indians; but it was the example of the Soviet Union that was most influential. The Soviet model fascinated many, not only because of the successes of the Five Year Plans in purely economic terms, but also because it appeared that many evils of the capitalist industrial revolution had been averted in the Russian case. As far as that country was concerned, Gandhi's critique of industrialism appeared to be invalidated. Many, and not only on the Left, thought that India could draw inspiration from the Soviet experiment of a centrally planned economy. From the 1920s, the most outspoken advocate of planning in India was the erstwhile dewan of Mysore, Sir M. Visvesvaraya, who had inspired the bold policy of aid to industry followed in that progressive Indian state.[17] There were basic differences between Visvesvaraya's capitalist conception of planning and that of the Leftists, however; some synthesis was achieved within the National Planning Committee (NPC) created by the Congress in 1938.[18]

What the capitalists achieved by participating in the NPC was to obtain recognition of the role of the private sector within a 'socialistic' (or, rather, state capitalistic) framework of economic organization. They were shrewd enough not to oppose frontally the trend towards state capitalism ('socialism' in Congress parlance) and chose to fight the Leftist menace from within the NPC. During 1938 through 1940, they succeeded in preventing the adoption of the most radical measures proposed by the Congress Left (such as widespread nationalization schemes). After 1940, taking advantage of the paralysis of the NPC due to the Second World War and the imprisonment of Congress leaders, the capitalists created their own post-war economic development committee within which they prepared a scheme for the economic development of India, known as the Bombay Plan. Their philosophy is summarized with admirable clarity in the following extract of a letter from by J.R.D. Tata to Sir Purshottamdas Thakurdas:

> The inevitability of a change in the direction of a socialist economy even in a country like India must now be recognised and leaders of industry would be well advised to take this into account and be prepared to make such adjustments as may meet all reasonable demands before the socialist movement assumes the form of a full-fledged revolution. The most effective way in which extreme demands in future may be obviated is for industrialists to take thought while there is yet time as to the best means of incorporating into the capitalist structure whatever is sound and feasible in the socialist movement. One of the principal tasks of the committee will therefore be to examine how far socialist demands can be accommodated without capitalism surrendering any of its essential features.[19]

By managing to produce the Bombay Plan in 1944, much before the NPC could finish its work, Indian capitalists pre-empted any attempt at imposing a radical programme of national economic trans-formation. Faced only with a hastily produced 'Gandhian' plan, the Bombay Plan was given recognition as a quasi-official blueprint for the future economic development of India. Congress thus left it to the capitalists to define the main outline of the economic policy of independent India. Does this mean that the Congress had become a simple tool of the capitalist class? The truth is quite complex. The Congress moderate leadership consisted of people who had very limit-ed notions of economics and who thought that the management of economic affairs should be entrusted to those most competent. Basical-ly it was the inability of either the Gandhians or the Leftists to propose any alternative programme that ensured the success of the capitalists.

Thus changes in Congress economic ideology, the gradual departure from Gandhian 'orthodoxy' that occurred during the 1930s and 1940s, had positive consequences for Congress–business relations. Within a trend of state interventionism, the private sector succeeded in having its place fully recognized. The pragmatism of Congress leaders, not only moderates such as Patel or Rajendra Prasad, but even a 'leftist' such as Nehru, was a major factor in the emergence of that kind of compromise. The governmental experience acquired by Congress between 1937 and 1947 contributed in no small way to the final victory of this pragmatic approach to business. This aspect deserves closer study.

## The Impact of Governance

During the few years when it held power in the majority of the provinces (first in 1937–9 and then again in 1946–7) as well as during the brief period of the interim cabinet in 1947, the Congress acquired some experience in dealing with business interests. Three areas of policy played a major role in shaping Congress–business relations: (1) financial policy, (2) economic policy, and (3) labour policy.

The Congress provincial governments as well as the Congress–Muslim League interim cabinet had limited resources at their disposal[20] and had, of course, to contend with great economic expectations from many different quarters. Because land revenue was inelastic, indirect taxation most unpopular, and agricultural incomes practically non-taxable, governments could increase their resources only by taxing more heavily the incomes of the more affluent urbanites, among whom merchants and capitalists figured most prominently. The reduction in excise revenues due to the adoption of a policy of prohibition was an added constraint. Faced with financial difficulties, Congress governments thus tended to look to business profits for this source of extra revenue. In the United Provinces in 1939, the Congress ministry sought to impose an employment tax levied exclusively on employers of labour.[21]

In the 'people's budget' adopted in 1947 by the interim cabinet, finance minister Liaqat Ali Khan of the Muslim League proposed a 25 per cent business tax on profits exceeding Rs 100,000 and a graduated tax on capital gains.[22] These proposals, widely interpreted as a 'clever' piece of Muslim League demagoguery intended to create confusion in the Congress camp,[23] were initially approved by Congress members of the interim cabinet, including Nehru.[24] In the case of both forms of taxation described above, however, business reactions, especially Birla's, were so violent that the Congress had to retract its steps. The 1947 budget proposals were quickly watered down from 25 to 16.66 per cent, and the proposal for a capital-gains tax was shelved, by referral to a select committee.[25] Taxation could have been a powerful instrument of social change, but the Congress used it with great caution in relation to business.

In their economic policies Congress governments were similarly faced with delicate choices. Efforts to help the deprived sectors of society through rural promotion and encouragement of cottage industries had to be accommodated within a framework that tended to favour vested interests. One signal failure of Congress provincial governments from 1937–9 and 1946–7 was in the area of small industries and cottage production, which should have benefited by the special role assigned to them in Gandhi's vision. Congress governments did enact some legislative measures in favour of these sectors, and they profited by increased budgetary outlays, but the cumulative impact was practically nil. Any attempt at intervening more openly to aid these sectors met with strong resistance from entrenched business interests. A proposal, for example, by the Bombay Congress ministry in 1939 to allot quotas of production to the handlooms and the mills was rejected by textile millowners.[26] In 1947 a more radical attempt by the Madras Congress ministry to prohibit the erection of new mills and reserve to the handlooms any future increase in production raised such a storm that the Congress government was obliged to discharge the minister responsible.[27] Congress policy in favour of the rural sectors and cottage industries thus never assumed the radical character it had in Gandhian reconstruction schemes: the large-scale transfer of resources advocated, for instance, in the Gandhian plan was never even initiated.

It was in labour policy, however, that provincial governance had the most effect on the Congress. A certain amount of state control of the economy necessarily meant some control of the labour process.[28] Indian capitalists were ready to accept that as part of the 'package deal' they made with the Congress. Workers held different views on the question and fiercely resisted attempts by the state and the Congress (the two gradually merged) to control the trade union movement. Their resistance had the effect of giving a marked anti-labour bias to labour legislation passed by Congress provincial governments in 1937–9 and 1946–7, culminating in the two Bombay Trade Dispute Acts of 1938 and 1946.[29] It became increasingly difficult for Congress leaders to accommodate the existing working-class movement within their policy framework. They started to make attempts to reshape this movement, therefore, and the outcome of their policy was a split in trade unions and the creation, after Independence, of the Indian National Trade Union Congress (INTUC). This Congress-controlled federation tended to become the privileged partner of big business.

Confronted with the realities of governance before even enjoying full power, Congress was progressively led to reducing its commitments to the underprivileged masses. A shift occurred in its long-term plans for an overall reconstruction of Indian society. Less ambitious projects, based more on the existing economic realities of a fragmented and highly inegalitarian Indian society, became Congress policy. Indian capitalists, guaranteed their important place, were asked to step up investment and were offered in return the prospects of greater profits.

## Conclusion and Alternative Paradigms

It is only recently that historians of the freedom movement, especially those of a Marxist persuasion, have paid attention to the relationship between Indian capitalism and the nationalist movement. Previously, authors such as Kosambi and R.P. Dutt, writing on the eve of, or just after, Independence, drew attention to the increasing role of what they perceived as an Indian 'bourgeoisie', but the impact of their views was confined to Leftist political circles.[30]

A view that gained wider currency was propagated in the 1970s by a school of Indian historians represented, in particular, by B. Chandra,[31] who perceives Indian capitalists as a progressive and anti-imperialist 'national bourgeoisie', a natural and essential component of the broad 'anti-feudal' and 'anti-imperialist' front constituted under the leadership of Gandhi and the Congress Party. In this view the link between the nationalist leadership and the capitalist class was a positive process, which was made evident in the capacity of Indian nationalism to unite all the social classes in the fight against foreign domination.[32]

A more recent trend in Indian Marxist historical writing, in contrast, stresses the limitations of the Indian bourgeoisie without treating it as 'compradore'.[33] For these authors, the bourgeoisie could establish only a limited 'hegemony' over the national movement, given an alliance with propertied elements in the countryside. The concept of 'passive revolution', borrowed by these authors from Gramsci, by which they define the Indian freedom struggle, serves to emphasize that neither the masses, in spite of their mobilization, nor the bourgeoisie, because of its own weaknesses, could give the national movement clear direction for the radical transformation of the country in either a capitalist or socialist direction. The process was basically one of limiting popular initiative and maintaining the movement within limits that objectively suited bourgeois interests whatever the subjective views of the leaders were.

I see two major problems with this interpretation of the Indian national movement. The first relates to the concept of an Indian bourgeoisie. To speak of hegemony even in a limited sense is to assume that the hegemonic class exists as a constituted and relatively coherent force. In the case of pre-1947 India, this seems doubtful: there were undoubtedly bourgeois elements and groups, but they do not appear to have coalesced into a class.[34] Indian capitalists were capable of displaying some unity when they felt challenged, as they did in the immediate pre-Independence period with the rise of Leftist groups, but they still found it very difficult to define common long-term positive objectives.

Moreover, to draw a comparison between the case of India and that of a Western country such as Italy is to assume a basic similarity in the relationship between the economy and the political order. In India, however, the dominant ideology—which still had a powerful hold on the minds of even the members of the westernized elite—treated the economy as a simple function of the social and political order, and not as an autonomous domain. The attitude of Congress leaders to Indian capitalists must be placed within this context. They believed in the primacy of politics over economics and therefore did not attach much importance to the precise nature of the economic regime of an independent India. They thought that the economy would somehow 'follow' and that once the fetters of foreign domination were removed, it would become robust. Of all the major nationalist leaders, only Jawaharlal Nehru did not share this view of the economy as a simple function of power and was conscious of some of the problems of generating development in a backward country such as India. This is why Indian capitalists who had openly condemned his 'socialistic' views in 1936 came to regard him in a new light from 1938 onwards and, after Independence, developed a comfortable relationship with him.

The view of the economy as a simple function of the political order that most Congress leaders shared favoured capitalist interests as well as set limits to their pretensions. They benefited by the political leaders' general ignorance of economic problems that allowed the capitalists to easily bend the emerging 'socialistic' structure to their own advantage. At the same time, however, they had to accept that power was a kind of superior entity situated beyond them and that ultimately imposed its choices on them. Furthermore, businessmen were perceived as an important source of funds for the party. In a later stage their expertise on economic affairs was sought by leaders who possessed little knowledge and experience in that field. Governmental experience also alerted the Congress leaders to the importance of business interests in society. Their attitude to labour problems was also largely shaped by the difficulties encountered by the Congress provincial governments. Short-term constraints were more important than long-term ideological trends in influencing Congress economic and social policies. Does this mean that the search for an all-embracing paradigm is doomed to failure? Not necessarily, but the search must perhaps proceed along another path.

Rather than postulating a priori that India followed the same route as other countries, perhaps a wider look at Indian historical experience would yield interesting results. What kind of relationship existed between merchants and rulers in precolonial Indian state formations? Are there not some similarities between precolonial states and the postcolonial state in this respect?

Recent works on eighteenth-century India, in particular C.A. Bayly's study of northern India, have drawn attention to an ongoing process of 'commercialization of power' in the successor states to the Mughal empire.[35] The main forms of this commercialization were the farming of revenue collection to merchants and financiers and the granting of state monopolies to great banking houses. During that period in the major state formations of northern India capital became closely integrated with the state. The influence acquired by merchants is illustrated by the political role of the house of Jagat Seth in Bengal and of bankers in Hyderabad state.[36] At the same time the merchants had no direct access to political power. Their relationship was to the ruler rather than to the state as such, and a change of ruler could have dramatic consequences for the fortunes of even the most powerful merchant houses.

A look at the present-day Indian state reveals striking similarities with precolonial state formations. Is it not possible to see in institutionalized corruption, the financing of political parties, especially the ruling party, by business houses, and state financial support to private 'monopolies', the modern equivalents of the farming of tax revenue or of the granting of state monopolies to private firms? In other words, is not power in modern India undergoing a process of 'commercialization' largely similar to the one witnessed in the pre-British era? An Indian economist has stressed the resemblances between present-day and old monopolies, emphasizing also that the appropriation of the labour process in modern India still displayed many premodern traits.[37] The continuing importance of personal rapport between big businessmen and governing elites is also noticeable.

In stressing those elements of continuity between precolonial merchant–ruler relationships and present-day connections between Indian big business and the ruling Congress party, I am not trying to argue that there has been no change at all and that the British period was but a small parenthesis. First, it should be recalled that the trend towards commercialization of power reached its climax under Company rule. Even under Crown rule, a close relationship remained between the colonial state and British business in spite of the impersonal style of government adopted by the British rulers. In that sense the British period represented no real break, and the colonial state retained strong Indian features. The close relationship established between Indian business and the government of independent India was as much a heritage of the British period with its close integration between private business and the colonial authorities as a resurgence of precolonial features. However, the highly personalized aspect of the business–government connection is clearly derived from a traditional view of the relationship between merchant and ruler. Even at the ideological level, the neomercantilist conception, which served as an integrative framework for the approaches of both big business and the Congress to economic policy, probably has some roots in ideas that were already in existence before colonization ideas, which perhaps inspired to some extent Tipu Sultan's policies in Mysore.[38]

I do not propose to substitute a merchant–ruler paradigm for the capitalist class–bourgeois party paradigm within which much of the analysis of the relationship between Indian business and the Congress has been embedded. Rather, I wish to draw attention to some of the problems raised by that kind of an analysis that would benefit from taking into account certain long-term continuities in Indian historical processes. I think that, from the 1920s onward, the Congress party was increasingly given by Indian businessmen the status of an aspiring ruler, and benefited from it. Its leaders were sufficiently pragmatic to make the adjustments that allowed them to accommodate the sectional interests of Indian business within the broad framework of a national liberation struggle. The acquisition of governmental experience after 1937, even on a limited scale, accelerated this process, which led to a compromise, the terms of which have not greatly changed in the post-1947 period despite the Congress choice of a 'socialistic' road for India.

## Notes

1. A.D.D. Gordon, *Businessmen and Politics: Rising Nationalism and a Modernizing Economy in Bombay, 1918–1933* (New Delhi: Manohar, 1978); Claude Markovits, *Indian Business and Nationalist Politics 1931–1939: The Indigenous Capitalist Class and the Rise of the Congress Party* (Cambridge: Cambridge University Press, 1985).

2. *Indian National Congress Resolutions 1885–1934*, Madras, 1935.

3. Ibid.

4. See Christine Dobbin, *Urban Leadership in Western India: Politics and Communities in Bombay City, 1840–1885* (London: Oxford University Press, 1972). For two contrasting views of the political attitudes of business during the 1890–1905 period, see Bipan Chandra, *The Rise and Growth of Economic Nationalism in India* (New Delhi: People's Publishing House, 1966), p. 753, and D.A. Washbrook, 'Law, State and Agrarian Society in Colonial India', *Modern Asian Studies* 15 (July 1981), pp. 649–721.

5. A.P. Kannangara, 'Indian Millowners and Indian Nationalism before 1914', *Past and Present* 40 (1968), pp. 147–64.

6. See Gopal Krishna, 'The Development of the Indian National Congress as a Mass Organization, 1918–1923', *Journal of Asian Studies* 25 (May 1966), pp. 413–30.

7. See M. Nehru's letter to Lalji Naranji, dated 21 April 1928: 'An alliance between the Congress and capitalists who are bent on profiting by the sufferings of the nation is an impossible one.' Copy of the letter in Purshottamdas Thakurdas Papers, file 40, Nehru Memorial Museum and Library, Delhi.

8. For a detailed account, see Markovits, *Indian Business*, chapter III.

9. Gordon, *Businessmen and Politics*.

10. D. Chakrabarty, 'Conditions for Knowledge of Working-Class Conditions: Employers, Government and the Jute Workers of Calcutta, 1890–1940', in Ranajit Guha (ed.), *Subaltern Studies*, vol. II (New Delhi: Oxford University Press, 1983), pp. 259–310. See also M.D. Morris, *The Emergence of an Industrial Labour Force in India: A Study of the Bombay Cotton Mills 1854–1947* (Berkeley and Los Angeles: University of California Press, 1963), chapter X, pp. 178–97.

11. See S. Amin, 'Gandhi as Mahatma: Gorakhpur District, Eastern UP, 1921–1922', in Ranajit Guha (ed.), *Subaltern Studies*, vol. III (New Delhi: Oxford University Press, 1986), pp. 1–61.

12. Some were kept by Thakurdas in his files. See Thakurdas Papers, file no. 107.

13. On this aspect, see Chandra, *Economic Nationalism in India*.

14. See A.K. Bagchi, *Private Investment in India 1900–1939* (Cambridge: Cambridge University Press, 1971), pp. 50–3.

15. See, for instance, some of Premchand's novels, in particular *Godan.*

16. It has also to be taken into account that khaddar did not directly compete with Indian mill cloth but used mill-made yarn.

17. M. Visvesvaraya, *Planned Economy for India* (Bangalore: Bangalore Press 1934).

18. Markovits, *Indian Business,* chapter VI.

19. J.R.D. Tata to Purshottamadas Thakurdas, 8 December 1942, Thakurdas Papers, file no. 291.

20. Under the 1935 Constitution, ultimate control over Indian finances was vested in the viceroy, and the transfer of resources to the provinces was very limited.

21. Claude Markovits, 'Indian Business and the Congress Provincial Governments 1937–9', *Modern Asian Studies* 15 (July 1981), pp. 487–526. [Chapter 2 of this volume.]

22. See *The Times of India* (Bombay), 1 March 1947.

23. See Sumit Sarkar, *Modern India: 1885–1947* (New Delhi: Macmillan, 1983), p. 436.

24. On this episode, see the first-hand testimony (although evidently biased in favour of the Muslim League) of Chaudhuri Muhammad Ali in his *The Emergence of Pakistan* (New York: Columbia University Press, 1967), pp. 104–14.

25. *Times of India,* 26 March 1947.

26. See 'Evidence of the Millowners' Association, Bombay, before Bombay Economic and Industrial Survey Committee' at its 35th meeting, on 7 August 1939, in Thakurdas Papers, file no. 212.

27. The minister was T. Prakasam. See *Times of India,* 15 March 1947.

28. Markovits, *Indian Business.*

29. On this aspect, see C. Revri, *The Indian Trade Union Movement: A Historical Outline, 1880–1947* (New Delhi: Orient Longman, 1972).

30. D.D. Kosambi, 'The Bourgeoisie Comes of Age in India', *Science and Society* 10 (Fall 1946), pp. 392–8; R. Palme Dutt, *India Today* (Bombay: People's Publishing House, 1947).

31. See B. Chandra, *Imperialism and Nationalism in India* (Delhi: 1979).

32. The main problem with this view is that it makes a certain number of basic assumptions about Indian capitalists and their unity of purpose and opposition to imperialism and 'feudalism' that are not supported by the evidence available. I have examined these views in some detail in my *Indian Business.*

33. For a particularly lucid exposition, see Sumit Sarkar, *'Popular' Movements and 'Middle-Class' Leadership in Late Colonial India: Perspectives and Problems*

*of a 'History from Below'* (Calcutta: K.P. Bagchi, 1983). See also Guha, *Subaltern Studies*, vols I and II.

34. On the anti-Nehru manifesto of 1936, see my *Indian Business*, chapter IV.

35. C.A. Bayly, *Rulers, Townsmen and Bazaars: North Indian Society in the Age of British Expansion, 1770–1780* (Cambridge: Cambridge University Press, 1983).

36. See Karen Leonard, 'Banking Firms in Nineteenth Century Hyderabad Politics,' *Modern Asian Studies* 15 (April 1981), pp. 177–201.

37. See N.K. Chandra, 'Monopoly Capital, Private Corporate Sector and the Indian Economy: A Study in Relative Growth, 1931–1976', *Economic and Political Weekly* 14 (August 1979), p. 1270.

38. See Ashok Sen, 'A Pre-British Economic Formation in India of the Late Eighteenth Century: Tipu Sultan's Mysore', in Barun De (ed.), *Perspectives in Social Sciences*, vol. I (Calcutta: Oxford University Press, 1977), pp. 46–119.

2

# INDIAN BUSINESS
# AND THE CONGRESS PROVINCIAL
# GOVERNMENTS 1937–1939*

THE LATE 1930s SAW A DEFINITE TURN IN POLITICAL DEVElopments in India. Following the abandonment of Civil Disobedience in 1934, a prolonged period of internal peace helped the Congress, until then a broad-based movement with a general commitment to fight foreign rule, evolve into a more organized party capable of aspiring to political dominance. In the process, its relations with different social forces took a more definite shape. While in the past the Congress had clung to the myth of an Indian society free of internal conflicts and united in opposition to the British, the growth of social conflicts in town and countryside forced it to take into account the competing aspirations of various groups.

Assuming office in seven provinces in July 1937 under a regime of qualified provincial autonomy introduced by the 1935 constitution, the party found itself confronted with the difficult task of accommodating these competing interests within a framework in which only limited financial resources were available; financial control at the centre remained firmly in British hands,[1] and provinces had largely inelastic

*From C.J. Baker, G. Johnson, and A. Seal (eds), *Power, Profit and Politics: Essays on Imperialism, Nationalism and Change in Twentieth-Century India* (Cambridge University Press, 1981), pp. 481–526.

sources of revenue. Among the interest groups which were making demands on the Congress ministries the most powerful was the Indian business class, which had expanded at a relatively quick pace during the period 1932–7, and which found itself increasingly alienated from the conservative economic policies followed by the Government of India. By the 'Indian business class' we mean here Indian big business, that is the small elite of big traders, financiers, and industrialists which was largely concentrated in a few centres like Bombay, Ahmedabad, Calcutta, Kanpur, and Coimbatore. Though far from constituting a homogeneous group, these businessmen displayed certain characteristics which set them clearly apart from the mass of small traders, moneylenders, brokers, and petty entrepreneurs which formed the bulk of the Indian merchant classes. They differed from the lesser interests in the size of their financial resources, the range and scale of their activities (from foreign trade to big industry), and their organizational skill. They had captured the leadership of most of the regional trade associations and had established in 1927 the first all-India business association, the Federation of Indian Chambers of Commerce and Industry (FICCI), which was the closest thing to a lobby in India. This group had been a major source of funds for the Congress campaigns since the 1920s, and it had acquired some influence on the Congress High Command. While the businessmen expected to derive some advantages from the advent of the Congress ministries, they were at the same time apprehensive of the policy the latter would follow in labour matters.

How could the Congress accommodate capitalist demands along with the growing populist pressures and postures which were in evidence both outside and inside the party? Conversely, would businessmen, who had always been careful of keeping good relations with the British, and had used nationalist agitations mainly as a means of extracting concessions from them, adjust to a situation in which some power of patronage had passed from the hands of the British into those of the Congress? These were some of the questions raised by the advent of the Congress ministries. After 1937 the British, though they were less in evidence, had not altogether disappeared from the

Indian scene and therefore the political attitudes of the Indian businessmen during the 1937–9 period were determined by a complex inter-
play of national and provincial factors. Though this study will focus
on the relations between Indian business and the Congress in the
major Congress-ruled provinces (thus leaving aside Bengal and its
strong Marwari business community) the impact of all-India trends
will not be ignored.

## Relations between Congress and Business before<br>the Advent of the Congress Ministries

Relations between the Congress and business at the national level
had grown closer during the 1920s and the first phase of the Civil
Disobedience movement (1930–1), but were severely strained in
1932–4. During these years, business support for the movement remained limited, while the Indian business class split over the issue of
imperial preference and the Ottawa agreement. Though the small-
and medium-scale traders in Bombay embarked upon an effective
boycott of British business and directly confronted the authorities in
1932–3, even the most pro-Congress faction in big business, represented by a section of the Calcutta Marwaris led by G.D. Birla and by the
Ahmedabad millowners, favoured the end of the agitation. Bombay
big business openly broke with the Congress, and tried to use the
Ottawa agreement to its own advantage by forming alliances with
groups of British capitalists to fight more dangerous competition from
Japan (in cotton textiles) and Belgium (in the iron and steel industry)
in the Indian market. The Lees–Mody pact concluded in 1933 between
the representatives of the Bombay cotton mills and of Lancashire epitomized the new course of Bombay business politics. The divisions
within the ranks of the Indian capitalists persisted even after the abandonment of Civil Disobedience by the Congress, but they became
less pronounced as Bombay business grew aware of the new moderation of the Congress leadership and found it increasingly difficult to
conciliate its interests with those of Lancashire.[2] In 1936 common
opposition to the Congress Left drew both factions of big business
closer to the dominant group of the Congress leadership.[3]

The decision by the Congress High Command to contest the 1937 elections in the provinces under the new regime of provincial autonomy showed that the Congress was ready to accept at least partly the new constitution. It exposed the basic weakness of its Left wing, which had been preaching boycott of the elections. Business circles generally welcomed the Congress decision and some financial aid was promised to the party.[4]

However, since the elections were fought on a provincial basis, the attitudes of businessmen were largely dictated by their relations with the Congress organizations at the provincial level, and not only by the rapport they had established with the High Command. The situation, thus, varied considerably from province to province. Prior to 1937, under the so-called 'dyarchy' regime, non-Congress provincial governments had only limited powers, but industry and civil works were among the transferred subjects and had conveyed some powers of patronage. In some provinces, the non-Congress forces in power had strengthened their links with the business class by giving businessmen ministries and other favours. This was, for instance, the case in the Madras Presidency, where a large section of the local capitalist class had been integrated with the power structure of the Justice Party.[5] Similar trends, though less conspicuous, had emerged in other provinces, particularly in Bombay and in the United Provinces. As a result, relations between business and the Congress provincial organizations were often strained. Actually one must distinguish between two levels of politics. At the lower level, that of the locality, traders and merchants seem to have increased their influence within the Congress in the post-1934 period, mainly through their control of financial resources.[6] But larger capitalists, that is, both big traders and industrialists, whose operations affected the entire economy of a province, generally kept aloof from Congress provincial politics, though there were of course exceptions. This explains partly the difficulties which the provincial Congress organizations had in raising funds for the election campaign and their need to appeal to the High Command for help. Thus, in a letter to Rajendra Prasad, the Congress leader of the United Provinces complained of lack of funds in his province,[7] adding that he thought that other Congress provincial organizations were similarly handicapped. In Bombay city, not much money was raised either.[8] In Bihar, Seth Dalmia, the big Marwari industrialist, gave some help, but on a limited scale.[9]

In spite of these difficulties, the Congress scored impressive victories in most of the provinces and showed that, outside the Muslim-majority provinces, it was the dominant political force in India. It won an absolute majority in six of the eleven provinces (Bihar, Central Provinces, Madras, Northwest Frontier Province, Orissa, and the United Provinces) was close to it in Bombay, emerged as the single largest party in Assam, and fared badly only in the three Muslim-majority provinces of Bengal, the Punjab, and Sind, in which it nevertheless won most of the general (non-Muslim) seats. An analysis of the election results gives interesting indications about the political complexion of Indian businessmen.

A first set of conclusions can be drawn from a careful reading of the results of the elections in the seats reserved for Indian commerce. Under the new regime, a total of twenty-three seats in ten Provincial Assemblies[10] were reserved for Indian commercial, mining, and industrial interests (including two seats reserved for Indian tea planters in the Assam legislature). Of these, the Congress Party contested only six and won three. Eight other seats went to businessmen known for their pro-Congress leanings, while a further seven seats were won by known anti-Congressites, three of whom were elected contesting against a Congress candidate. The remaining seats went to businessmen without known political leanings, though some of them might have been Congress sympathizers. Table 1 shows the results of the commercial seats in each province.

This table shows wide differences in the political behaviour of businessmen in various provinces. In Madras, where industry was still dominated by British capital (with the exception of Coimbatore, which was the largest centre of the textile industry in the province), the opposition to the Congress from large Indian trading and money-lending interests was demonstrated by the failure of the Congress Party to secure any of the reserved seats. In the Nattukottai Nagarathar Association constituency, the Congress candidate was defeated by

TABLE 1

Results of 1937 Provincial Elections: Seats Reserved for
Indian Commerce

| I | II | III | IV | V | VI | VII |
|---|---|---|---|---|---|---|
| Assam | 3 | | | | | 3 |
| Bengal | 5 | | | 3 | 2 | |
| Bihar | 2 | | | 2 | | |
| Bombay | 4 | 1 | 1 | 2 | 1 | |
| Central Prov. | 2 | 2 | 1 | | 1 | |
| Madras | 2 | 2 | 0 | | 2 | |
| Orissa | 1 | | | | | 1 |
| Punjab | 1 | | | | | 1 |
| Sind | 1 | 1 | 1 | | | |
| United Prov. | 2 | | | 1 | 1 | |

I name of the Province; II no. of seats reserved for Indian Commerce; III no. of seats contested by the Congress; IV no. of seats won by the Congress; V no. of seats won by pro-Congress businessmen; VI no. of seats won by anti-Congress businessmen; VII no. of seats won by others.

*Sources:* A Brief Analysis of the Election Results. Issued by the Political and Economic Information Department of the All-India Congress Committee (AICC). Reproduced by N. Mitra (comp.), *Indian Annual Register, 1937*, vol. I, pp. 168 ff (Calcutta, 1937), and *Indian Yearbook 1937–38* (Bombay, 1938).

Muttiah Chettiar, a merchant-prince and banker, the head of the Nattukottai Chettiar community, which dominated the financial scene in south India and had huge interests abroad. He had been a minister under the Justice Party regime, and became the leader of the Justicite opposition to the new Congress regime. The Congress also lost the seat for the Southern India Chamber of Commerce. If one keeps in mind that in the 1934 elections to the Central Legislative Assembly, the Congress had secured its only seat in a constituency reserved for Indian commerce in Madras, the 1937 results will undoubtedly appear as a setback. In the Central Provinces also, the anti-Congress feelings of one section of the traders and industrialists were shown by the defeat of the Congress candidate from the Berar commerce seat (which included Nagpur, the only big commercial and industrial centre in the province) at the hands of one of the biggest Marwari millowners of the province.

The United Provinces results revealed the political division among Indian businessmen in this largely agricultural province in which Kanpur was the only big industrial centre. Sir J.P. Srivastava, a Kanpur industrialist who was a supporter of the Hindu Mahasabha and a determined adversary of the Congress (he had been a minister under dyarchy and contested the election on the ticket of the National Agriculturist Party, which represented the most reactionary faction of the United Provinces zamindars), was elected to one of the seats reserved for the Upper India Chamber of Commerce, a British-dominated commercial association. In the joint constituency formed by the United Provinces Chamber of Commerce and the Merchants' Chamber of the United Provinces, Lala Padampat Singhania, a pro-Congress business magnate of Kanpur, defeated in a straight fight another magnate, Rameshwar Prasad Bagla, who was an opponent of the Congress.[11]

In Bombay, the Congress contested only the seat reserved for the East India Cotton Association and won it. Pro-Congress businessmen were elected in the Ahmedabad Millowners' Association and Indian Merchants' Chamber constituencies. But in the Bombay Millowners' Association constituency, Sir S.D. Saklatvala, of the Tata group, was returned unopposed. Both the Millowners' Association and the Tata group had in the past followed an anti-Congress line, and though they had become more cautious lately, they could not be counted as supporters of the party. In Bengal, there was a clear-cut division. Out of five members elected from the reserved constituencies, three could be considered pro-Congress. They were the two nominees of the Bengal National Chambers of Commerce and the one of the Indian Chamber of Commerce. Among them was Nalini Ranjan Sarkar, who became Finance Minister in the non-Congress ministry formed after the elections but who was known to be close to the B.C. Roy faction of the provincial Congress. The other two members elected for commerce, from the Muslim Chamber of Commerce and the Marwari Association, were opponents of the Congress. Finally, the Congress and its allies had their greatest victories in Bihar and Sind, where they won all the commercial seats.

The overall results thus reveal a fair amount of support for the Congress from the electorate in the reserved constituencies (which represented the upper strata of the Indian business community), despite the existence of strong pockets of opposition in two or three provinces. Other indications about businessmen's participation in the political process are to be found in an analysis of the results of the elections to the non-commercial seats. It was customary for some big businessmen having an interest in politics to seek election from either urban or rural seats. In the 1934 elections to the Central Legislative Assembly, some businessmen were elected to such seats,[12] generally as independents. No precise data is available on the number of business-men who tried to get elected in the 1937 elections, but one must draw attention to the following facts. Two figures of local big business who contested on non-Congress tickets suffered crushing defeats at the hands of the Congress in two rural constituencies of Kanpur district.[13] The only representative of big business who was elected as an independent in the face of Congress opposition was Lalchand Hira-chand who stood successfully from a rural constituency in Maharash-tra. Being the son of Walchand Hirachand, one of the biggest Indian capitalists in Bombay, he could rely on the vast rural clientage provided by his father's sugar factory situated in the area.

Apart from the sugar magnates, few businessmen could draw upon a client network in the countryside, and this seriously limited their possibilities of getting elected in rural constituencies without the sup-port of a party machinery. With the multiplication in the number of voters brought about by the enlargement of the franchise,[14] electioneer-ing was no more only a question of resources, but necessitated organiza-tion, which only a political party and not an individual could muster. This is demonstrated *a contrario* by the electoral successes of some big Muslim merchants who contested on Muslim League tickets from Muslim rural seats.[15] The reasons why the Muslim League was more generous than the Congress in giving tickets to businessmen were twofold: firstly, the Muslim League had less resources and talent than the Congress; secondly, contesting on a League ticket did not expose a businessman to the active hostility of the British authorities, while siding too openly with the Congress might have had dangerous consequences.[16] Also, the growing communal alignment among Indian businessmen favoured the League more than the Congress.[17]

There was, thus, no perceptible increase in the direct participation of businessmen in electoral politics. Businessmen tended to work more behind the scenes and tried to use the financial weapon to influence the Congress.[18] But the overwhelming victories won by the Congress in most of the provinces did not leave them much room for manoeuvring. The prevailing economic and social conditions under which the new Congress ministries, formed in July 1937, had to operate, caused them further anxieties.

### The Environment of Provincial Autonomy: Major Constraints on Congress–Business Relations in the Provinces

When the Congress ministries were formed in seven provinces, the Indian economy had just started to recover from the effects of the unprecedented depression of the early 1930s. The depression resulted in a fall in land revenue, which was the single largest source of revenue for the provincial governments,[19] and thus had a disastrous impact on provincial finances. While the central government had been able to overcome a financial crisis by 1932,[20] the provincial governments remained in a difficult situation throughout the 1930s. Their inability to find new sources of revenue to supplement those in existence prevented them from making any significant contribution towards economic development. The share of civil works in the total expenditure of all the provincial governments actually fell during the first half of the 1930s, and the allocation for industries (a purely provincial subject since the 1919 reforms) remained at a measly 1 per cent.[21] In this context, the devolution to the provincial governments of increased responsibilities in matters of economic development and social welfare under the 1935 reforms was bound to remain purely theoretical, unless accompanied by an increase in the financial resources of the provinces.

A small step in that direction had been made when the Government of India had accepted the recommendations of the Indian Financial Enquiry Committee of 1936,[22] headed by Sir Otto Niemeyer. The Niemeyer Award, as it came to be known, had allotted to the provinces 50 per cent of the revenue yielded by the income tax, the levy of which remained a prerogative of the central government. But it had been decided that during five years part of the transferable amount would be retained by the Centre for the consolidation of its own finances. The overall transfer of resources was therefore very limited. In the way the allocation had been made between the different provinces, the poorest ones, such as the newly-formed provinces of Orissa and Sind, had been favoured at the expense of the more developed ones, such as Bengal and Bombay, which were deemed to have sufficient resources. The business community in the latter provinces had reacted very unfavourably to the Niemeyer Award, protesting that lack of resources would hamper the work of the ministries.[23] Despite these hostile reactions the Niemeyer Award had the merit of offering some prospect of financial relief to the beleaguered governments of the poorest provinces.

Another innovation introduced by the 1935 reforms had been the freedom given to the provincial governments to borrow money directly from the market without having to go through the cumbrous financial machinery of the central government. Yet borrowing could be no more than an expedient; to attract investors, the provincial governments had to offer conditions at least as interesting as those given by the Centre, which meant that in the future the repayment of the debts incurred would necessitate a raising of the permanent revenue. All in all, existing conditions restricted considerably the possibilities of the provincial governments. Unless they managed to cut down notable administrative expenditure (which would necessarily mean a direct clash with a powerfully entrenched bureaucracy) or to raise new revenue (which, given the inelasticity of land revenue, meant increased indirect taxation, never a popular measure), there was not much scope for a radical change in provincial policies. An added constraint was Gandhi's prohibitionist fad, which threatened to reduce one of the major sources of provincial revenue.

Financial constraints were not the only factor to influence business–Congress relations in the provinces. Labour problems also played an increasing role, due to the rapid growth of labour militancy in India from the mid-1930s and the increased political weight of the trade unions.

India's labour movement, which had grown steadily throughout the 1920s, had suffered a setback at the end of the 1920s and during the early 1930s, because of repression, internal splits, and the unfavourable impact of the depression on workers' struggles. From 1935 onwards, the movement had started regaining strength. The number of registered unions and their membership showed an upward trend, strikes became more frequent, and the two largest federations of trade unions initiated a process of gradual rapprochement.[24] As the trade union movement grew in strength, it was able to make its weight felt in politics. The provincial elections in 1937 witnessed attempts at an adjustment between the Congress and the trade unions over the sharing of the seats reserved for labour. While this was not possible everywhere, nevertheless the Congress was able to capture approximately half of the seats reserved for labour in the provincial assemblies.[25] To get workers' votes in the elections to the general urban seats, the Congress made big promises to them in its electoral manifesto. This attitude paid off, as shown by the victories of the Congress candidates in most of the towns with a sizeable working-class population.[26] The advent of Congress ministries in the majority of the provinces no doubt raised great expectations among workers and prompted them towards greater militancy. During 1937, the labour scene in India was dominated by the great strike of the Calcutta jute workers, which affected an industry dominated by British capital, and received encouragement from the Congress. The Calcutta strike was a clear warning that labour unrest was growing, and there was not much likelihood that the Congress-ruled provinces of Bombay, Madras, and the United Provinces, which had a sizeable industrial labour force,[27] would be spared. As a matter of fact, the new Congress ministry in the United Provinces was immediately confronted with a general strike of the millworkers in Kanpur.

Capitalists, particularly the large section which had manufacturing interests, were naturally disturbed at the growing incidence of strikes, and they were aware that Congress propaganda had helped nurture discontent among the workers. Despite handsome profits made in 1936–7,[28] they still entertained fears of a recession. Already the sugar industry, which had gone through an unprecedented boom in 1932–6, had been affected by an overproduction crisis, mainly due to unregulated competition among mills. Another distressing factor was the new depression which had started to affect the industrial countries. All this made Indian capitalists little inclined towards making concessions to workers and suspicious of the efforts made by the Congress to woo labour.

The new Congress ministries therefore were faced with a difficult task: they had to try to conciliate the interests of two groups which had tended to support them in the elections, both of which equally hoped that Congress rule would bring them benefits. The ministries were in danger of being subjected to contradictory pressures from above and below. The Congress High Command, with which the capitalists wielded more influence than the trade unions, was likely to pressurize them towards taking a stand against labour; while local Congress organizations, more responsive to direct pressure from workers, would advocate support for their demands. The provincial governments would be hard put to find a middle way.

Apart from the problems posed by labour unrest, the Congress ministries would also have to arbitrate between the demands of urban and rural interests. Though conciliation was possible in many cases, as linkages were numerous between urban capitalists and big landlords in the countryside,[29] there was nevertheless the possibility that urban and rural interests would increasingly compete for scarce resources. Some capitalists were undoubtedly scared that, buttressed by Gandhi's well-known and increasingly radical rural bias, the Congress ministries would follow a course of hostility towards modern industry and would restrict the opportunities for the urban interests to enlarge themselves.[30] Given the difficult conditions in which the Congress ministries came to power, it is not surprising that business interests harboured some misgivings about their future course of policy. Generally speaking, no capitalists were offered ministerial posts by the Congress,[31] which preferred to rely on its own party workers, even if their technical qualifications were limited. This could only add to the diffidence of the capitalists. The only section which really showed enthusiasm at the advent of the Congress ministries was the Marwari group led by G.D. Birla. Birla and his friends had most of their interests in Bengal, a non-Congress province, and in the Indian States.[32] Therefore they could afford to take a long-term view of developments and see the new ministries as one more step towards a peaceful transfer of power at the Centre.[33] The capitalists who had the bulk of their interests in the Congress-ruled provinces, and particularly those in the Bombay Presidency, were more closely concerned with the policies of the Congress ministries.

### Economic and Social Policies of the
### Congress Ministries in the Initial Phase
### (Summer 1937–Spring 1938)

The single biggest factor to influence the course of relations between Indian business and the newly formed Congress ministries was labour unrest. The advent of popular ministries encouraged workers in the Congress-ruled provinces to press for the redress of grievances which had been accumulating for the previous few years. Though most authors emphasize the economic aspects of labour demands in that period,[34] there is no doubt that political changes also played a role in the new upsurge in labour militancy. The election manifesto issued by the Congress in 1936 had promised to secure for workers 'a decent standard of living, hours of work and conditions of labour in conformity, as far as the economic conditions in the country permit, with international standards, suitable machinery for the settlement of disputes between employers and workers, protection against the economic consequences of old age, sickness and unemployment, and the right . . . to form unions and to strike for the protection of their interests'.[35] V.V. Giri, himself a trade unionist and the Labour and Industries Minister of Madras, testified in his memoirs to the great expectations raised among workers by the advent of the Congress governments.[36] In most provinces the new ministries were soon confronted with an unprecedented wave of labour disputes; 1937 and 1938 were peak years in terms of incidence of labour trouble; one has to go back to 1928–9 to find comparable unrest. What is also significant is that while in 1937 Bengal was the province most affected by disputes, due to the long strike in the jute mills, in 1938 the focus of the disturbances tended to shift to the Congress-ruled provinces, particularly Madras and the United Provinces. In 1937 Bengal accounted for more than two-thirds of all man-days lost in India due to industrial disputes, but in 1938 its share had fallen to less than one-third. Conversely, the share of the five Congress-ruled provinces of Bihar, Bombay, the Central Provinces, Madras, and the United Provinces rose from less than one-third to more than two-thirds of the total.[37] Table 2 shows the changes in the location of disputes over 1937 and 1938.

In most Congress-ruled provinces, the number of disputes and of workers involved in them did not actually increase over 1937 and 1938, but the number of man-days lost multiplied spectacularly, an indication that strikes lasted longer. In 1938, half of the disputes ended in a settlement which was at least partly satisfactory for the

TABLE 2

Industrial Disputes in Selected Provinces in 1937 and 1938

| I | II | III | IV | V | VI | VII |
|---|---|---|---|---|---|---|
| Bengal | 166 | 365,699 | 6,090,883 | 157 | 162,888 | 2,698,742 |
| Bihar | 14 | 14,946 | 222,509 | 21 | 27,471 | 1,103,130 |
| Bombay | 88 | 109,858 | 897,211 | 111 | 62,188 | 694,118 |
| Central Prov. | 5 | 9,701 | 222,094 | 14 | 18,260 | 307,043 |
| Madras | 61 | 60,980 | 656,404 | 52 | 65,290 | 2,226,049 |
| United Prov. | 15 | 63,350 | 704,940 | 14 | 53,851 | 2,046,868 |
| All India | 379 | 647,801 | 8,982,257 | 399 | 401,075 | 9,198,708 |

I Province; II no. of industrial disputes in 1937; III no. of workers involved in 1937; IV no. of man-days lost in 1937; V no. of disputes in 1938; VI no. of workers involved in 1938; VII no. of man-days lost in 1938.

*Sources:* C. Revri, *The Indian Trade Union Movement. An Historical Outline* (Delhi, 1970), pp. 217–19. *Labour Gazette*, Bombay, June 1939, p. 768.

workers.[38] Among causes of disputes, wage demands came first, but significantly, demands for the recognition of trade unions were on the increase.[39] This reflected the spectacular growth of the trade union movement in 1937–8. The number of registered unions and their membership increased by 50 per cent in one year, an unprecedented fact in the history of the Indian labour movement.[40] Though the progress of unions was greatest in Madras, followed by the United Provinces, in other Congress-ruled provinces such as Bombay or Bihar, it was less than in Bengal.[41]

In the Congress-ruled provinces, Indian capital was generally dominant, and therefore bore the brunt of the labour unrest. In Madras and the United Provinces, where British-controlled mills employed approximately half of the workforce in the cotton textile industry,[42] the strikes tended to affect the Indian capitalists as much or even more than their British colleagues. In Madras, most of the strikes took place in or around Coimbatore where there were few British mills. In the United Provinces, the Kanpur strikes hit both the Indian and British millowners. The nationality of the owners made visibly little difference to the striking workers.

Turning now to the policy of the Congress ministries in labour matters, their dilemma is nicely, though somewhat naively, summed up by a labour historian, who writes:

> The [Congress] organization as a whole did not desire to alienate the vested interests. It was keen on retaining their friendship and cooperation. The Congress ministries were, therefore, faced with a difficult task; they had to do something to satisfy workers' demands but they had to see at the same time that employers did not get too angry or annoyed.[43]

Actually the Congress High Command was very conscious of the predicament in which the ministries found themselves, but it decided that, to avoid a bigger explosion on the labour front, concessions had to be made quickly to the workers. In October 1937 the Congress Labour Committee, after holding consultations with the labour ministers from the Congress-ruled provinces, passed a series of resolutions[44] aiming at the implementation of the programme of labour welfare chalked out in the Congress election manifesto. Yet the committee took care not to fix any time limit for the implementation of these measures and left each government free to choose the pace of the reforms. It limited itself to giving general guidelines.

The Congress provincial ministries responded by setting up enquiry committees to look into the question of wages in the textile industry. Such committees were formed in Bombay, the Central Provinces, and the United Provinces. They were non-official bodies, in which representatives of capital and labour sat beside political workers and academics. These committees were subjected to contradictory pressures from the unions and from the employers' associations. They generally recommended wage increases which, though substantial, amounted to no more than a partial compensation for the wage cuts made during the depression. Their recommendations could be described as moderate, and in accepting them, the Congress governments showed that, though they were committed to trying to better the lot of the workers, they had no desire to hit capitalist interests too hard. In the case of Kanpur, the enquiry committee appointed by the Congress government also recommended the recognition of the union, the Mazdoor Sabha, by the employers. The insistence in Kanpur on the recognition of the union was no doubt due to the fact that it was controlled by Congress workers who were close to the ministry.[45] Elsewhere the question of recognition of the unions was left in abeyance, pending the establishment of a new legislation on trade disputes, which some governments were contemplating for the near future. On the whole, the Congress ministries showed commendable moderation in dealing with uncompromising capitalists. In spite of it, they could not avoid antagonizing capitalist interests.

Apart from the labour policy, the economic and fiscal policies followed by the Congress ministries during their first months of tenure of office also had a direct impact upon their relations with Indian capitalists. These policies were generally characterized by great caution bordering on conservatism. The new Congress ministries barely introduced any change in the budgets prepared by the caretaker governments which had assumed office during the few months of constitutional bickerings prior to the final acceptance of office by the

Congress. The boldest step taken by some of the ministries was the issuing of provincial loans which were very successful with the public.[46]

The only exceptions to this cautious policy were the energetic measures taken by the Bihar and United Provinces governments to solve the overproduction crisis in the sugar industry of those two provinces. Firstly, a joint sugarcane conference, in which the representatives of the growers, manufacturers, and traders took part, was convened by the two governments in Lucknow at the end of September.[47] Following it and after various consultations with the interests directly concerned, the Government of Bihar passed in the Assembly a sugar factories control bill, which was soon followed by a similar bill passed by the United Provinces Assembly. Those bills aimed at regulating the supply of cane to the mills, in a way which would ensure remunerative prices for the cultivators and check overproduction. The Congress governments of Bihar and the United Provinces wanted basically to satisfy their rural clientele, especially the middle peasantry which had taken to sugarcane cultivation on a big scale, but they also wanted to conciliate the manufacturers who were a powerful lobby, especially since they had formed in 1937 a combine called the Sugar Syndicate. Therefore they introduced in their bills a clause which forced all sugar mills to join the syndicate.[48] This particular clause was irksome to some sugar millowners who had stayed away from the syndicate[49] but it helped to ensure a high degree of coordination among the producers. The bills proved beneficial to the sugar industry of Bihar and the United Provinces as well as to the growers. The only victim was the consumer, who had to pay a higher price for his sugar. In the case of the sugar industry, the Congress governments acted as mediators between two groups, the growers and the manufacturers, whose interests were easy to conciliate, but who had found it difficult to come to a direct agreement.

In other provinces, initial measures in favour of Indian industry included a review of the purchasing policies of the various government departments, with the aim of increasing the purchase of swadeshi goods,[50] and the appointment of various committees on industrial policy.[51]

The intentions of the Congress ministries in matters of economic and fiscal policies were made clearer at the time of the preparation of the new budgets for 1938–9, which were the first genuine Congress budgets. By then the financial situation of the provincial governments had slightly improved, following the payment of the first instalment by the Centre from the income-tax receipts.[52] Yet this increase would have to be partly used to compensate for the expected loss in excise revenue due to the introduction of prohibition in some provinces.[53] Therefore there would not be much scope for a large increase in expenditure, unless a government was ready to resort to deficit budgeting. The United Provinces government was the only Congress government which presented a deficit budget for 1938–9.[54] Other provincial governments pursued a more orthodox policy.[55] Generally the bulk of the small increases in expenditure went to education and rural development, two very Gandhian subjects, and industry got very little.[56] The Premier of the United Provinces, Pandit Pant, did not hide his rural bias. In a talk to merchants at the end of 1937, he stressed that industrialization would not solve the problem of unemployment to any appreciable extent in his populous province, and pledged to give priority to agricultural development.[57] In most provincial budgets, the bulk of the projected increases in aid to industry was directed towards the cottage and small-scale industries, particularly to the production of khaddar.[58]

The policies followed by the Congress governments during their first months in office were generally not very different from those followed by the non-Congress ministries during the dyarchy regime, nor did they differ widely from those followed by the non-Congress governments in the few provinces where the Congress had not come to power. The Congress governments made some concessions to the workers, largely to defuse a tense situation on the labour front, increased to some extent expenditure on rural development and cottage industries to consolidate their power base in the countryside, and generally let the bureaucracy operate with a more or less free hand.[59] But this cautious policy failed to satisfy the capitalist interests which had hoped for a more active industrial policy. It also created fears that their interests would be endangered. We shall now turn to the response of the business class to Congress policy in the provinces.

## The Initial Business Response

While analysing the responses of the Indian capitalists to the policies followed by the Congress provincial governments, one should not overlook the fact that they were dictated not only by provincial events, but also by the state of Indo-British economic relations, in particular by the trade negotiations which were being held between the two governments. The aim of these negotiations was to conclude a new agreement in place of the Ottawa agreement denounced by the Indian Central Legislative Assembly in 1936.[60] Indian businessmen were represented in those negotiations by Birla, Kasturbhai Lalbhai,[61] and Thakurdas as unofficial advisers to the Government of India. As long as there seemed to be a reasonable chance of reaching a satisfactory agreement with Britain on this question, businessmen were keen to avoid antagonizing the British authorities by extending too open a support to the Congress ministries. The trade negotiations influenced the attitude of the Indian capitalists in another more direct way: any increases in the wages of textile workers, such as were recommended by the various enquiry committees in some of the Congress-ruled provinces, were bound to result in an increase in the production cost of Indian cotton textiles and therefore to render imported textiles more competitive on the Indian market. Indian cotton millowners, still the largest group among Indian capitalists, could not at the same time accept a reduction in the duties on British textiles entering India (a concession which the British Board of Trade urged them to make, in exchange for more advantageous conditions to Indian goods in the UK) and bear increased internal costs of production. This extraneous factor explains largely why Indian capitalists so stubbornly opposed any concessions to workers in matters of wages and therefore came to an open clash with the Congress governments.

Relations between the Congress and business became particularly strained in the United Provinces because of continuous labour unrest among the textile workers in Kanpur. In that town most of the mills were controlled by British capitalists, yet there was a lot of Indian capital invested in them. Besides, two of the biggest cotton magnates, Sir J.P. Srivastava and Lala Padampat Singhania, were Indian, the latter also one of the leaders of FICCI and a well-known supporter of the Congress. When the Pant ministry was formed in July 1937, a general strike had been going on in Kanpur for several weeks. After some initial hesitation, the new ministry decided to ask the millowners to make one major concession to the workers by recognizing the Mazdoor Sabha. The capitalists, both British and Indian, who had formed the Employers' Association of Northern India to defend their interests against labour,[62] were most reluctant to accord recognition; they alleged that the Mazdoor Sabha was not a genuine union but a political organization preaching the overthrow of the capitalist system. Eventually they were forced to give in to government pressure, but they resented it considerably.[63] In fact, they never forgave the United Provinces Congress government for having sided with the workers. A few years later in the course of a private conversation Sir J.P. Srivastava revealed that the Indian industrialists of Kanpur, all Hindu, became thereafter such bitter opponents of the Congress ministry that they went to the length of subsidizing the Muslim League in the province.[64] Another result of the strike was the appointment of the Cawnpore Labour Enquiry Committee to look into the question of wages in the textile industry. While the committee was doing its work, the millowners under the pretext of an incident in a mill, withdrew their recognition of the Mazdoor Sabha.[65] Therefore, when the committee submitted its report in April 1938 recommending a 21 per cent increase in wages in the textile industry (it only amounted to a restoration of three-fifths of the wage cuts made during the depression), the situation was tense, and the rejection of the report by the Employers' Association triggered a new general strike which lasted almost two months. Once again the question of the recognition of the Mazdoor Sabha became the main issue of contention between the two parties. During this second strike, the government, under pressure from the local Congress organization, gave some support, though half-hearted, to the strikers,[66] and eventually the millowners had to give in again, though in the course of their negotiations with the ministry they managed to make their recognition of the Sabha conditional upon changes in its internal constitution. The attitude of the government came in for strong criticism even from Singhania, a Congress supporter,[67] and in the United Provinces relations between Indian business and the Congress remained tense.

In the United Provinces, the Indian capitalists took a very uncompromising line in their dealings with the industrial workers and resented the attempts at arbitration made by the Congress ministry, because they thought that the government was biased in favour of labour. There are specific reasons for the failure of the Congress and the capitalists to find an adjustment. One of the reasons was the weight of the British in the capitalist class of the United Provinces, and the close links between them and Indian capitalists. British capitalists had no reason to be particularly friendly to a Congress ministry, and their stand influenced their Indian colleagues. Another factor leading to confrontation was the strong position enjoyed by the Congress Socialists and other Leftist elements in the Congress provincial organization. These forces were able to pressurize the ministry into taking a stand in favour of the workers, thus further antagonizing the capitalists.

In other Congress-ruled provinces Indian businessmen generally followed a less uncompromising line, but this did not prevent limited clashes with the provincial governments. In the Bombay Presidency, where the bulk of the cotton textile industry was concentrated, the Congress ministry immediately set up a Textile Enquiry Committee to review the wage situation in the textile centres of the province. Businessmen complained that they were not sufficiently represented on the committee, and they opposed the demands of the unions for a sizeable increase in wages, under the pretext that the financial situation of the mills was precarious.[68] The proposals of the committee, embodied in the interim report released in February 1938,[69] were a compromise between the extreme demands of labour and the negative stand taken by the millowners. The immediate increases granted were not negligible[70] and they seemed to satisfy most workers, if not the most militant section of the working class. The millowners, according to the Governor of Bombay, Sir Roger Lumley, 'took some time in making up their minds',[71] but faced with the possibility of a general strike, they had no choice but to accept the recommendations of the committee. Yet the *Indian Textile Journal,* the mouthpiece of the Bombay millowners, did not hesitate to accuse the Bombay government of having played upon the threat of a strike to force them into accepting those recommendations.[72]

According to Lumley, the millowners, in exchange for their acceptance of the report, were able to extract from the ministry the promise that it would not introduce any new labour welfare measures for at least one year.[73] The Bombay government also committed itself to seeking an agreement with the Centre and other provincial governments for the standardization of wages in the textile industry on an all-India scale, so that the millowners in the Bombay Presidency would not find themselves handicapped *vis-à-vis* their upcountry competitors, the millowners of other provinces and the Indian States who did not have to contend with similar burdens.

Though in March 1938 Lumley could write about the new outlook in Bombay that 'the prospect of serious labour trouble in the mills' had 'faded away',[74] and could rightly ascribe the change in the labour situation to the advent of a Congress ministry, the price paid by the millowners for industrial peace was indeed heavy. The foreseeable increase in the production costs of Indian textiles reduced the chances of reaching an agreement with Lancashire over the question of the duties on British textiles, and thus the Indo-British trade negotiations, the final success of which had become dependent on a direct agreement between Indian and British textile manufacturers,[75] were more or less doomed to failure.

In other Congress-ruled provinces, capitalists faced with similar labour unrest also made concessions on wages. This was the case in Coimbatore where, following a strike in the mills, the Madras government referred the problem to a court of enquiry whose rulings were accepted by both parties, and in the Central Provinces where an enquiry committee was set up on the Bombay model.

Thus in those Congress-ruled provinces which had a textile industry, the millowners were forced to make some concessions to labour in order to avoid more widespread trouble. Generally the Congress ministries took an attitude which, though only mildly sympathetic to labour, was enough to create suspicions among the capitalists that the Congress was becoming hostile to them. Actually it could be argued that by pressurizing the industrialists into giving in to moderate labour demands, the Congress saved them from a more dangerous confrontation. But most Indian capitalists were not farsighted enough to perceive this, and they tended to see only the immediate cost incurred by them from the policies of the Congress governments.

There were also differences in the responses of the capitalists, which were directly linked to the state of their relations with the Congress organizations in their respective provinces. In that respect, the United Provinces and Bombay represented two extreme cases. In the United Provinces, relations between local big business and the Congress had been strained for a long time, and among Congress national leaders it was Nehru, not a great friend of the capitalists,[76] who wielded the greatest influence. The labour trouble in Kanpur brought these already strained relations to a breaking point. In Bombay, big business, particularly the Ahmedabad millowners, had played a great part in Congress politics for many years, and benefited from close links with Patel, who kept a careful watch on the activities of the Bombay ministry. Ready access to the ministry allowed local capitalists to negotiate when problems arose and often reach some kind of compromise. Indian capitalists, generally dissatisfied with the labour policies of the Congress ministries, could not find great compensations in their economic policies. It is not that they had exaggerated expectations in that matter. They were very conscious of the many limitations under which the Congress ministries had to function, but they pointed out that even within such a restricted framework as that of provincial autonomy the ministries had powers 'which they could exercise for the development and progress of trade and industry'.[77] Speaking in March 1937 at the annual conference of Indian insurance companies, the Bombay business magnate Walchand Hirachand had expressed the hope that in the future Congress governments would be able 'to act in such a way . . . as to directly benefit Swadeshi enterprises'.[78] Yet, the actual policies of the Congress ministries during their first months in office disappointed even their supporters in the business class. In March 1938, the *Indian Textile Journal* came out with a severe condemnation of the industrial policy of the Congress governments and asked: 'Would the Congress play into the hands of the enemies of the industrial advancement of the country?'[79]

The discontent in business circles with the policy of the Congress in the provinces manifested itself in the tendency by big business groups to step up investment in the non-Congress provinces and even more in the Indian States. The exact extent of this movement is difficult to gauge but a few striking examples suggest that it was not altogether negligible.[80] Even pro-Congress businessmen, like Lala Padampat Singhania of Kanpur, increasingly preferred to set up new factories in the Indian States where wages were lower, labour legislation almost non-existent, and taxation practically nil. Apart from the immediate profit motive, such investments were also a clear, though discreet, way of conveying to the Congress leadership that the policies followed by the Congress ministries were antagonizing Indian capitalist interests.

What was also significant of the mood in Indian business was that in the face of the growing challenge from labour and the ambiguous attitude of the Congress, capitalists tended to close their ranks and forget old enmities and feuds. In Kanpur, the millowners, British and Indian, pro-Congress and anti-Congress, displayed remarkable unity in their fight against the Mazdoor Sabha and in their difficult negotiations with the Congress ministry. In the Bombay Presidency, the old rivalry between the textile manufacturers of Ahmedabad and Bombay city became less apparent. The Ahmedabad millowners used their own good relations with the ministry and Patel to negotiate on behalf of the entire textile industry of the province. Sectional differences among capitalists were becoming less acute and all-India organizations such as FICCI were strengthening themselves. In what amounted to a spectacular break with a ten-year-old policy, the Tatas, the biggest Indian business group joined the FICCI in 1937. Their move was directly related to the advent of the Congress ministries: the Tatas, who had the bulk of their interests in the Congress-ruled provinces of Bombay, Bihar, and the Central Provinces, wanted to benefit from the privileged relationship existing between the FICCI and the Congress. But at the same time it testified to the growing trend of unity among Indian capitalists in a threatening environment.

It seems that by the spring of 1938 the Congress High Command became aware of the danger of letting its good relations with the Indian business class be threatened by the policies of the provincial ministries. Pressure from the top leadership probably explains in part the shift which became noticeable in the labour and economic policies of the Congress ministries at that time.

### The Shift in the Policies of the Congress Governments and the Improvement in Relations between Congress and Business

In the spring of 1938, the Congress governments started making efforts at placating capitalist interests and at improving their relations with the business world. The persistence of labour unrest in the Congress-ruled provinces even after substantial wage increases had been granted to the workers was a decisive factor. Congress politicians became increasingly suspicious of the motivations of the labour leaders in launching agitations, and they started to view communist infiltration as the root cause of all the trouble. This led to a new policy in the matter of trade unions. Previously, the Congress leadership had sought adjustments with the existing organizations, particularly the All India Trade Union Congress (AITUC) and the National Trade Union Federation (NTUF), the two biggest federations, which had set up a joint council in 1938 to coordinate their activities. But neither of these organizations was controlled by elements close to the Congress leadership: the AITUC was led by a coalition of Congress socialists and communists while the NTUF was the preserve of moderate politicians linked to the Servants of India Society. They were therefore not amenable to direct pressure from the Congress High Command and the latter had thus no way of directly controlling the labour movement. In the spring of 1938 the Congress leadership decided to set up a new movement which would be under their control, and would be organized on the model of the Ahmedabad Mazdoor Mahajan, a Gandhian union which had established amicable relations with the employers in that big textile centre. In an interview to the *Bombay Chronicle* Patel stressed the necessity of having workers' organizations which did not believe in the policy of class struggle, and he chided the existing unions.[81] Congress leaders made use of the Gandhi Sevak Sangh to create the nucleus of the future Hind Mazdoor Sabha (HMS) which became for a few years the labour branch of the Congress, prior to the creation of the Indian National Trade Union Congress (INTUC). Not surprisingly the Bombay government was in the forefront of the attempts at setting up new, more docile unions. The Minister for Local Government, L.M. Patil, proclaimed the intention of the Bombay Provincial Congress Committee to start their own working class organizations.[82] The Bombay Chief Minister, B.G. Kher, came under attack from trade unionists for using government money in order to help form pro-Congress unions.[83] But the main thrust in the new labour policy of the Congress governments was towards the introduction of a new legislation on labour relations, which would help to establish durable industrial peace in the provinces, and thus check the flow of capital towards the Indian States.

The existing legislation, both central and provincial, had been effective in checking the growth of the trade union movement but it had no proper machinery for the settlement of industrial disputes. New legislation was mainly aimed at remedying this defect. The Madras government, dismayed by the spate of labour conflicts in this traditionally peaceful province, was the first one to move in that direction. On 22 April 1938 the Labour Minister, V.V. Giri, presented the draft of a bill under the name of Madras Industrial Disputes Investigation and Settlement Act.[84] In Madras it never reached the statute book, but it served as the basis of similar attempts in other provinces. In Bombay, the Congress ministry took up the matter seriously and 'improved' considerably Giri's initial draft. In September 1938 they submitted to the Provincial Legislature the Bombay Trade Disputes Act, which was the most complex and effective piece of legislation ever devised in India for the settlement of industrial disputes. Though a provision for compulsory arbitration initially introduced by the framers of the bill was deleted from the final version,[85] the bill included a provision for a compulsory delay which could extend to several months before a strike or a lockout could begin, a measure which drew applause from the Governor of Bombay himself.[86] Introducing the bill in the Bombay Legislative Assembly, Kher made clear the intention of his government 'to promote legislation aiming at the prevention of strikes and lockouts as far as possible'.[87] Though the bill was theoretically aimed as much at lockouts as at strikes, it was nevertheless obvious that its framers were above all interested in stopping strikes. In any case, as lockouts were generally declared in retaliation to strikes, it could be assumed that if there were no more strikes the incidence of lockouts would tend to be less. The intention of curbing strikes was openly avowed by the Chief Minister who, in his Assembly speech, condemned labour unrest in the strongest terms and proclaimed that 'his government stood for class collaboration and not for class conflict'.[88]

Though the framers of the bill pretended to keep a balance between capital and labour, a detailed examination of its many clauses brings out the fact that it was heavily weighted in favour of the capitalist side. For instance, though strikes and lockouts were apparently put on the same footing, only strikes were penalized and not lockouts.[89] The penalty for illegal strikes, which was six months' imprisonment, was extremely high. There was also a complex clause regarding the registration of trade unions about which Nehru who, surprisingly enough, stated in a confidential note that 'on the whole the Act seemed a good one',[90] remarked that 'company unions' were 'definitely encouraged and given very great advantages over independent unions'. He also criticized the encouragement given in the bill to occupational unions, underlining that it would 'lead to the formation of numerous petty unions, usually on caste and community lines'.

The bill met with strong opposition in the Legislative Assembly from trade unionists, Ambedkar's independent labourites, and the Muslim League, but the government was in such a hurry to have it passed that it did not even allow the formation of a Select Committee to look more closely into its merits. Eventually the bill was passed on 5 November 1938 amidst angry scenes.[91] The haste with which the government acted showed that they wanted to put the bill into effect as soon as possible in order to establish their control over the labour movement in Bombay.

Yet the immediate effect of the passing of the bill was to provoke a general strike in the Bombay Presidency in protest against the 'Black Act', as well as demonstrations of solidarity in the other provinces. In Bombay city, the strike was joined by approximately half of the mill-hands, but it failed to gain much support in Ahmedabad and Sholapur.[92] The determined way in which the police under the Congress Raj dealt with the strikers[93] shocked the public,[94] but it showed that the ministry was determined to curb labour unrest at any cost.

The firm stand taken by the government against the general strike earned it the approval of the Bombay capitalists, who had had their own initial reservations regarding some of the clauses of the bill.[95] They could now forget them and look forward to an improvement in the labour situation in the province. The turn in government labour policy was soon epitomized by its attitude to the Bombay seamen's strike of December 1938. Not only did it refuse any kind of support to the strikers, but it even adopted harsh repressive measures against them.[96] The fact that many seamen in Bombay were employed by Scindia, the big navigation company led by Walchand Hirachand who had links with the ministry, might also partly account for the special callousness displayed by the Congress ministry.

The new attitude of the Congress governments *vis-à-vis* labour, much in evidence in Bombay, manifested itself also in other Congress-ruled provinces. In the United Provinces, after the conditional recognition of the Mazdoor Sabha by the employers and its capture by communist elements, labour trouble remained endemic in Kanpur, but the Congress ministry ceased to show sympathy to the workers.[97] In Bihar, where conflict erupted in the Dalmia and Tata factories, which employed the bulk of industrial labour in the province, the government tried to reassure capitalists and contemplated the introduction of a trade disputes act on the Bombay model.[98]

During 1939, as compared to 1938, although there was a slight increase in the number of industrial disputes in India, the number of workers involved and days lost showed a downward trend, and strikes tended to be shorter in duration.[99] It is difficult to know if the new legislation in Bombay had an impact, since it came into operation only at the end of the year. What is clear is that the rapid pace of growth of the trade union movement in 1937–8 did not continue.[100]

If there were no spectacular strikes comparable to the Kanpur strike of 1938, a disturbing trend from the capitalists' point of view was the appearance of a new phenomenon, the stay-in strike. The first one took place in a Bombay textile mill in April 1939, and was strongly condemned by the provincial government.[101] It then spread to Madras and the Chief Minister, Rajagopalachari, indicted it in the severest terms in the Legislative Assembly.[102] Both ministries insisted upon the illegal character of such actions, but the existing legislation was not equipped to deal specifically with stay-in strikes. Therefore, in 1939, though there was some improvement on the labour front, industrial peace remained an elusive goal.

While the new labour policy adopted by the Congress ministries did not succeed in radically curbing labour unrest, it was nevertheless a welcome development for Indian capitalists. It showed that their fears of seeing the Congress adopt a line of hostility to capitalist interests were unfounded. The Congress was in fact striving for conciliation of different class interests: once it had given some satisfaction to the workers, it naturally tended to conciliate business interests. The Congress Left was not strong enough to oppose that policy, although in one or two provinces it could influence government policy to a certain extent and make more difficult an adjustment with the capitalists.

There were also encouraging signs in the economic policies of the provincial governments, although concrete advantages gained by businessmen from such policies remained necessarily limited. The High Command increasingly tended to intervene on behalf of capitalist interests with the various provincial governments. Thus in July 1938 Patel, in a circular addressed to all the Congress chief ministers,[103] urged them to ensure all government business with genuine swadeshi companies. He also asked them to put pressure on the textile industry and other protected industries to do the same. In February 1939, the AICC assured a big Indian chemicals firm that their instructions to the provincial governments were 'to patronise Indian industries in preference to foreign industries'.[104] In August 1939, Patel intervened personally with the Bombay Chief Minister to prevent the granting of a licence for the electrification of Gujarat to a big British firm.[105] In Bombay the provincial government gave its guarantee to a few industrial projects, and thus helped their promoters to raise capital for them.[106] The Madras Cabinet, urged by Patel, helped a big cement combine to get a licence for the exploitation of a mineral quarry.[107] During the last phase of the Congress rule in the provinces, closer links were established between capitalist interests and Congress politicians, particularly in Bombay, but naturally there is little factual evidence available on such matters.

The improvement in the relations between Indian business and the Congress provincial governments facilitated the work of the National Planning Committee set up by the Congress at the end of 1938. Actually the decision of setting up such a committee was taken at a conference of industries ministers of the provincial governments. Business observers also took part, and Indian big business was fully associated with the work of the committee, which benefited from the active collaboration of the Congress ministries.[108] The conference also considered the possibilities of taking some immediate measures for the development of medium-scale industries in some of the provinces. An All India Planning Commission was entrusted with the task of drafting a programme of immediate action,[109] but its work was cut short by the war and the resignation of the Congress ministries.

The rapprochement between Indian business and the Congress was facilitated by the breach which took place between the unofficial advisers and the Government of India in the Indo-British trade negotiations. It started with the failure of the direct talks held in Simla in May 1938 between a Lancashire delegation and the representatives of the Indian textile industry.[110] Then after a few more months of protracted negotiations, in September 1938 the unofficial advisers advocated rejection of the last offer of the British Board of Trade; and the final negotiation resulting in the March 1939 agreement took place only between officials, the business community not being associated any more in the process.[111] The policies of the Congress ministries had a direct effect on the negotiations, insofar as they refused to give the advisers any guarantee that they would not impose any more burdens upon the textile industry, thus preventing the latter from making concessions to Lancashire which would have permitted a settlement with the Board of Trade.[112]

The March 1939 agreement drew unanimous condemnation in India from political as well as from business circles. It helped to further consolidate the rapprochement between business and the Congress at the national level; but from the end of 1938 onwards financial difficulties in the provinces had put the relations between Indian business and the Congress governments under fresh strain and threatened to cancel all the gains made during the previous period.

### The Final Phase of the Congress Ministries: New Strains in Congress–Business Relations

Towards the end of 1938, the Congress provincial ministries faced an impending financial crisis, and they resorted to measures which alienated capitalist interests to a certain extent. The framing of the new budgets for 1939–40 forced the ministries to take a closer look at the precarious condition of their finances, due on the one hand to the loss of revenue caused by the introduction of prohibition, and on the other hand to the necessity of increasing expenditure if projected measures for rural upliftment were to be effectively implemented. During the debate on the budget in the United Provinces Legislative Assembly in March 1939, Sir J.P. Srivastava pointed out that in the last twenty months the provincial government had incurred supplementary expenditure up to Rs 1.6 crores, while the loss in its excise revenue due to prohibition amounted to Rs 0.4 crores. Therefore supplementary resources of 2 crores had to be found, of which approximately 1.3 crores were already provided by the levy of various small taxes and duties, but there remained a balance of Rs 0.7 crores.[113] Though the United Provinces was a special case, even a financially sound province like Bombay was looking for new sources of revenue.[114] The Congress ministries had therefore no alternative but to increase taxation, however unpopular such a move was bound to be. The only choice which they could exercise was regarding which categories of the population would have to bear the burden of the increase. Though Bihar and Assam, two almost exclusively agricultural provinces, tried to introduce an agricultural income tax, Congress ministries in other provinces sought to avoid taking such a step which would create opposition to the party in the countryside, especially among the landholding classes which were the main power base of the Congress regimes. Therefore they decided to shift the main burden towards the less inflammable and less strategic urban areas.

The possibilities of levying new taxes were severely limited by the constitution, which reserved the levy of income tax of any kind to the Central Government. The United Provinces government tried to get around the difficulty by introducing an employments tax, which was an indirect way of taxing the incomes of merchants and employers of labour. Not surprisingly their proposal met with determined opposition from the trading and industrial interests of the province. After the employments tax bill had been passed by the Assembly on 16 April 1939, a protest conference was convened, in which prominent businessmen participated.[115] A few days later a memorandum was sent to the Viceroy by seven associations representing the bulk of commercial and industrial capital in the province, underlining that the tax was *ultra vires* of a provincial government, and asking the Viceroy to refer the case to the newly established Federal Court.[116] The last months of Congress rule in the United Provinces saw the local business class put up a stiff fight against the financial policy of the Congress ministry.

In other Congress-ruled provinces the ministries generally followed a more cautious policy, and the projected increases in taxation were less, but even the modest proposals regarding taxation of urban incomes were strongly resented by the business class. In Bombay the ministry sought to increase the electricity duty, and to introduce an urban immovable property tax, as well as a sales tax on petrol and cloth.[117] In Madras the Rajagopalachari ministry moved a bill for the imposition of a general sales tax, which the Chief Minister defended openly on the ground that part of the burden of taxation had to be shifted from the cultivator to the urban trader.[118]

In Bombay, business opposition to the financial policy of the ministry centred around the urban property tax and the sales tax on cloth. Opposition to the former ran high, because of the speculative boom which had been taking place in Bombay for many years and which had incited many traders to invest heavily in urban properties. A renowned economist defended the proposal on the ground that it would help to curb unhealthy speculation, and would act as an incentive to investment in industry, thus ultimately proving a boon to capitalist interests;[119] but these sophisticated arguments cut no ice with the merchant classes which continued to agitate against the bill until the resignation of the ministry.[120]

The sales tax on cloth raised an even stronger storm in the textile industry, although in that case also it was argued by a pro-Congress economist that since the tax would be levied on imported cloth as well, it would not have an adverse effect on the local mills.[121] The unexpectedly violent reaction of the millowners to this relatively minor issue could be explained by the difficult situation in which the textile industry in the Bombay Presidency found itself in 1939, after a few years of continuous prosperity. The major causes of the new difficulties seem to have been the bad crops which reduced the purchasing power of the peasantry, the renewed vigour of the Japanese offensive on the Indian market,[122] and the increased competition from upcountry mills in India where the cost of labour was lower than in the Bombay Presidency. In July 1939, in Bombay city alone four mills had been forced to close down, making 18,000 workers idle, while most of the mills had ceased to work a full double-shift.[123] This difficult situation led the millowners to fiercely oppose all attempts at imposing supplementary burdens on them. In March 1939, Kasturbhai Lalbhai a friend of the Congress, delivered a scathing attack on the policies of the Congress governments towards the textile industry.[124] From April 1939 onwards, Lumley saw evidence of a 'widening breach between Congress and the millowners'.[125] The latter tried to avoid giving their workers the supplementary wage increase to which they had committed themselves in accepting the recommendations of the Textile Labour Enquiry Committee, but they could not bring the government to support them, and eventually had to pay up.[126] Failure to avoid an increase in their labour costs prompted the Bombay and Ahmedabad millowners to try to obtain the agreement of the entire textile industry to a scheme of reduction of output.[127] But millowners in other regions, less hit by the crisis, refused to countenance the scheme and the industrialists of western India were left in the lurch.[128]

They were more successful in their fight against the proposal for the fixation of a minimum wage, which the Textile Labour Enquiry Committee, still working on its final report, was known to be contemplating. In August 1939, Gulzarilal Nanda, Parliamentary Secretary to the Government of Bombay, and the real power in matters of labour policy, hinted, while the committee was still sitting, that in view of the difficult situation in the textile industry, the government would oppose any move tending to put up wages.[129]

With the worsening of the situation in September 1939, the millowners sought more radical measures. Thus the Ahmedabad millowners obtained the agreement from Patel to a 20 per cent cut in wages, to be implemented after discussions with the unions.[130] Yet the same Patel restrained the Bombay government from sanctioning a 20 per cent increase in the price of cloth, as demanded by the industry.[131] Therefore just on the eve of the war, which suddenly ended the crisis, the situation in the textile industry of the Bombay Presidency was so chaotic that it tended to affect adversely the relations between the largest group of capitalists in the province and the Congress ministry.

Apart from the United Provinces and Bombay, other provinces also witnessed a deterioration in the relations between Indian business and the Congress. In Madras, where there was tremendous opposition to the sales tax proposal from the merchant community, a new provincial loan met with little success, a fact which the Governor of the province attributed to the hostility of capitalist interests to the Congress ministry.[132] In Bihar, renewed trouble in the Tata factories created a tense atmosphere.[133]

The financial difficulties which the Congress ministries had to face made an adjustment between the overall compulsions of governmental action in the provinces and the sectional interests of Indian business more and more difficult. Even in Bombay, which of all the provinces had the government best disposed towards capitalist interests, tension was mounting. When its immediate interests were at stake, as was the case in the textile industry crisis of mid-1939, even the most pro-Congress section of the capitalist class, the Ahmedabad textile manufacturers, did not hesitate to violently attack the ministry and tried to pressurize it into taking unpopular measures. On the other hand even the most pro-capitalist among the Congress politicians, such as Patel, could not find any way of avoiding a clash with capitalist interests, without at the same time renouncing the basic tenets of their political faith, including prohibition, which was partly responsible for the aggravation of the financial crisis in the provinces. Patel must have been aware of all this when in July 1939 he mentioned for the first time the possibility of the Congress ministries resigning, if military expenditure was not drastically reduced and if the provinces were not granted a greater share of the income tax receipts.[134] Undue prolongation of the experiment of autonomous provinces without adequate financial resources would have led to a further deterioration in relations between the Congress and business in the provinces, which in its turn would have endangered the emerging alliance between the Congress and Indian big business, as symbolized by their collaboration in the National Planning Committee. The interests of both the capitalists and the Congress, therefore, required an end to this uneasy situation. This explains why the capitalists took with equanimity the news of the resignation of the Congress ministries under the pretext of Linlithgow's rash move in committing India to the war without prior consultation with the Assembly. While they had nothing to gain from a continuation of Congress rule in the provinces, the prospect of easy war profits became alluring. It was once again important to establish good relations with the British authorities, and a large section of the Indian business class set to the task. The Congress ministries went down unsung and unregretted. Yet with the benefit of hindsight, we can see that the 1937–9 period was decisive in placing the relations between the Congress and business on a more assured footing. It is worthwhile attempting a detailed assessment of it.

## Conclusion

The advent of the Congress governments in most of the provinces of India did not result in major changes in economic and fiscal policies, which were basic to the prosperity of Indian capitalists, since control of finances and customs remained in British hands. The impact of the new governments was felt mainly in the realm of labour and agrarian relations, two domains in which provincial governments had powers to legislate. It was also felt, though to a lesser extent, in the field of industrial policy. Large sections of the Indian capitalist class remained unaffected by the direct impact of the Congress ministries. Those businessmen who were engaged mainly in foreign trade, and also those who had the bulk of their interests in the non-Congress provinces and in the Indian States (including a large section of the Marwari community, the largest of the Indian business communities) did not suffer or gain as a result of the policies of the Congress. Given those limitations, the period under review saw significant developments which had a lasting influence on the relations between Indian business and the Congress.

The most important result of the period of provincial autonomy was a definite shift in the labour policies and ideology of the Congress. While in the previous period, starting with the Karachi declaration on fundamental rights, the Congress had tended to be vaguely sympathetic to workers' demands but had not been deeply involved in the labour movement (with the exception of Ahmedabad), it now found itself suddenly confronted with an unprecedented wave of labour unrest sweeping the entire country. Congress response to labour unrest was largely shaped by the fact that it had already established a relationship with the capitalists and could ill afford to upset it, since in the event of a new struggle with the British, it would again need financial help from the businessmen. Though the Congress governments made some concessions to the workers, they mainly aimed at keeping the labour movement within definite bounds. To achieve this, Congressmen were drawn into intervening more actively in the affairs of the labour movement. There they clashed with other organized groups, particularly with the Communists, who were not very strong but had pockets of influence mainly in Bombay and Kanpur. As a result of this confrontation, the Congress labour policy became dominated by a fear of Communist infiltration, which drove them towards following a policy of greater moderation. For the Congress, labour policy became largely synonymous with labour administration; struggles were seen as unnecessary and dangerous and direct peaceful dialogue between employers and workers was favoured as the only solution to all problems. The Bombay Trade Disputes Act expressed the essence of the Congress philosophy of labour relations: conciliation was to be favoured at all costs. Though this approach tended to work to the advantage of the capitalists, it could also clash with their interests, since in some cases they themselves sought confrontation and were prevented from achieving it. Yet the Congress blueprint for industrial relations was clearly designed to favour capitalist interests, and the Indian business class, which prior to 1937 had harboured fears that the Congress would not be able to control labour, could feel reassured that a Congress Raj would be as effective as the British Raj, if not more so, in dealing with the working class.

In other fields also the policies pursued by the Congress ministries helped to dispel fears entertained by the capitalists. For instance, widespread apprehensions about nationalization of public services and key industries were set at rest by the policy of collaboration with private enterprises pursued in the Congress-ruled provinces.

The question of capitalist attitudes to the policy of rural upliftment followed by the Congress ministries is, however, more complex. Rajat Ray has argued that this policy was basically in the interest of the capitalists, since it ultimately aimed, by raising the standard of living in the countryside, at enlarging the internal market for industrial goods.[135] Yet, apart from the fact that it could be seen as a diversion of scarce resources which could have been utilized more efficiently in giving direct aid to industrial development, another inherent danger in this policy was underlined by the President of the United Provinces Merchants' Chamber. He expressed fears that, if not supported by appropriate measures to relieve indebtedness, the rural upliftment drive of the Congress governments might result only in an increase of social tension by raising expectations without being able to satisfy them.[136] Basically capitalists, though they might be interested in agricultural development, had a stake in the preservation of the social status quo in the countryside, and any attempt at disturbing it even mildly, as in the United Provinces with the 1939 Tenancy Bill, was looked upon with suspicion. The enlargement of the internal market was a secondary consideration compared to social peace. Yet the emergence of a wealthy tenantry in some regions like Gujarat was a welcome development, provided this group did not compete too directly with urban capitalists for governmental resources. In any case further research into the problem of rural–urban linkages, a neglected field, is needed before we can form a clearer picture of the situation.

As far as the related question of large versus small-scale and cottage industries is concerned, things are not very clear either. Though it can be rightly argued that there was no fundamental opposition of interests between the cotton mills and the handlooms (since the latter were largely fed with yarn from the mills), it should yet be noted that in Bombay, the millowners resisted attempts by the provincial ministry to allot production quotas to the mills and the handlooms, and to reserve a share of the market to cottage production.[137]

By the end of the 1930s despite the setting up of the National Planning Committee, the options of the Congress in matters of economic policy were far from clear and priorities had not been sorted out. Questions of relations between agriculture and industry, large- and small-scale industries, the place of foreign capital, were still unresolved. Congress economic thought was still in a state of flux, with 'Gandhians' and socialists battling about modern industrialization, and it took a few more years before a clearer picture started to emerge. Within a general framework marked by a growing trend of moderation in social matters, there were nevertheless significant nuances, in the way different Congress ministries tried to grapple with the problems. In that respect, Bombay and the United Provinces represented two opposite poles. In the United Provinces a trend of mildly radical populism was noticeable in some of the policies of the Congress government and it led to a permanent estrangement of vested interests from the ministry. In Bombay, by contrast, the Congress government displayed a strong anti-labour, pro-capitalist, and pro-rich peasant bias. Madras was a slightly special case, for the 'radical conservatism'[138] of the Chief Minister, Rajagopalachari, strongly influenced the policy of the provincial ministry and gave it a pro-rich peasant tinge more pronounced than elsewhere, while urban interests felt neglected. Business responses, therefore, varied from one province to another. In Bombay a close relationship developed between big business and the ministry, though it was endangered towards the end of the period by financial difficulties. Even British business expressed its satisfaction at the course of policy followed by the Congress ministry.[139] On the contrary, in the United Provinces big business was in the forefront of the opposition to the Congress government. In Madras also a trend of opposition was clearly noticeable. Everywhere Muslim businessmen tended to oppose the ministries and to align with the Muslim League.

Though Congress provincial governments were not always successful in accommodating Indian capitalist interests and could not prevent conflicts from arising between them and sections of the business class, an overall view of the two years of Congress rule in the provinces reveals that a certain amount of stabilization did occur in relations between business and Congress. While during the war many businessmen reverted to a policy of close collaboration with the British authorities in order to benefit from the war orders, the business class as a whole did not break with the Congress during the war period, and when the party made its final bid for power, businessmen found themselves in a position to influence developments to a certain extent.

The first years of Congress rule after 1947 witnessed a pattern in the relations between the Congress and business which bore some similarity to the one which had emerged during the period of provincial autonomy.


## Notes

I am grateful to Dr Sumit Sarkar for his comments on an earlier draft of this paper. The remaining errors of judgement are of course mine.

1. See B.R. Tomlinson, *The Political Economy of the Raj: The Economic of Decolonization in India 1914–1947* (London, 1979), p. 131.
2. This brief account of the politics of Indian business in 1932–6 is based on my unpublished Ph.D. dissertation, 'Indian Business and Nationalist Politics from 1931 to 1939: The Political Attitude of the Indigenous Capitalist Class in Relation to the Crisis of the Colonial Economy and the Rise of the Congress Party', Cambridge, 1978.
3. See ibid., pp. 166–71.
4. In February 1936, G.D. Birla held a series of talks with the Congress Parliamentary Board. He estimated the needs of the Congress for the election campaign at Rs 5 lakhs, of which he proposed to raise a large amount from the business community. See Bhulabhai Desai diary, entries for 2 and 10 February, Bhulabhai Desai Papers, Nehru Memorial Museum and Library (NMML), New Delhi .
5. David Arnold, *The Congress in Tamilnad: Nationalist Politics in South India, 1919–1937* (Delhi, 1977), p. 158.
6. This trend is noticed for the United Provinces in G. Pandey, *The Ascendancy of the Congress in Uttar Pradesh 1926–1934: A Study in Imperfect Mobilization* (Delhi, 1978), p. 57, and in Arnold, *The Congress in Tamilnad*, p. 168, for Madras.
7. Pandit Pant to Rajendra Prasad, 11 May 1936, intercepted letter. Government of India, Home (Poll.), 14 May 1936, National Archives of India (NAI), New Delhi.
8. Two of the most influential figures in Bombay big business, the cotton magnates and financiers Sir Purshottamdas Thakurdas and his cousin Sir Chunilal Mehta, pointedly refused to contribute. B.R. Tomlinson, *The Indian National Congress and the Raj, 1929–1942: The Penultimate Phase* (London, 1976), p. 82.
9. Ibid.
10. There was no seat reserved for commerce in the Northwest Frontier Province Assembly.

11. Singhania defeated Bagla by 101 votes to 67. P. Reeves et al., *A Handbook to Elections in Uttar Pradesh 1920–1951* (Delhi, 1975), p. 308.

12. Among them was Sir Cowasji Jehangir, a big Parsi financier and industrialist, who was elected from Bombay Central (Non-Muhammedan Urban).

13. They were Vikramjit Singh, a big Kanpur merchant and one of the leaders of the United Provinces Chamber of Commerce who contested on a Hindu Sabha ticket, and Lady Kailash Srivastava, Sir J.P.'s wife, who stood as independent. Reeves *et al., Elections in Uttar Pradesh.* p. 273.

14. The total number of voters grew from 7 to 36 millions. The really poor remained excluded, but there was an extension of the franchise to the urban working class and lower middle classes, and to the middle peasantry. See Tomlinson, *Indian National Congress and the Raj*, p. 71.

15. Among them A.H. Ispahani in Bengal and Ibrahim Rahimtoolla in Bombay.

16. Many Indian businessmen were heavily dependent upon government orders and contracts.

17. Muslim businessmen, who faced increasing competition even in their traditional fields from Hindus, tended to close ranks in the 1930s and to support the Muslim League. Hindu businessmen on the other hand, especially those living in the Muslim-majority provinces of Bengal and the Punjab, found the Congress too soft with the Muslims, and many supported the Hindu Mahasabha.

18. Thus businessmen pressurized the Congress into removing from their list of candidates some trade unionists whom they found too radical. In Bombay, the trade unionist Nimbkar lost the Congress ticket because of big business pressure. See *Times of India,* 11 November 1936. In Bihar, Seth Dalmia obtained the removal of a man who had organized a strike in his mills from the list of Congress candidates. Tomlinson, *Indian National Congress and the Raj*, p. 83.

19. In 1929–30, land revenue accounted for 33.2 per cent of the total revenue of all provincial governments, while the second largest single item, excise, accounted for 22.2 per cent. Tomlinson, *Political Economy of the Raj*, Table 4.5, p. 156.

20. See Markovits, 'Indian Business and Nationalist Politics', pp. 62–3.

21. Between 1929–30 and 1934–5, the share of civil works in the total expenditure of the provincial governments fell from 10.9 to 8.6 per cent. During the same period, industries dropped from 1 to 0.9 per cent. Tomlinson, *Political Economy of the Raj*, p. 156.

22. *Report of the Indian Financial Enquiry Committee* (London, 1936).

23. In an interview to the *Times of India,* 2 May 1936, Sir Purshottamdas Thakurdas had underlined that, during five years, there would be 'no

elbow-room discernible for nation-building activities to Ministers in the provinces', unless they raised new taxes.

24. C. Revri, *The Indian Trade Union Movement: A Historical Outline* (Delhi, 1972), pp. 204 ff.

25. Out of 38 labour seats, the Congress contested 20 and won 18. It won all the labour seats in Madras and the United Provinces, while in Bombay it contested and won only two of the seven reserved seats.

26. The only exception was the Bombay Presidency, where Ambedkar's Independent Labour Party won some of the urban working-class seats.

27. In 1937, out of 1,675,869 factory workers in India, the largest number was in Bengal, 566,458, followed by Bombay, 435,207, Madras, 186,630, and the United Provinces, 153,484. *Indian Yearbook, 1938–39* (Bombay, 1939), p. 538.

28. According to the index of variable yield securities published in Statistical Research Branch, *Review of the Trade of India, 1938–39* (Calcutta, 1939), dividends paid by joint-stock companies reached a record index of 137 in March 1937 (1927–8 = 100).

29. Many zamindars, besides Indian princes, held shares in Indian joint-stock companies. Some zamindars had themselves promoted sugar mills in northern India in collaboration with merchants. Conversely, many Indian capitalists, especially in northern and eastern India, were large-scale land-holders.

30. Such fears had been voiced in particular by Sir H.P. Mody, the spokesman of the Bombay textile industry and the Tatas, as early as in 1935 in an interview to the *Times of India*, dated 14 August 1935.

31. The only exception was in Madras where Yakub Hasan, a big Muslim merchant, was given the Public Works portfolio.

32. Though Birla himself had sugar mills in the United Provinces.

33. In a letter dated 25 May 1937 to Laithwaite, private secretary to the Viceroy, Birla expressed the hope that 'if once the Congress realises the potentiality of constitutionalism', it would 'stick to it to the end', Linlith-gow Papers, India Office Library (IOL), London, Mss Eur F. 125, vol. 118.

34. See Revri, *Indian Trade Union Movement*, p. 222 and V.B. Karnik, *Indian Trade Unions: A Survey* (Bombay, 1966), pp. 110 ff.

35. Quoted in Kanji Dwarkadas, *Forty-five Years with Labour* (Bombay, 1962), p. 50.

36. V.V. Giri, *My Life and Times* (Madras, 1976), vol. I, p. 130.

37. Computed on the basis of Table 2.

38. Out of 387 disputes in which settlements were arrived at during the year, in 181 or 46.77 per cent, the workers were successful in gaining con-cessions. In 51 or 13.18 per cent, they were completely successful and in

130 or 33.59 per cent only partially successful. *Labour Gazette* (Bombay, June 1939), p. 770.

39. Revri, *Indian Trade Union Movement*, p. 220.

40. The number of registered unions increased from 262 in 1937, of which 219 submitting returns had a membership of 257,308, to 420 in 1938, of which 343 submitting returns had a membership of 390, 112. Ibid., p. 234.

41. Ibid.

42. In 1939, 51.4 per cent of workers in the textile mills of the United Provinces and 49.2 per cent in those of Madras were employed in British-controlled mills. Computed on the basis of Annual Statement of Mills, included in *Bombay Millowners' Association: Annual Volume 1939* (Bombay, 1940).

43. Karnik, *Indian Trade Unions*, p. 110.

44. Resolutions of the Congress Labour Committee, Wardha, 25–26 October 1937, reproduced in *Indian Annual Register, 1937*, vol. II, p. 378.

45. On the labour movement in Kanpur, see S.M. Pandey, *As Labour Organizes. A Study of Unionism in the Kanpur Textile Industry* (Delhi, 1970).

46. In August 1937, five provincial governments, including the Punjab government but excluding Bombay, raised loans. See India Office Records (IOR), Financial collections, F/7/323, IOL.

47. See Proceedings of the joint sugarcane conference convened by the governments of the United Provinces and Bihar and held at Lucknow on 29 and 30 September 1937, in Rajendra Prasad Papers, NAI, File XIII/37, Collection I, sr 106.

48. This brief account of sugar policy in Bihar and the United Provinces is based on a memorandum submitted to the National Planning Committee by the United Provinces Government Industries Department, particularly on pp. 107–8. Copy in AICC Papers, NMML, 1939, File G-14.

49. See G.D. Birla to Rajendra Prasad, 21 December 1937, Rajendra Prasad Papers, File XII1/37, Collection I, sr 127.

50. See for instance *Two Years of Congress Rule in Madras*, published by the Madras Legislature Congress Party, undated, p. 38.

51. In Bombay the government set up an industrial advisory board, the role of which was never very clear, and appointed in March 1938 an Economic and Industrial Survey Committee, to review the position of small industries in the province. See Government of Bombay to Sir Purshottamdas Thakurdas, 23 March 1938, Thakurdas Papers, NMML, File 212.

52. While the Finance Minister in Bombay had predicted a deficit of Rs 10½ lakhs for the financial year 1937–8, there was a final surplus of Rs 18½ lakhs, due to the payment of Rs 27 lakhs by the Centre from the income tax. *Times of India*, 26 February 1938.

53. Prohibition was first introduced in 1937 in the Salem district of the Madras Presidency on an experimental scale, then extended to other districts of the Presidency and other provinces, particularly Bombay.

54. See details of provincial budgets in annual issues of the *Indian Yearbook*.

55. In Madras the Congress ministry presented regularly surplus budgets. Ibid.

56. In Bombay the budget presented in the Assembly for 1938–9 included supplementary expenditure of Rs 34 lakhs on education, Rs 39 lakhs on rural development and only Rs 7½ lakhs on industry. *Times of India*, 26 February 1938.

57. *The Pioneer*, 13 November 1937.

58. See *Two Years of Congress Rule in Madras*, p. 33: 'With a view to encourage the production of handloom cloth, the Madras Sale of Cloth Act was enacted and the Khadi (Name Protection) Act was extended to the Province.' Rs 2 lakhs was set apart for khadi production in each budget, and grants were given to the All-India Spinners Association.

59. Thus Giri complains in his Memoirs that the Premier of Madras, Rajagopalachari, tended to favour the British ICS officers and give them a free hand. Giri, *My Life and Times*, p. 118.

60. For a detailed analysis of these negotiations, see Markovits, 'Indian Business and Nationalist Politics', pp. 191–7, and Chatterji's article in Baker, Johnson, and Seal (eds), *Power, Profit and Politics*.

61. A big Ahmedabad millowner and a close friend of Gandhi.

62. See Pandey, *As Labour Organizes*, pp. 54 ff.

63. In a communiqué, the employers said that they felt 'that they should not have been forced by government to recognize the Mazdoor Sabha as long as it remains constituted as at present'. *The Pioneer*, 12 August 1937.

64. In *The Viceroy's Journal* (London, 1973), p. 102, entry for 30 November 1944, Lord Wavell writes: 'Srivastava [then a minister in Wavell's cabinet] . . . today told me that after the Congress success at the polls and assumption of office in the United Provinces in 1937, the leading industrialists—all, I think, Hindu—got together and decided to finance Jinnah and the Muslim League and also the Mahasabha, as the extreme communal parties, to oppose Congress who they feared might threaten their financial profits.'

65. *The Pioneer*, 30 November 1937.

66. On 19 May 1938 Pandit Pant, receiving a workers' delegation, chided them for their lack of discipline. *The Leader*, 21 May 1938. But on 23 May, the United Provinces Congress Committee passed a resolution supporting the strikers and thereafter the attitude of the ministry to the strike changed. Ibid., 25 May 1938. On 12 June the government asked

for the implementation of the recommendations of the report. Ibid., 14 June 1938.

67. *The Leader*, 29 June 1938.

68. See Evidence of the Bombay Millowners' Association before the Textile Enquiry Committee, *Indian Textile Journal*, 15 December 1937, p. 84.

69. See *Textile Labour Enquiry Committee*, vol. I, Preliminary Report (Bombay, 1938).

70. They were fixed at 9 per cent in Ahmedabad, where wages were the highest in India, at 11.9 per cent in Bombay, and at 14.3 per cent in Sholapur, the third big textile centre in the province, where wages were particularly low.

71. Lumley to Linlithgow, report no. 12, 15 March 1938, Linlithgow Papers, vol. 51.

72. *Indian Textile Journal*, 15 March 1938, p. 192.

73. Lumley wrote to Linlithgow: 'My information is that the decision of the millowners was not reached without some very plain speaking by the Congress Ahmedabad millowners to the ministers. I understand that these millowners, in heated interviews, pointed out that they had supplied in the past a large part of the Congress funds and that they were now receiving in return from the Congress governments very heavy burdens to bear. They extracted from the Ministers and from Sardar Vallabhbhai Patel a promise that further legislation providing sickness benefit and old-age pensions for the workers, the cost of which would be mainly borne by the millowners, should not be put into operation for at least a year.' Report no. 12, 15 March 1938, Linlithgow Papers, vol. 51.

74. Lumley to Linlithgow, ibid.

75. For a detailed account, see Markovits, 'Indian Business and Nationalist Politics', pp. 191–7.

76. In 1936 many Bombay capitalists had condemned his socialist views, and though in the following period he had become more moderate, he was nevertheless still suspect in the eyes of many businessmen.

77. M.C. Ghia, Vice-President of the Indian Merchants Chamber, in a speech at a function in Bombay in honour of B.G. Kher, *Times of India*, 26 July 1937.

78. *Times of India*, 8 March 1937.

79. *Indian Textile Journal*, 15 March 1938, p. 200, 'The State and Industries'.

80. Business groups which invested in the Indian States in 1937–9 included: Singhania (in Bhopal), Srivastava (in Rampur), Tata (in Baroda), Sassoon (in Travancore). This list is not exhaustive.

81. *Bombay Chronicle*, 29 March 1938.

82. Quoted in Revri, *Indian Trade Union Movement*, p. 232.

83. Patel wrote to Kher in a letter dated 9 July 1938: 'the trade-union people have already begun to howl at you for employing men at government expense to organize labour unions rival to the trade-unions organized, by non-officials.' Kher Papers, NMML, File 6.

84. Copy enclosed in Giri to Kripalani, 14 July 1938, AICC Papers, NMML, File PL 3(1),1939.

85. Dwarkadas, *Forty-five Years with Labour*, p. 79.

86. Lumley to Linlithgow, Report dated 15 September 1938, Linlithgow Papers, vol. 51.

87. Bombay Legislative Assembly debates, 2 September 1938, quoted in *Indian Annual Register*, 1938, vol. 11, p. 149.

88. Ibid., 4 September 1938, ibid., p. 157.

89. For a detailed analysis of the main provisions of the bill, see Revri, *Indian Trade Union Movement*, p. 226 ff.

90. 'Confidential note on Bombay. Trade Disputes Act', 14 December 1938, Nehru Papers, NMML, File 150.

91. *Times of India*, 6 November 1938.

92. Lumley to Linlithgow, report dated 15 November 1938, Linlithgow Papers, vol. 51.

93. The police opened fire upon demonstrators in different places in town, resulting in several dead and many injured. *Times of India*, 8 November 1938.

94. The government had to agree to the setting up of a committee to enquire into the disturbances.

95. Lumley wrote to Linlithgow in his report dated 15 September 1938 that the millowners feared that the 'cumbrous machinery' set up by the Act would make it difficult for them to introduce changes in their way of operating their factories. Linlithgow Papers, vol. 51.

96. See Karnik, *Indian Trade Unions*, pp. 114–15.

97. In July 1939, the relations between the provincial trade union Congress and the provincial government reached the breaking-point, following a letter sent by the government to the Mazdoor Sabha, in which they had objected strongly to the preaching of class hatred by trade unions. *The Leader*, 14 July 1939.

98. *The Leader*, 8 December 1938.

99. In 1939, there were 406 disputes, involving 409,075 workers and resulting in the loss of 4,992,795 man-days. Revri, *Indian Trade Union Movement*, p. 260.

100. Membership of registered trade unions showed little change between 1938 and 1939. Ibid., p. 234.

101. Dwarkadas, *Forty-five Years with Labour*, p. 56.

102. Ibid.
103. Patel to Kher, 1 July 1939, Kher Papers, File 6.
104. AICC to Alembic Chemical Works, 4 February 1939, AICC Papers, File G-72, 1938.
105. In a letter to Kher, dated 3 August 1939, Patel urged the Chief Minister to refuse the licence to the British firm of Killick Nixon which already held the license for Ahmedabad. Kher Papers, File 6. Yet such interventions directed specifically against British firms were very rare
106. In a letter to Kher dated 5 July 1939, Manu Subedar, of the Indian Merchants' Chamber, protested against the stand of the Bombay government in giving its guarantee to the capital sunk in 'one or more industrial venture'. Kher Papers, File 6.
107. C.M. Kothari, a Gujarati businessman of Madras, wrote to his friend Thakurdas in a letter dated 17 March 1938: 'there was a regular tussle in the Cabinet meeting to give the lease [of Trichinopoly] to Narayandas Girdhardas [a Madras businessman] and not to C.P. company [part of the Associated Cement Companies combine] and everyone of the ministers was in favour of giving the same to him, except Rajaji and Dr. Subborayan. In that meeting Rajaji read a letter from Vallabhbhai mentioning amongst other things that the lease may be given to C.P. Cement Co. as the company has necessary capital.' Thakurdas Papers, File 206.
108. The Madras ministry was the only one to show a reluctance to collaborate. Giri, *My Life and Times*, p. 161.
109. There is a detailed account of the conference in *Indian Annual Register*, 1938, vol. II, pp. 288–92.
110. Markovits, 'Indian Business and Nationalist Politics', p. 197.
111. Ibid., pp. 229–32.
112. See the correspondence between Thakurdas, one of the unofficial advisers, and Iyengar, Secretary to the Government of Bombay, Finance Department, in August 1938. In a letter dated 18 August Thakurdas wrote: 'if the textile industry is to make the sacrifice indicated in the proposals [of the Board of Trade ] under piece goods and prints, obviously they will not be able to stand any more burden which provincial governments in India may have in mind to put on them'. Copy in Kher Papers, II, File 3. In a letter dated 25 August, Iyengar replied that it was impossible for the ministers to commit themselves in advance on the final outcome of the labour enquiry committee and that they considered 'that the terms of the Indo British pact must be judged on the basis of the facts as they are today'. Copy enclosed in Irwin, Secretary to the Governor of Bombay, to Puckle, Secretary to the Viceroy, Linlithgow Papers, vol. 52.
113. United Provinces Legislative Assembly debates, 13 March 1939, quoted in *Indian Annual Register*, 1939, vol. I, p. 220. The budget presented for

1939–40 made for a deficit of Rs 38 lakhs, of which Rs 30 lakhs was to be covered by the employments tax.

114. Lumley to Linlithgow, 26 December 1938, Linlithgow Papers, vol. 52.

115. *The Leader*, 19 April 1939.

116. Memorandum submitted by the Upper India Chamber of Commerce, the United Provinces Chamber of Commerce, the Merchants' Chamber of the United Provinces, the Indian Sugar Producers' Association, the Employers' Association of Northern India, the Kanpur Sugar Merchants' Association, the Kanpur Sugar Brokers' Association. *The Leader*, 20 April 1939.

117. See Lumley to Linlithgow, report dated 15 February 1939, Linlithgow Papers, vol. 52.

118. In a speech in the Madras Legislative Assembly on 16 March 1939, quoted in *Indian Annual Register*, 1939, vol. I, p. 182. On this occasion Rajagopalachari castigated merchants and traders for their refusal 'to pay even one pie out of one rupee'.

119. C.N. Vakil in *Times of India*, 21 February 1939.

120. An added factor was that many property-holders were Muslims, which gave the agitation a communal turn.

121. V.K.R.V. Rao, in *Bombay Chronicle*, 21 February 1939.

122. In 1938–9, sales of Japanese piece goods showed an increase of 40 per cent over the figures for the previous year. Computed on the basis of data in A.K. Bagchi, *Private Investment in India* (Cambridge, 1972), p. 238.

123. 'Indian Textile Industry in the Doldrums', *Indian Textile Journal*, 15 July 1939, p. 392.

124. In an interview to the *Times of India*, 3 March 1939, he complained that the provincial governments were 'out to crush' the cotton textile industry.

125. Lumley to Linlithgow, report dated 15 April 1939, Linlithgow Papers, vol. 52.

126. Lumley to Linlithgow, report dated 15 May 1939, ibid.

127. *Indian Textile Journal*, 15 July 1939, p. 392.

128. Ibid., 15 August 1939, p. 431.

129. Gulzarilal Nanda to Bombay Provincial Congress Committee, quoted in *Indian Textile Journal*, 15 August 1939, p. 430.

130. Ibid., p. 431. One wing in the Ahmedabad Millowners' Association led by Kasturbhai Lalbhai agreed with Patel's proposal to hold discussions with the unions, while another section, headed by Sakarlal Balabhai, advocated unilateral measures.

131. Patel to Kher, 17 September 1939, Kher Papers, File 6.

132. Erskine to Linlithgow, 6 July 1939, Erskine Papers, IOL, London, Mss Eur. D 596. In a reply dated 12 July, ibid., Linlithgow expresses his surprise

at Erskine's views and points out that most likely the international situation is the main cause of the shyness of the investing public in Madras.

133. See A.R. Dalal's call to the Bihar government to intervene to restore peace in Jamshedpur. *The Leader*, 14 August 1939.

134. *The Leader*, 23 July 1939.

135. Rajat Ray, *Industrialization in India, 1914–1947: Growth and Conflict in the Private Corporate Sector* (Delhi, 1979), p. 70.

136. *The Leader*, 5 March 1938.

137. See Evidence of Bombay Millowners' Association before Bombay Economic and Industrial Survey Committee, 35th meeting, 7 August 1939, Thakurdas Papers, File 212.

138. See A.H.R. Copley, *The Political Career of Rajagopalachari, 1937–1954: A Moralist in Politics* (Delhi, 1978), for an analysis of Rajaji's views.

139. See the speech of the Chairman of the Bombay Chamber of Commerce, A. MacIntosh, in *Bombay Chamber of Commerce, Annual Volume 1938* (Bombay, 1939), p. xxvii.

3

# BUSINESSMEN AND THE PARTITION OF INDIA*

HE VAST AND STILL GROWING LITERATURE ON THE PARTI-
tion of India does not place much emphasis on its economic
aspects, and the role of businessmen remains one of the most
obscure points in the story. It is not claimed here that the attitudes of
the Indian capitalists were a central factor in the most dramatic event
in the modern history of the subcontinent. The underlying causes of
Partition are to be sought in long-term trends and policies which,
after a certain point in time, were beyond the control of any of the
actors involved. Therefore, even if Indian big business had, on grounds
of economic rationality, unanimously opposed Partition, it would
not have been able to prevent it. The interesting point, however, is
precisely that, on the whole, Indian big business did not oppose Partition, but, at least from 1942 onwards, seems to have been increasingly favourable to it. This is true not only of Muslim businessmen,
but also of their non-Muslim colleagues. On the first point, an apparent rationale is furnished by W.C. Smith's thesis of the contrast between a relatively advanced Hindu bourgeoisie and a retarded Muslim
capitalist class. But the second point is more puzzling.

*From D. Tripathi (ed.), *Business and Politics in India: A Historical Perspective*
(New Delhi: Manohar, 1991), pp. 284–307.

The great weakness of all existing rationalizations including Smith's is that they do not sufficiently disaggregate the data, that they tend to treat both the Muslim and non-Muslim capitalists as more or less homogeneous entities, while in fact there were major internal differences within these two categories. The emphasis of this chapter will, therefore, be on presenting a picture as disaggregated as is possible on the basis of the limited empirical evidence available to the author. But, before embarking upon that kind of study, it is necessary to make a few preliminary remarks of a general nature on the kind of framework most appropriate for analysing the relationship between Indian business and communal politics. This has been done in the first section of this chapter. The second section will deal with developments in communal politics in the period prior to 1942, while the third section will consider the attitudes of businessmen in the years immediately preceding Partition. The final section sums up the conclusions derived from this analysis.


# I


While communalism in India has been generally defined as a middle-class movement and a middle-class ideology, little attention has been paid to the role played in its emergence by merchants and capitalists. Actually there seems to be a sort of consensus that communalism as a distinct and somewhat articulate ideology evolved in the late nineteenth century among non-capitalist middle-class elements, such as government servants, professionals, and sections of intelligentsia and spread during the twentieth century both to the lower classes and the emerging capitalist bourgeoisie. Forms of community consciousness were, however, undoubtedly present among various strata even before the advent of colonialism[1] and they are germane to the later elaboration of a communalist ideology. Various movements of religious reform throughout the nineteenth century were manifestations of that community consciousness but could not be described as full-fledged statements of a communalist view of society.

What is of relevance to our topic is that merchant communities often seem to have been closely connected to some of these movements. Unfortunately, little is known of the attitude of Muslim business people to the various movements of 'Islamicization' which, throughout the nineteenth century, sought to 'purify' Indian Islam and to bring about some homogenization of beliefs and practices among a very diverse and heterogeneous religious community.[2] It is interesting to note, however, that the first specifically 'Muslim' association in India, the Anjuman-i-Islam, was created in the 1870s in the major commercial city of Bombay, and that two of the richest and most prominent local Muslim businessmen were closely associated with its birth.[3] More is known about the contribution of some Hindu merchant communities to the growth of various shades of Hindu 'revivalist' movements, particularly in northern India. Recent studies[4] have pointed to the important role played by trading communities in the Cow Protection Agitation of the 1890s in the United Provinces and Bihar. Hindu commercial men appear to have been actively involved in financing the various cow protection societies and to have had often a prominent part in their organization. Pre-existing links between some north Indian merchants and the Arya Samaj (the Hindu revivalist sect), which played an important role in the genesis of the movement, facilitated their involvement. Similarly the movement for the propagation of Hindi, with its strong anti-Muslim overtones, got support from Hindu businessmen in many localities of northern India.[5]

The interpretation of these facts, however, remains a problem. 'Religious' community consciousness was only one of the variegated forms of community consciousness which developed in India during that period. Other groupings, which tended to emphasize divisions within the religious communities rather than their unity, also became important foci of loyalty for many Indians, Hindu and Muslim alike. One has only to think of the tremendous surge in caste-based organizations in India under the stimulus of the population censuses. Merchants were not the last ones to organize on that basis. Therefore, 'Hindu' or 'Muslim' was only one of the categories which a trader or a businessman could use to define his social identity. The advantages to be derived from its use would be primarily of a symbolic nature, such as a rise in the self-esteem of men who did not occupy a very exalted position in the accepted social hierarchy. But it did not obliterate other forms of consciousness. To take one example, in undivided India, a businessman who was a Muslim by religion had many categories to choose from in order to define his social identity: he could identify himself primarily as a member of a small community, sect or quasi-caste (that is, in Gujarat as a Bohra, a Khoja, or a Memon, to mention three groups to which most of the prominent Muslim businessmen of western India belonged, with further subdivisions into Daudi and Sulaimani Bohra, Ismaili and Itna'ashari Khoja, Kutchi and Halai Memon); or he could emphasize the regional connection and see himself as a Gujarati, a Bengali, or a Tamilian; he could also stress a feeling of corporate identity (merchant vs non-merchant) which was highly developed in the towns and cities of Gujarat and northern India.[6] With the rise of Indian nationalism, there was also a growing tendency among Indian businessmen to stress the indigenous–expatriate divide, especially since they were subjected to various disabilities in comparison with European and particularly British businessmen.[7] Lastly, of course, a Muslim businessman could identify himself primarily as a Muslim, because of either a deep religious faith (not a very common occurrence though, according to a keen observer of Indian Muslim society[8]) or a desire to differentiate himself from his Indian non-Muslim colleagues. Needless to say, these identities were mutually overlapping, and whether the emphasis was put on one or another did not depend only on individual strategic choices. There is no reason, however, to assume a priori that, because a businessman was Muslim by religion, he saw himself first and foremost as a 'Muslim businessman'.

Therefore, as far as political alignments are concerned, one could not automatically infer that Muslim businessmen would support Muslim communal movements and organizations after the 1909 reforms established separate electorates and the Muslim League started putting forward its claim to represent a specific 'Muslim' interest in politics. Nor could it be inferred that non-Muslim, and particularly Hindu businessmen, would necessarily adopt a 'nationalist' outlook.


## II

To this day, the most influential statement regarding the relationship between the economic role of Muslims in India and the growth of Muslim communal politics remains the one put forward in 1943 by W.C. Smith in his *Modern Islam in India.* A radical critic of capitalism, Smith saw in the specific kind of capitalism which evolved in India under colonial conditions, a fertile ground for the development of communalism.[9] Specifically concerned with Muslim communalism, he defined it in its most recent phase as 'the nationalist ideology ad-opted by the emergent and precarious Muslim middle class in its struggle against domination within India by the much more developed Hindu middle class'.[10] Although he was ideologically opposed to com-munalism, Smith tended to rationalize Muslim communalism as the response of an emergent but still weak Muslim bourgeoisie to the at-tempt by an already entrenched Hindu bourgeoisie to thwart its growth. He did not, however, muster any empirical evidence to prove his point regarding the 'retardation' of the Muslim capitalist class. His views have recently been challenged by Bipan Chandra who stresses that, at least prior to the 1940s, 'Hindu bourgeoisie' and 'Muslim bourgeoisie' were not meaningful categories.[11] His refutation of Smith's thesis, however, is not based on a detailed empirical study of the role of Muslim and non-Muslim capitalists in the Indian economy.

In a recently published study I have presented some data on the position of Muslim businessmen in the Indian economy, drawn mainly from the 1921 census and various primary and secondary sources.[12] Treating, for convenience's sake, 'Muslims' as one category, I have concluded that, during the first half of the twentieth century, Muslim businessmen still occupied fairly important positions in the commer-cial life of India in spite of wide regional variations. I have stressed the contrast between the situation in the regions which at a later stage formed Pakistan, in particular Bengal and the Punjab, where Muslims, although a majority in the population, did not occupy dominant positions in trade and finance, and in other regions where a numerically small Muslim population often played an important role in the commercial life. On an all-India basis their main area of weakness, albeit a crucial one no doubt, was finance. It appears also that Muslim representation in the ranks of large-scale industrialists, although not insignificant in the 1920s, tended to decrease in the 1930s.[13]

It seems that the 1930s represented a watershed in the perception that many Muslim businessmen had of their role in the economic life of India. Before that date, they do not seem to have nursed a particular sense of grievance, as shown by the fact that they did not create separate commercial associations but participated, often actively, with their Hindu, Jain, and Parsi colleagues, in major Indian commercial bodies.[14] Nor were partnerships between Muslim and non-Muslim businessmen a totally unknown feature in the principal commercial and industrial cities of India. It is true that there are not many instances of that kind of partnership, at least outside Bombay. But it should be remembered that in India business partnerships were generally family- or kinship-based, which in any case restricted possibilities of cross-communal associations. Marwaris for instance chose only Marwaris as business partners, but did not exclude Muslims more than Parsis or members of other Hindu communities. This kind of exclusiveness operated also within the Muslim community: thus in western India Khojas rarely formed business partnerships with Memons. A common religion was no strong bond in the business world of India, which was fragmented along the lines of caste and kin.

From the 1930s onwards, however, attempts were made by some Muslim businessmen to forge business linkages with co-religionists belonging to other groups and regions. These attempts were not very successful before the 1940s when, at the prompting of Jinnah and the Muslim League, there developed a movement specifically aimed at creating the so-called 'Muslim enterprises'.[15] Although it achieved some results, this movement does not seem to have been received with great enthusiasm by at least a section of the Muslim business elite.

More successful and of more far-reaching importance was the movement which developed from 1932 onwards to create separate Muslim associations. Starting with the foundation in 1932 of the Muslim Chamber of Commerce in Calcutta, it gathered momentum throughout the 1930s and 1940s and at the time of Partition the number of such bodies had grown enormously.[16] The reasons for this mushrooming of Muslim commercial associations are, however, far from clear. The Muslim Chamber of Commerce in Calcutta was created to take advantage of the political reforms in Bengal: under the new regime one seat in the provincial legislature was reserved for a Muslim commercial association. Since none existed, a few prominent Muslim businessmen of Calcutta, such as M.A.H. Ispahani and Adamji Haji Dawood,[17] moved in to fill the vacuum. But it is not easy to discover what their real motivations were. They did not raise, as could have been expected, the bogey of 'Marwari domination' of business in Calcutta; on the contrary, they tended to overestimate the strength of Muslim business interest there.[18] And it is interesting to note that, prior to 1942, the Muslim Chamber of Commerce did not raise any specific 'Muslim' issues; actually its resolutions largely paralleled those passed during the same period by the Indian Chamber of Commerce.[19] It also seems that some members of the new Muslim Chamber continued with their membership of the Indian Chamber.

The creation of the Muslim Chamber thus need not be seen as a clear sign of an increasing polarization in the Calcutta business world along 'communal' lines. The more plausible interpretation is in terms of factional conflict: big Muslim businessmen such as Ispahani and Adamji, like some of their Hindu colleagues, increasingly resented the heavy-handed leadership exercised by the Birla brothers, G.D. Birla in particular, over the Indian Chamber and their autocratic methods. By creating a separate chamber, they could escape their domination; 'Muslim' came in handy as a label, since it could also bring in political advantages, but the term hardly had any 'communal' meaning. Once that kind of movement was launched, however, it acquired a dynamics of its own, which was beyond the control of its promoters, and the creation of separate Muslim commercial bodies did contribute to dividing the business world along communal lines. The process culminated with the creation in 1945 of a Federation of Muslim Chambers of Commerce and Industry which was conceived by Jinnah as a counterpart of the Federation of Indian Chambers of Commerce and Industry (FICCI) which had increasingly tended to align itself with the Indian National Congress.[20]

Post-Partition accounts of that period, coming in particular from Pakistan, have tended to stress the existence of a growing gap between Muslim and Hindu businessmen.[21] It is true that most of the spectacularly successful businessmen of the 1930s and 1940s happened to be Hindus.[22] As I have shown elsewhere,[23] however, there is no hard evidence that, as opportunities in the trading sector diminished under the impact of the world depression, Muslim businessmen were systematically barred from entry into industry by entrenched Hindu interests. The absence of large Muslim banks has often been cited as a major handicap for would-be Muslim industrialists. But banks did not play a major role in financing industries in India; most capital for industry was raised through credit networks which remained largely 'informal' and were generally controlled by some specialized communities like the Marwaris. It cannot be demonstrated convincingly that the controllers of credit in India, who were mostly Hindus, discriminated against Muslim businessmen because they were Muslims. Such an assertion, to be plausible, would have to be based on a statistical study of all cases of refusal of credit for industrial projects, a study which is of course impossible.

In history facts are, however, often less important than perceptions, even though distorted. Although its empirical foundations were, to say the least, flimsy, the idea seems to have gained ground in some Muslim business circles that Hindus were doing their utmost to prevent Muslim businessmen from succeeding and, as the years went by, this kind of crude rationalization became accepted as an undisputed truth. It led to increasing demands for 'positive discrimination' in favour of Muslim business interests which were difficult to accommo-date within a unitary political framework. In this way, Muslim separat-ism, the demand for a political separation of the Muslim-majority areas from the rest of India, acquired an economic dimension.

This was, however, a late development. Prior to the 1940s, the idiom of communal politics in India was steeped in the preoccupations of the landed elite and of the non-capitalist middle classes. Problems of unequal educational entitlements with their purported consequen-ces at the level of competition for scarce jobs in the government and service sector and of delicate landholder–tenant relationships figured much more prominently in discussions of the 'communal question' than views on the structure of industrial credit. The existence of links between businessmen and 'communal' politicians did not mean that communal 'lobbies' articulated business interests in a coherent fashion. In that respect, there were significant regional differences. The Punjab and Bengal were two specific cases, and they deserve a separate treat-ment. In the Punjab, the 1919 reforms had resulted in the coming to power in the province of a coalition of 'rural' interests in which Muslim landholders occupied a dominant position. The urban interests, mainly Hindu traders and moneylenders, had been pushed aside and they resented the orientation of provincial politics and the 'rural bias' of the provincial government Although Hindu and Sikh landholders were very much part of the Unionist Party power structure, the urban–rural divide was given a clear communal twist by the political represent-atives of the urban commercial classes. The cities and towns of the Punjab were Arya Samaj strongholds and politicians like Lala Lajpat Rai, who had close links with the sect, became the spokesmen of the urban Hindu interests in the province. In the Punjab the dominant Hindu business interests, thus, became clearly identified with a com-munal outlook in politics.

Sir Gokul Chand Narang, head of one of the largest business groups in the Punjab (with large interests in the sugar industry), was also one of the most outspoken representatives of Hindu communalist views. As far as the much smaller Muslim business class of the Punjab is concerned, it seems to have solidly supported the Unionist ministry which in its turn bestowed favours on it. Although no detailed study of this is available, an indication of the trend is the rapid and spectacular rise of the Muslim firm of Wazir Ali, headed by Sir Syed Maratib Ali,[24] which became the largest contractor of military canteens in the Punjab, a hugely profitable activity in a province which sheltered so many garrisons. Since Punjabi regionalism was the main platform of Muslim politicians in the province,[25] local Muslim businessmen did not show much interest in all-India Muslim politics and, even after 1937, did not support the Muslim League. In the richest agricultural province of India, however, the landholding interest always remained paramount, and urban businessmen played only a marginal role.

Things were different in Bengal, the other Muslim-majority province, because of the weight of Calcutta and of its business interests. In this old stronghold of Indian nationalism, the death of C.R. Das in 1925 opened an era of gradual decline for the Congress and growing assertion of communal forces in politics.[26] While British firms still occupied a dominant position in the business world of Calcutta till the 1940s, an increasingly important role was played by Indian businessmen, particularly Hindu Marwaris, and also non-Bengali Muslims of various origins.[27] Although provincial politics was dominated by the *bhadralok* of Calcutta and the rising Muslim *jotedars* of eastern Bengal, the various factions contending for control of the province had to seek some business support to fill their coffers. No study of the involvement of businessmen in Bengal politics is available, but one can focus briefly on three businessmen who played an important role at various moments.

G.D. Birla emerged in the mid-1920s as the most influential leader of the Calcutta Marwaris, displacing the more conservative and pro-British Rai Badridas Goenka. Although Birla was a staunch nationalist and a follower of Gandhi in all-India politics, he maintained close links with the conservative Hindu leader Pandit M.M. Malaviya, whose friends in Bengal opposed a compromise between Hindus and Muslims in the province.[28] In 1934 Birla sided with Malaviya in opposing the Communal Award, which gave Muslims the majority of seats in the provincial legislature, and criticized Gandhi's stand.[29] His outlook on Bengal affairs, therefore, was close to that of the Hindu communalists and the Hindu Mahasabha, although he had at an early stage severed his links with the latter organization. It seems that many Calcutta Marwaris feared that a Muslim-dominated provincial government might take measures detrimental to their interests. Nevertheless, when the Fazl-ul-Huq ministry, the first Muslim-dominated ministry in Bengal, was formed after the 1937 provincial elections, the finance portfolio was given to N.R. Sarker, a Bengali Hindu businessman-politician (with large interests in insurance), who had close links with the Marwari business community, particularly G.D. Birla. In spite of its radical stand, the Huq ministry did nothing to upset the powerful Marwari business interests of the province. But the Marwaris remained suspicious of Muslim intentions.

As far as Muslim businessmen are concerned, their main representative in Bengal politics was the Cambridge-educated M.A.M. Ispahani, scion of an illustrious family of Persian origin. He represented the Young Party on which Jinnah increasingly relied to intervene in the faction-ridden world of Bengal Muslim politics. In the 1940s Ispahani emerged as the main financier of the Muslim League and a major figure in all-India Muslim politics. In spite of a growing communal polarization of politics, there was more room in Bengal than in the Punjab for an accommodation between Hindu and Muslim business interests. The existence of an active urban Muslim commercial class based in Calcutta made a difference: the growing West Bengal–East Bengal divide did not totally coincide with the communal alignment. Nevertheless, in so far as the Marwari businessmen were gaining in strength (largely at the expense of British interests)[30] and self-assurance, there was a possibility that they would increasingly resent the prospect of Muslim political domination of the province.

In the two large Muslim-majority provinces, Hindu and Muslim businessmen developed divergent appreciations of the problem of centre–province relations. Given their close links with the provincial governments, Muslim businessmen favoured greater provincial autonomy, especially in financial and economic matters, while their Hindu colleagues put their hopes in a strong central government, because Muslims would necessarily wield less influence with it than Hindus.

In the other provinces, where Muslims were not in a majority, but where Muslim businessmen often played an important role in commercial life (particularly in the Bombay and Madras presidencies), communal considerations were not central to the politics of business, be it Hindu, Parsi, or Muslim. In the United Provinces, which was the birthplace of Muslim separatism, businessmen do not figure prominently in accounts of the growth of the movement,[31] which drew support mainly from landlords, urban professionals, and government servants. In the Bombay Presidency, a Hindu–Muslim divide in the commercial world was revealed for the first time during the Civil Disobedience movement when the pro-government stand of most Muslim traders formed a clear contrast to the pro-Gandhian enthusiasm of the majority of the Hindu commercial class.[32] It does not seem, however, to have created a permanent rift within the commercial community along the Hindu–Muslim divide: the business world of western India was too complex and interdependent, with the Parsis in particular still playing an important role.

A new conflict arose in 1936 around the question of the separation of Sind from the Bombay Presidency. The local Hindu business community opposed the move, which was bound to result in the creation of one more Muslim-dominated province, and some Bombay businessmen supported their stand.[33] In spite of this, communal politics did not deeply penetrate western India, and Muslim traders continued to be active in the Indian Merchants Chamber in Bombay.

The 1937 provincial elections revealed that the Muslim League, reorganized by Jinnah from 1934 onwards, had more support among the commercially oriented Muslim communities of the Bombay and Madras presidencies than in the predominantly rural and agrarian communities of the other provinces.[34] But the League, in spite of its claim to represent a specific 'Muslim' interest in all-India politics, was still operating within the broad ideological framework of Indian nationalism and did not advocate separatism. It therefore appears that the Muslim business communities of western and southern India, which were the most active and the richest in the subcontinent, still conceived their future within a unitary India and were not averse to a strong Centre, since, because of the sheer law of numbers, they had little hope of playing a decisive role in provincial politics.

The transformation of the Muslim League during the 1937–47 period from an organization seeking guarantees for Muslim interests within a unitary structure of government into a spokesman for the separation of Muslim-majority areas was a complex and gradual process. Actually it has been argued in a recently published book that Jinnah's aim remained till the very end a united India with a strong Centre in which Muslims would have parity of representation with Hindus and that he eventually settled for a separate Muslim state as only the second-best option.[35] According to this view, he used the separatist demand formulated in very ambiguous terms in the famous Pakistan resolution of 1940 as a bargaining counter to obtain concessions from the British and the Congress. But, whatever were Jinnah's ultimate intentions, the demand for Pakistan gathered a momentum of its own, and, from 1942 onwards, its shadow loomed large over India's political landscape. Businessmen, Muslim and non-Muslim, increasingly had to take it into account and to define their position with regard to it.

III

Prior to 1942 the British had always thought of the political future of India in unitary terms and therefore the possibility of a partition of the country had never been seriously entertained by anyone. The first intimation that partition might be a practical possibility came with the Cripps Mission offer of the 'provincial option' to resolve the Indian deadlock. A. Jalal has shown that it aimed mainly at driving a wedge between Jinnah and the Muslim leaders of Bengal and the Punjab, who were more interested in getting increased freedom of action for their own provinces than in obtaining concessions for Muslim interests in a united India.[36] Jinnah was saved from an open breach with those leaders by the opposition that the provincial option met from both

Linlithgow and the Congress leadership. Of all the Congress leaders, only the astute Rajagopalachari understood that Cripps' proposal offered a way to break the 'communal' deadlock by dividing the Muslim camp, but his advice was ignored.[37]

It is nevertheless interesting to note that one of the Congress's main business supporters, G.D. Birla, tended to echo Rajaji's views in a letter written to Gandhi's secretary in July 1942. Birla wrote:

> You know my views about Pakistan. I am in favour of separation and I do not think it is impracticable, or against the interest of Hindus or of India. As long as we will quarrel, there is no salvation of India. Besides, we should not forget that the Muslims—every one of them— now want it. Even the Congress Muslims are no longer exception. How could then we resist?[38]

Birla gave an interpretation of the Pakistan movement in purely 'communal' terms and did not mention its regional dimension. It shows that, contrary to what has been asserted by some,[39] he clearly thought of the problem in communal terms. This led him to overlook the deep divisions within the Muslim camp that Rajaji was precisely keen on exploiting. But he clearly understood that Muslim demands had become a fact of the political life of India and that they could not be brushed aside.

That is precisely what his fellow businessman Lala Shri Ram, the big Delhi industrialist who also thought in communal terms, failed to grasp. In a private letter written in September 1942, in the aftermath of the Quit India movement, he took the line that 'we [the Hindus? the Congress?] should not pay any price for Independence to the Muslims, either in the way of Pakistan or increase in percentage of seats in the Centre or residual power in the Provinces'.[40] Shri Ram was advocating a line of total rejection of all the demands put forward by Muslim politicians. It was certainly closer to the dominant stand of the Congress than Birla's conciliatory approach. The president of the Bombay Millowners' Association publicly defended the same strong unitary line.[41] It seems, therefore, that there was a clear division of opinion in the ranks of non-Muslim big business regarding the question of Partition, which was reflected in the inability of FICCI, the mouthpiece of the dominant business interests, to define a clear position in the matter.

There is nothing surprising in this, given the complexity of the issues involved. From a strictly economic point of view, partitioning India did not seem to make much sense. Thus Sir Ardeshir Dalal, a member of the Tata board and one of the most influential figures in Bombay big business, argued the economic case against Partition in a pamphlet released in February 1943 entitled 'An Alternative to Pakistan'. Stressing that Pakistan would be a poor country, he added:

> With innumerable problems . . . to be handled and a burden of debt difficult to repay, it will cut itself off from the great economic and industrial future which a self-governing India may look forward to. There will be a great urge to impose heavy custom duties on goods from 'Hindustan' to fill its depleted coffers and that in itself will not only hinder industrial progress but might be a fertile source of trouble between the two states.[42]

In conclusion, Sir Ardeshir urged Hindus to make sacrifices to placate Muslims so as to keep the country united. He proposed a plan for a federation in which the constituent units would have important powers. Dalal's views partly reflected the specific interests of the Tata group, the most 'national' of all the Indian business groups since the market for its products was the entire country. But with the growing integration of the Indian market brought about by customs protection and wartime restrictions of imports, most big business groups had an interest in the preservation of the subcontinent as one market.

For instance, the Ahmedabad millowners sold a lot of cloth to Bengal and separation of that area could be harmful to the prosperity of their mills. There was a lot of 'Hindu' capital invested in factories in the Muslim-majority provinces. Birla controlled two large jute mills in Calcutta and one cotton mill in the Punjab; Shri Ram had a cotton mill in Lyallpur in western Punjab and one sewing-machine factory in Calcutta; the Associated Cement Companies (controlled by Hindu,

Parsi, and British businessmen) had several plants in the Punjab and Sind; the Narang group and Lahore Electric were two major Hindu-controlled operations in western Punjab. For 'Hindu' big business, however, the losses would be minimized if Calcutta, with its large trade and many industries, remained in 'Hindustan', but this required a partition of Bengal between the Hindu west and Muslim east which would hurt Bengali feelings and may not be easy to bring about. Muslim businessmen in the areas which would not go to Pakistan might also face great difficulties, unless they were ready to migrate to the Muslim-majority areas, a move that was not so easy to contemplate. Their colleagues in the Punjab and Sind were the only ones who could really expect immediate gains from a political separation of their provinces. For Muslim businessmen in Bengal, who were mostly Calcutta-based, a lot depended on whether Calcutta would or would not go to a Muslim-dominated Bengal.

In spite of these economic problems, there seems to have been increasing support to partition from most businessmen especially from 1945 onwards. The essential reason, more than the intrinsic merits of the case, was the absence of an attractive alternative. For Jinnah's cherished dream of a unitary state with parity between Hindus and Muslims was rapidly fading in the face of determined Congress opposition. The only way to avoid Partition seemed now to be the acceptance of a loose federal regime with a weak central government having limited powers and limited finances, most powers and revenue going to the provinces. That is what Maulana Azad advocated in 1945[43] and Jinnah seems to have rallied to the idea in 1946 when he realized that he would never get parity at the centre.[44] Big business, especially the dominant non-Muslim interests which were behind the 1944 Bombay Plan, found such a prospect distasteful. They wanted a strong centre, and their blueprint for the economic development of independent India assumed the existence of a unitary India, in which a central plan could be implemented without hindrance from powerful provincial governments.[45]

A practical step in that direction had been the Industrial Policy Statement of April 1945, the last significant economic measure taken by the colonial government, which transferred responsibility for most large-scale industries from the provinces to the centre,[46] reversing the trend inaugurated by the Montagu-Chelmsford reforms of 1919. For big business, there was no question of going back on this and allowing provincial interests to interfere in the definition of economic policy. It is significant that a resolution passed at the FICCI session of March 1947 explicitly criticized the Cabinet Mission plan of 1946 for the vagueness of its formulations regarding the powers of the central government.[47] At the same session a resolution on 'the powers and policy of the government of the Indian Union' was adopted recommending that the central government be given all powers in matters of monetary policy, custom duties, protection, defence, and communications.[48]

To achieve a unitary India with a strong centre, big business was ready to pay a price in the separation of the Muslim-majority provinces, provided the non-Muslim areas of Bengal and the Punjab were incorporated into the Indian Union. This solution, a separate Muslim country, also suited Muslim businessmen in Sind and Punjab, since it promised to free them from the stranglehold of Bombay non-Muslim big business. The prospect was less attractive to Muslim businessmen in Calcutta since it meant they would have to migrate from the city where they had been operating for long. But they had no other choice than to accept it, since the alternative prospect of a united independent Bengal was, as we shall see, even more distasteful to them. As for Muslim businessmen in the rest of India, many of them, although not all, seem to have reconciled themselves to a migration which seemed to offer new economic opportunities.[49] Therefore, Partition eventually emerged as the solution most responsive to the needs and aspirations of a very large section of big business, Muslim as well as non-Muslim, because it combined the attractions of a strong unitary structure which appealed to non-Muslims and of the separation of Muslim-majority areas which satisfied the Muslims.

The most delicate question was, nevertheless, the partition of Bengal, because Bengalis were sentimentally opposed to it, and this popular opposition found an echo among some politicians. The Muslim League leader H.S. Suhrawardy thus sought to reach an agreement with a section of the Bengal Congress led by Sarat Bose on a pro-gramme of unity and independence for Bengal.[50] His attempt was, however, sabotaged both by a section of the provincial Muslim League and by the all-India Congress leadership,[51] although Jinnah on his part appeared ready to condone it. It seems that big business, both Muslim and Hindu, had a hand in the failure of Suhrawardy's attempt. Ispahani and Adamji, the two biggest Muslim businessmen of Bengal, had always sided with Suhrawardy's rivals in the complicated factional struggles which had rattled the Bengal Muslim League during the early 1940s, culminating in their dismissal from the ministry in 1943.[52] They did everything in their power to sabotage his efforts at conciliation. As for Hindu big business, it supported the campaign launched at the end of 1946 by the Hindu Mahasabha for the partition of the province.[53] Sarat Bose complained that in Bengal it was mainly the middle classes which were for partition,[54] and he must certainly have included businessmen among them. Businessmen seem to have feared that the only common platform which could unite Suhrawardy and Sarat Bose was radical populism, and Ispahani and Adamji pre-ferred to leave Calcutta rather than live in a populist Bengal, even if Suhrawardy claimed that he was acting within an Islamic tradition.

As Calcutta was eventually awarded to India,[55] the last obstacle to Partition in the eyes of Hindu big business was removed. Nothing could be done to save the big Hindu interests in the western Punjab and in April 1947 a huge flight of capital and personnel occurred from that area, which Jinnah's reassuring declarations could do nothing to stem.[56] With Calcutta in Indian hands and the Punjab and Sind stripped of most of Hindu capital, Birla was in a position to argue that the overall cost of Partition to non-Muslim business was slight. He could emphasize the fact that almost all the industrial assets of India were in the Indian Union[57] and that the trade balance between the two countries would be clearly favourable to India.[58] One worrying aspect was that the Calcutta jute mills would be cut off from their supplying areas of raw material in eastern Bengal. The situation could, however, be improved if jute cultivation developed in western Bengal and adjoining areas. For Muslim businessmen, the massive flight of

Hindu traders and moneylenders from the western Punjab, Sind, and eastern Bengal created a void which Muslim immigrant traders from Bombay, Calcutta and other areas could step into, notwithstanding that the economic prospects of Pakistan were uncertain.

A development not foreseen by businessmen on either side of the new border was that Partition would bring into being two mutually hostile countries and that the resulting escalation in the defence budgets of the two countries would tend to slow down their rate of economic growth. For it was considered likely at the time that there would be some form of common defence agreement between the two countries to face a potential threat from the north-west.[59]

How far did the attitudes and policies of businessmen influence the decisions of the major actors, that is, the British government, the Muslim League leadership, and the Congress High Command? Regarding the former's role, a close examination of the attitudes of British business and of the way it may have influenced government policies would be necessary, but it falls outside the scope of this study. Suffice it to mention here that British business in Calcutta clearly showed its preference for the inclusion of the city in the Indian Union,[60] a fact which may have influenced the policy of the British government in that matter.

As far as the two major Indian political organizations are concerned, there were some similarities in the way they interacted with big businessmen. In particular, a parallel has often been drawn between the role of Birla *vis-à-vis* the Congress and that of Ispahani in relation to the League. The League at the all-India level was, however, more dependent for its functioning on the contributions of a few wealthy business supporters than the Congress, which drew support from a wider range of interests in society. But, since the League derived most of its strength, especially in 1946–7, from regional sentiments, the nature of its central organization did not influence its policies to such an extent.

In the Punjab and Bengal, the two key Muslim-majority provinces which formed the backbone of Pakistan, the League's eventual political success was due to the rallying to it of the dominant Muslim rural interests. Its urban supporters, who were few in any case given the overwhelmingly rural character of the Muslim population in the two provinces, never played a major role. Even in Bengal the rising *jotedars* of eastern Bengal eventually mattered more than a few business magnates of Calcutta. The rural bosses of the western Punjab and eastern Bengal were motivated mainly by their hostility to urban interests which happened to be largely Hindu but they did not particularly relish the prospect of a massive migration of displaced Muslim businessmen from the Indian Union. They were regionalists more than 'communalists'. Muslim businessmen had more influence on regional 'Muslim' politics in the Bombay and Madras presidencies but were increasingly peripheral to the concerns of the Muslim League. Although the business supporters of the League at the all-India level may have played some role in Jinnah's retreat from his cherished dream of power-sharing with the Congress at the Centre as is suggested by A. Jalal,[61] their part was not crucial; Jinnah would in any case have been forced to lower his sights.

What, then, of the possible influence of non-Muslim big business over the final acceptance by the Congress of a partition the idea of which the nationalist party had obstinately resisted between 1942 and 1946? Given the fact that the most influential business supporter of the Congress, G.D. Birla, had been converted to the inevitability of Pakistan as early as 1942, it is tempting to speculate whether Birla's pressure did not have something to do with the change in the attitude of the Congress High Command in 1947, particularly since the main architect of the shift in Congress policy was Vallabhbhai Patel,[62] the crucial link between the Congress High Command and big business since the late 1930s.[63] Patel, however, had a mind of his own. He was in favour of a strong Centre, since he could hope to control it. Actually, in the absence of convincing evidence of big business pressure on Patel regarding the question of Partition, let us be content with signalling the existence of a clear coincidence of views between the strong man of the Congress and his friends from big business.

Also striking is the simultaneousness of the adoption by FICCI of its resolution on the powers of the Union at its session of March 1947 and the passing by the Constituent Assembly on 28 April of the first report of the Union Powers Committee. The latter, by putting forward a very extensive conception of the powers of the central government of the future Indian state, 'slammed the door shut on Jinnah and the League once and for all'.[64] Leaving aside the question whether they were or were not 'communal' in their outlook, big non-Muslim businessmen had very precise reasons for not relishing the prospect of a co-sharing of power between the League and the Congress at the centre. They feared the capacity of the League to exploit the internal contradictions of the Congress by proposing anti-business measures, as Liaqat Ali Khan had done in March 1947 at the time of the budget of the interim government.[65] Knowing how tenuous was the hold of the Right-wing leaders over the Congress organization, they were mortally afraid of the emergence of a 'populist' combination of Muslim and non-Muslim politicians which would have taken measures against big business interests. In this, there was also a clear coincidence of interests between non-Muslim big business and the Congress Right-wing leadership.

IV

Although many businessmen came to accept the Partition of India as the most satisfactory solution to the political deadlock, it is not suggested here that capitalists as a class were a major influence in the developments which led to it. Big business influence was probably crucial in so far as the fate of Calcutta was concerned, but in the Punjab urban capitalists were not the deciding factor.

Feelings of 'communal' solidarity, cutting across differences of caste and class, certainly existed among some businessmen, but they do not really provide a rationale for the behaviour of the business class. To argue, for instance, that Muslim business magnates in Bombay suddenly felt that they had more in common with the poorest peasants of East Bengal than with their Hindu or Parsi fellow businessmen of Bombay does not appear very sound. Attitudes towards Pakistan and Partition were determined more by considerations of personal advantage than by religious sentiments. This is not meant to imply that, from the economic point of view, Partition was a perfectly rational solution. Actually in strictly economic terms, it could be shown to be a zero-sum game, the gains of some being offset by the losses of others.

Those who gained most were undoubtedly some Muslim businessmen in the Punjab, Sind, and East Bengal, as well as some business immigrants from Bombay, Madras, and Calcutta who settled in Pakistan. They were able to take advantage of the void created by the massive departure of Hindu traders and moneylenders from the areas which went to Pakistan. They also benefited from the pro-business policy adopted by the authorities of the new country which were keen to foster industrialization in an almost exclusively agricultural country. But not all Muslim businessmen benefited from the establishment of Pakistan. The Muslim business communities remaining in the Indian Union faced a difficult situation as the more dynamic elements which were generally in a position of leadership left for Pakistan. And many Muslim businessmen who settled in Pakistan had lost almost everything they owned and had to start again from scratch. For non-Muslim businessmen who fled Pakistan and settled in India, there were the same problems, with the added difficulty that they entered a more competitive world, for in India the departure of Muslim traders had never created a void comparable to the one that existed in Pakistan.

The separation of rich agricultural areas deprived several Indian industries of a more or less captive market. Actually, Indo-Pakistani trade was very rapidly reduced to almost nothing, a development which had not been anticipated by Birla in 1947. Particularly hard hit was the Indian cotton textile industry which, after having lost a lucrative market in the Punjab and Sind, was faced with increased competition from the new Pakistani mills on the foreign markets to which it had turned to offset the loss of a part of its domestic market. The jute mills of Calcutta, having faced for a few years the problem of supply of raw material, also had to contend in the export market with the competition of the new mills of East Bengal which could exploit a large pool of cheaper labour.

In economic terms, Partition can ultimately be analysed as a response to the problem of the uneven pace of capitalist development in colonial India.[66] The formation of a new state allowed some of the least industrialized areas of India to create a minimal industrial infrastructure which had been denied to them by the workings of colonial capitalism. Those regions were under-industrialized not because they had a mainly Muslim population; other regions of the subcontinent with mainly Hindu populations (like Orissa or large tracts of central India) were no better off from that point of view. But, not having a Muslim population, they could not separate themselves and escape the domination of Bombay or Calcutta-based big business.

All the same, the inter-regional contradictions which were a powerful (although obviously not the only) factor in the Partition of India did not disappear with Partition. In the new independent state of Pakistan, capitalism developed in an even more unbalanced way than in colonial India; the Punjab and Karachi got most of the benefits while the peripheral regions, and in particular East Bengal, remained sadly neglected. The independence of Bangladesh was only the logical outcome of this whole process. On the other hand, in the Indian Union, the unitary structure which was created after 1947 has probably become one of the major obstacles to the economic development of the country and is increasingly criticized by regional capitalists. All this tends to show that the 1947 Partition could not be, contrary to what some big businessmen expected, a durable solution to the problem of growing regional economic imbalance which the colonial regime bequeathed to its successors.

## Notes

The author wishes to thank the Foreign Affairs Ministry of the Government of France for financial support to participate in the IIMA Seminar where an earlier version of this paper was presented.

1. See C.A. Bayly, 'The Pre-History of "Communalism"? Religious Conflict in India, 1700–1860', *Modern Asian Studies* IXX (1985), pp. 177–203.
2. On the various movements such as that of Sayid Ahmad of Bareilly and the *fara'izi*, see P. Hardy, *The Muslims of British India* (Cambridge, 1972), pp. 50–60. For a detailed account of developments in Bengal, see R. Ahmed, *The Bengal Muslims, 1871–1906: A Quest for Identity* (Delhi, 1981), pp. 39–105.

3. The Tyabji brothers, leaders of the Sulaimani Bohra community and Muhammad Ali Roghay, a Konkani Muslim belonging to a leading ship-owning family. C. Dobbin, *Urban Leadership in Western India: Politics and Communities in Bombay City, 1840–1885* (Oxford, 1972), p. 231.

4. As for instance, G. Pandey, 'Rallying Round the Cow: Sectarian Strife in the Bhojpuri Region, c. 1888–1917', in R. Guha (ed.), *Subaltern Studies II: Writings on South Asian History and Society* (Delhi, 1983), pp. 60–129.

5. Sec C.A. Bayly, 'Patrons and Politics in Northern India', *Modern Asian Studies* VII (1973), pp. 349–88.

6. On the corporate world of the north Indian merchants, see C.A. Bayly, *Rulers, Townsmen and Bazars: North Indian Society in the Age of British Expansion, 1770–1870* (Cambridge, 1983).

7. See A.K. Bagchi, 'European and Indian Entrepreneurship in India, 1900–1930', in E. Leach and S.N. Mukherjee (eds), *Elites in South Asia* (Cambridge, 1970), pp. 213–56.

8. W.C. Smith, *Modern Islam in India* (Lahore, 1946, 2nd reprint 1963), pp. 203–4: 'It is difficult to discover what, if anything, they mean when they say "Islam", except the Muslim community and loyalty to it . . . Usually they do not govern their lives by their religion in any other sense.'

9. He wrote: 'Capitalist society is favourable to the growth of communalism. Indian capitalist society is especially favourable to the growth of Muslim communalism'. Ibid., p. 199.

10. Ibid., p. 200.

11. B. Chandra, *Communalism in Modern India* (Delhi, 1984), p. 75.

12. C. Markovits, 'Les hommes d'affaires musulmans dans la premiere moitie du XXe siecle', *Purusartha* IX (1986), pp. 111–26 (chapter 4 in the present volume).

13. The 1930s witnessed in particular the collapse of the largest Muslim-controlled (although not exclusively Muslim-owned) industrial group in India, the Bombay-based Currimbhoy group with its large interest in cotton textiles.

14. An analysis of the names of the members of the major chambers of commerce in the principal cities of India shows a fair proportion of Muslim names. There were also Muslims in the committees of the various chambers and at times several chambers had a Muslim president.

15. On this movement, see H. Papanek, 'Pakistan's Big Businessmen: Muslim Separatism, Entrepreneurship and Partial Modernization', *Economic Development and Cultural Change* XXI (1972), pp. 1–32.

16. The *Muslim Yearbook of India and Who's Who* compiled by S.M. Jamal (Bombay, 1949) listed 88 Muslim commercial associations.

17. On Ispahani, see K. Macpherson, *The Muslim Microcosm: Calcutta 1918 to 1935* (Wiesbaden, 1974), pp. 120–51.

18. In a 'Note by the Muslim Chamber of Commerce on the Memorandum containing the Proposals of the Government of Bengal on the Delimitation of Constituencies for the Federal Legislation under the Reformed Constitution', it was claimed that Muslim traders controlled a large share of the import-export trade of Calcutta. See Muslim Chamber of Commerce, Calcutta, *Annual Report of the Committee for the Year 1935* (Calcutta, 1936), Appendix A, pp. 134–40. The hollowness of these claims was exposed in an article by N.K. Basu in the *Amrita Bazar Patrika* of 12 September 1935.

19. As shown by a systematic comparison of the resolutions passed by the two chambers between 1932 and 1942.

20. On the prolonged battle waged by Jinnah to convince the major Muslim business magnates to join the federation and the resistances he encountered, see M.A.H. Ispahani, *Qaid-e-Azam Jinnah as I Knew Him* (Karachi, 1976), pp. 119–25.

21. In particular M.A.H. Ispahani, 'Factors Leading to the Partition of British India', in C.H. Philips and M.D. Wainwright (eds.), *The Partition of India: Policies and Perspectives, 1935–1947* (London, 1970), pp. 331–59.

22. See C. Markovits, *Indian Business and Nationalist Politics 1931–39: The Indigenous Capitalist Class and the Rise of the Congress Party* (Cambridge, 1985), pp. 64–7, for some case studies.

23. Markovits, 'Les hommes d'affaires mussulmans . . .'

24. See the entry in the *Muslim Yearbook of India and Who's Who*. Sir Syed, born in 1884, managing proprietor of the firm of M/S Syed Ali & M. Wazir Ali, secretary of the All-India Canteen Contractors Association from 1922 to 1926, became a director of the Reserve Bank of India in 1935.

25. On Muslim politics in the Punjab, see D. Page, *Prelude to Partition: The Indian Muslims and the Imperial System of Control 1920–1932* (Delhi, 1982), in particular pp. 46, 72.

26. See J. Gallagher, 'Congress in Decline: Bengal 1930 to 1939', *Modern Asian Studies* VII (1973), pp. 269–325.

27. On Muslim businessmen in Calcutta, see Macpherson, *The Muslim Microcosm*, p. 22.

28. According to Page, *Prelude to Partition*, p. 130, G.D. Birla and Malaviya were behind the agitation of the Karmi Sangha to have C.R. Das's Bengal Pact rescinded.

29. See Birla to Gandhi, 14 April 1934, in which the business magnate asked the Mahatma to allow the members of the Swaraj Party 'to fight the Communal Award in their own way'. G.D. Birla, *In the Shadow of the Mahatma* (London, 1955), p. 127.

30. Although there remains a question mark as to the extent of Marwari control of the jute industry.

31. See F.C.R. Robinson, *Separatism among Indian Muslims: The Politics of the United Provinces Muslims, 1860–1923* (Cambridge, 1974).

32. The point is made in R. Kumar, 'From Swaraj to Purna Swaraj: Nationalist Politics in the City of Bombay, 1920–1932', in D.A. Low (ed.), *Congress and the Raj: Facets of the Indian Struggle, 1917–1947* (Delhi, 1977), p. 97.

33. See Purshottamdas Thakurdas Papers, file no. 72, 'Separation of Sind', Nehru Memorial Museum and Library, New Delhi.

34. In Bombay, the League won 20 of the 39 Muslim seats, and only one out of 86 in the Punjab. See A. Jalal, *The Sole Spokesman: Jinnah, the Muslim League and the Demand for Pakistan* (Cambridge, 1985), p. 32.

35. Ibid., pp. 59, 175.

36. Ibid., p. 75: 'By offering a provincial not a communal option, Cripps hoped to provide a powerful incentive for those very constituents on whom Jinnah's strategy depended to unhitch their wagons from the League's train.'

37. On 2 May 1942 the All-India Congress Committee rejected Rajagopalachari's resolution allowing separation of the Muslim provinces. Ibid., p. 83.

38. G.D. Birla to Mahadev Desai, 14 July 1942, in G.D. Birla, *Bapu, a Unique Association* (Bombay, 1977), vol. I, pp. 315–17.

39. Thus, Bipan Chandra writes in *Communalism in Modern India*, p. 71: 'The Indian capitalist class was not Hindu in any sense other than that its majority followed the Hindu religion. At no stage did any section of the Indian bourgeoisie think of itself or act objectively or subjectively as a Hindu (or Parsi) bourgeoisie or in communal terms.'

40. Lala Shri Ram to Sir Purshottamdas Thakurdas, 29 September 1942, Purshottamdas Thakurdas Papers, file no. 239.

41. In his presidential address at the annual session of the Bombay Millowners' Association, V.N. Chandavarkar declared that 'any scheme that was likely to result in the disintegration and disunity of the country was not likely to be welcomed'. Quoted in the *Times of India*, 25 March 1942.

42. A.R. Dalal, *An Alternative to Pakistan* (Bombay, 1943), p. 45.

43. Mentioned in Jalal, *The Sole Spokesman*, p. 135.

44. Ibid., p. 211.

45. See P. Thakurdas et al., *Memorandum Outlining a Plan of Economic Development for India* (Bombay, 1945).

46. The text of the statement is found in India Office Records, Economic and Overseas Department Collection, L/E/8/3618.

47. FICCI, *Proceedings of the 20th Annual Session of the Federation of Indian Chambers of Commerce and Industry* (Delhi, 1947), p. 138.

48. Ibid.

49. In April 1946, Chaudhary Khaliquzzaman mentioned to the Cabinet delegation that Muslim industrialists from Bombay might wish to transfer

their business to the Punjab. See 'Note on meeting of the Cabinet Delegation with Mohammad Ismail, I.I. Chundrigar, Chaudry Khaliquzzamman and Maulana Syed Abdur Rauf', 8 April 1946, reproduced in P.S.N. Mansergh (ed.), *India: The Transfer of Power, 1942–1947* (London, 1970–83), vol. VII, pp. 166–9.

50. Jalal, *The Sole Spokesman*, pp. 265–6.

51. A resolution passed by the Congress Working Committee on 8 March 1947 endorsed the demand for a partition of the Punjab, opening the way for the partition of Bengal. Reproduced in Mansergh (ed.), *Transfer of Power*, vol. IX, pp. 900–1.

52. The victory of Suhrawardy's faction over Nazimuddin's at the meeting of the Bengal Provincial League Committee in November 1943 led to Ispahani and Adamji's exit from the provincial cabinet. Jalal, *The Sole Spokesman*, p. 103.

53. S. Sarkar, *Modern India, 1885–1947* (Delhi, 1983), p. 436.

54. Sarat Bose to Patel, 27 May 1947, reproduced in D. Das (ed.), *Sardar Patel's Correspondence, 1945–50* (Ahmedabad, 1971–4), vol. IV, pp. 45–6.

55. In spite of the governor's efforts to have declared it as a free city. Jalal, *The Sole Spokesmen*, p. 266.

56. Capital flight from the Punjab was estimated to be as high as Rs 250 crore, and a Hindu banker declared: 'We are leaving Pakistan an economic desert.' See *Times of India*, 6 May 1947.

57. In a pamphlet brought out by G.D. Birla in 1947 under the title, 'Basic Facts Relating to Pakistan and Hindustan', it was underlined that Pakistan would get only 9 out of 389 cotton mills, none of the 108 jute mills, 10 of the 166 sugar mills, none of the 18 iron and steel mills, only 3 cement plants and none of the 16 paper mills. Quoted in *Times of India*, 7 June 1947.

58. Exports from India to Pakistan were estimated to amount to Rs 850 million (mainly cloth, coal, steel, and manufactured items) while exports from Pakistan to India amounted only to Rs 700 million (mainly cereals and raw jute, and some raw cotton). Ibid.

59. See M. Zinkin's note on Pakistan in Mansergh (ed.), *Transfer of Power*, vol. VI, pp. 801–5.

60. See Cabinet Delegation to India, Paper C.D.I.(1), ibid., vol. VI, p. 953.

61. According to her, the business supporters of the League strongly reacted to Nehru's press statement of 10 July 1946 in which he defended a strong centre capable of deploying 'central authority to restrict the freedom of action of Muslim-majority provinces in their provincial domains'. To them 'this meant the supremacy of the Tatas, the Birlas and the Dalmias in the competitive wilds of an independent India'. Jalal, *The Sole Spokesman*,

p. 210. It was clear that Jinnah and Nehru's ideas about the Centre were not compatible, and therefore some form of Pakistan was inevitable.

62. It was Patel who, on 25 April 1947, conveyed to Mountbatten that if the League was not ready to accept the Cabinet Mission's proposals, the Congress would demand partition. Mountbatten's interview with Patel, eighth miscellaneous meeting, 25 April 1947 in Mansergh (ed.), *Transfer of Power*, vol. IX. pp. 424–6.

63. See Markovits, *Indian Business and Nationalist Politics*, p. 181, on Patel's role as a 'privileged broker' of big business interests.

64. The wide definitions given to the three headings of 'Defence', 'Foreign Affairs', and 'Communications' allowed the central government to exercise its control over most economic activities and forbid the provincial governments to impose restrictions on the doings of any citizen of the Union. Muslim-majority provinces would therefore not have been permitted to discriminate against non-Muslim businessmen. See Jalal, *The Sole Spokesman*, pp. 261–2.

65. Liaqat Ali Khan, who was finance minister of the Congress-League interim government, introduced in the budget project proposals for taxation of high profits and a capital tax. He initially had the support of Nehru and Azad, but big business reaction was so strong that the Congress then stepped in to water down his proposals. The Congress–Hindu big business equation was thus planted in the minds of many, as Liaqat had probably anticipated. On this episode, see M.A.K. Azad, *India Wins Freedom* (Delhi, 1959), pp. 205–6 and C.M. Ali, *The Emergence of Pakistan* (New York, 1967), p. 105.

66. For an analysis of the problem, see A.K. Bagchi, 'Reflections on Patterns of Regional Growth in India during the Period of British Rule', *Bengal Past and Present* XCV (I): 180 (January–June 1976), pp. 247–89.

# PART II
# Entrepreneurship and Society

4

# MUSLIM BUSINESSMEN IN SOUTH ASIA *c.* 1900–1950*

THE RELATIONSHIP BETWEEN ISLAM AND CAPITALISM HAS been viewed mostly from the point of view of the 'centre' of the Muslim world,[1] less so from the perspective of its 'periphery', with a few exceptions such as those represented by Clifford Geertz's studies on Indonesia.[2] The specialists of South Asian Islam have generally paid little attention to the economic aspects of the life of the subcontinent's Muslim communities. As to the literature regarding the mercantile world of South Asia, it has little to say about the specific role of Muslims.[3] One likely explanation for that state of affairs is that the most successful amongst Indian businessmen have generally been Hindus (or Parsis), and rarely Muslims. However, the Muslim businessmen of pre-Partition India do not deserve to be totally obliterated from the record, as they have been. The development of a dynamic private business sector in post-1947 Pakistan is a timely reminder that, in the subcontinent, the entrepreneurial spirit was not a monopoly of the Hindus. Even in contemporary India, Muslims, while not occupying a prominent place in economic life, are far from being absent from the commercial and industrial world. It is therefore

*Translated from M. Gaborieau (ed.), *Islam et Société en Asie du Sud, Purusartha* 9 (Paris: Edition de l'Ecole des Hautes Etudes en Sciences Sociales, 1986), pp. 112–26.

worth having a look at the recent past of Muslim capitalism in South Asia and reflecting on the place of Muslims, and more particularly of Muslim businessmen, in the economic life of colonial India during the first half of the twentieth century.

Starting with the presentation of some basic data on the role of Muslims in the economic life of undivided India, this chapter will then focus on the emergence of a Muslim business elite. The specific problems of that elite will be examined, in particular its limited role in colonial industrial development. In conclusion, some remarks will be presented about the relationship between the Partition and Muslim businessmen.

## Some Basic Data on the Role of Muslims in the Economic Life of India before Partition

Using data from the 1931 Census of India, the last complete census before the Partition, the first point to note is the higher degree of urbanization of the Muslim population in comparison with the Hindu population (13.5 per cent as against 10.5 per cent), together with the existence of wide regional variations. In Bengal and Punjab in particular, two Muslim-majority provinces which accounted for a large part of the overall Muslim population of India, a smaller proportion of Muslims than of Hindus lived in the urban areas (3.7 per cent as against 11.8 per cent in Bengal, 12.2 per cent as against 17.8 per cent in Punjab). By contrast, in most areas where Muslims constituted a minority of the population, their urbanization rate was generally higher than that of the Hindu population. In many provinces and Indian States, it was higher than 25 per cent and sometimes close to 50 per cent.[4] It was, however, never higher than 50 per cent; even when it was fairly urbanized, the Muslim population always remained pre-dominantly rural. A broad contrast can thus be drawn between two different Muslim Indias: a compact one, corresponding to the Muslim-majority provinces and the Indian State of Jammu and Kashmir, with two-thirds of the total Muslim population, marked by a strong rural preponderance, and a more dispersed one, consisting of the provinces in which Muslims were in a minority, characterized by the existence of a significant Muslim urban population.

Since the 'first Muslim India' formed in 1947 the separate Muslim state of Pakistan, there is a tendency to conflate the specific economic problems of the regions which constituted it (primarily the western Punjab and eastern Bengal) with those of the entire Muslim community of the subcontinent. In those regions, including Sindh, which constituted Pakistan in 1947, it was a fairly urbanized Hindu minority which held the dominant positions in trade and finance, and thus the Muslim agriculturist generally was indebted to the Hindu bania. Besides, these areas, and in particular East Bengal, had very little modern industry. Hence the widespread belief that Muslim-majority areas were particularly at a disadvantage from an economic point of view. This hardly fits, however, with what is known of empirical facts. Firstly it seems that the Muslim peasantries of the western Punjab and eastern Bengal, far from being particularly impoverished, were slightly better off (prior to 1947) than most Indian peasantries. They were heavily indebted no doubt, but not more so than other peasantries. As to the fact that Muslim agriculturists were indebted to Hindu moneylenders, it would have assumed particular significance only if Hindus had lent money to Muslims at higher rates of interest than they charged Hindus, which is not an established fact. As to the industrial underdevelopment of Muslim-majority areas, it would also assume particular significance only if it could be demonstrated that no Hindu-majority region was similarly handicapped. To give only one instance, Orissa, of all the provinces of India the one with the highest percentage of Hindus in the population, was also one of the least industrialized, in spite of the presence of important mineral resources. The uneven character of industrial development in colonial India was not linked to the communal factor, but was rather an outcome of the heavy concentration of capital in a few port-cities and large inland trading centres, which in turn had resulted in a concentration of the industrial labour force in these few areas.

The idea that the Muslim minority as a whole was economically disadvantaged *vis-à-vis* the Hindu majority is not based on solid empirical facts. The commercial and financial domination exercised by Hindu banias over Muslim peasantries in Muslim-majority areas took special meaning only in the atmosphere of exacerbated communal tension of 1946–7 Bengal and Punjab. In other areas of the subcontinent, it was sometimes the case that a highly urbanized Muslim minority played a role in economic life which was out of proportion to its sheer numbers.

The data allowing us to evaluate more precisely the degree of participation of Muslims in commercial and industrial life are unfortunately of a very fragmentary nature. The 1921 Census of India is the last one to include data on the distribution of professions between the various religious communities, and its reliability is in doubt, given the difficulty of gathering data on such facts. Since there are no comparable data in the 1931 and 1941 Censuses, only a limited comparison with the earlier 1911 Census is possible to give an idea of the trend. Some of the 1921 data regarding the proportion of Muslims in the trading population are presented in Table 1, together with data

## TABLE 1

Percentage of Muslims in Population Engaged in Trade
(both workers and dependents) in Selected Provinces and
Indian States according to the 1921 Census of India

| Province or State | Percentage of Muslims in total urban population | Percentage of Muslims in population engaged in trade |
| --- | --- | --- |
| Bengal | 27.5 | 24.3 |
| Bombay | 20.7 | 26.0 (only males in 'cities') |
| Hyderabad | 34.0 | 12.5 |
| Madras | 13.1 | 21.5 (only males) |
| Punjab | 51.6 | 28.6 (only 'cities') |
| United Provinces | 37.5 | 40.4 |

*Source*: Computed from Table V, 'Towns arranged territorially with population by religion' and Table XX, 'Distribution by religion of workers and dependents in different occupations' in the volumes for the different provinces and Indian States in *Census of India 1921*.

on the proportion of Muslims in the urban population, the underlying assumption being that most traders lived in the urban areas.

The six territorial units examined fall into two distinct categories. In Bengal, Hyderabad, and Punjab, the proportion of Muslims engaged in trade was lower than that of Muslims in the urban population, while it was the opposite in Bombay, Madras, and the United Provinces. Within the first group, a clear contrast existed also between Bengal and Punjab: in the former province, the urban Muslim population was relatively small and consisted mostly of traders and craftsmen, while in Punjab, where the urban Muslims were more in evidence, there was a large non-trading Muslim middle class, which was practically absent in Bengal. As to Hyderabad, the weakness of the Muslim trading group is explained by the predominance of landowners and clerical personnel in the Muslim population of the towns, which is in turn related to the dominant position occupied by Muslims in that Indian State. In Bombay, Madras, and the United Provinces, it appears that the Muslim minority, which was fairly urbanized, also had an orientation towards trade.

Looking at various branches of trade, Muslim specialization appears strong (albeit with significant regional variations) in the trade in leather and skins,[5] as well as in the trade in 'luxury articles' (an ill-defined category), noticeable in the trade in textiles,[6] and weak in all other branches, especially banking and finance. These statistics, however, give no indication as to the turnover of the different branches and do not allow for an estimate of the share of Muslims in sectoral output.

On the basis of the data presented here, no more precise conclusion can be drawn than that in the 1920s Muslims had a place which was not negligible in the commercial life of India, in particular in the larger centres. Since there are few indications as to later trends, outside Bombay,[7] it is impossible to know whether the trend towards a fall in Muslim participation in trade, which is observable there, applied elsewhere also.

As far as the manufacturing industry is concerned, data are more abundant and mostly more reliable. The 1921 and 1911 Censuses give two kinds of informations. The first one concerns the religious affiliation of owners of private industrial establishments (not belonging to joint-stock companies), that is, more or less corresponding to the category of small- and medium-scale industries. They are reproduced in Table 2 for the whole of India.

The ratio, which remained stable between 1911 and 1921, stood at approximately 4.5 to 1 in favour of Hindus, as against 3 to 1 in the overall population, a difference which is not very significant. Nothing unfortunately is known of the trend after 1921.

A second kind of data, more comprehensive, bear upon the religious affiliation of the managers of all industrial establishments, whether privately owned or owned by joint-stock companies. In 1921, Hindus managed 8,079 establishments, Muslims only 1,373, that is, a ratio of 6 to 1 in favour of Hindus, the difference with the previous data being mostly due to the weight of the 'organized' sector in which Hindu predominance was much greater. It is also clear that some establishments owned by Muslims were managed by Hindus. Looking in detail at various branches, Muslims are seen to occupy a leading position only in leather and skins, while in the closely related sector of footwear, Hindus dominated, which reveals a lack of vertical integration in the

TABLE 2

Number of Industrial Establishments by Religious Affiliation
of Owners All-India, 1911–21

| Census year | Number of establishments owned by Hindus | Number of establishments owned by Muslims |
|---|---|---|
| 1911 | 1,818 | 400 |
| 1921 | 7,153 | 1,629 |

*Source*: Computed from Table XV–E—Part III, 'Statistics of Industries: Particulars of Ownership of Factories, etc.', in the volumes for various Provinces and Indian States in *Census of India 1911* and Table XXII, 'Industrial Statistics, Part III—Industrial Establishments classified according to the class of Owners and Managers', in the volumes for various Provinces and Indian States in *Census of India 1921*. For 1911, data are not available for Baluchistan, Cochin, Northwest Frontier Province, and Punjab; for 1921, data are not available for Baluchistan and Northwest Frontier Province.

activities of Muslim industrialists. Muslims occupied a significant position in only a few other sectors: timber, furniture, tobacco, and cigarettes. They also occupied a position which was not insignificant in the cotton textile industry, by far the largest industrial branch in India at the time.

A look at widely scattered data concerning other branches[8] leads to the conclusion that during the 1921–47 period, small- and medium-scale Muslim entrepreneurs had some success, but were unable to increase their relative share of the industrial sector of the economy.

It is therefore in trade more than in industry that a Muslim business elite can be found. The next section focuses on this elite.

### A Muslim Business Elite?

There is no systematic study of big Muslim merchants and capitalists in pre-Partition India. There are useful indications, however, both in a study by Hanna Papanek of big Pakistani businessmen[9] and in the writings of Kenneth Macpherson on the Muslims of Tamil Nadu and Calcutta.[10] *Who's Who*[11] and biographical dictionaries[12] are also a precious source of information on individual businessmen. If one adds scattered data from various provenance, there is enough to allow for at least a partial reconstruction of the profile of the pre-Partition Muslim business elite.

A first question relates to its place within the wider business elite. While Europeans remained dominant in big business in India at least till the eve of the Second World War, an indigenous business elite started taking shape from the middle of the nineteenth century onwards and grew quickly in the post-First World War period, being thus able to gradually challenge the European domination of external trade, finance, and industry.[13] This elite, in which Parsis at first played an important role, became increasingly dominated by Hindu (and Jain) businessmen of merchant caste background, mostly Gujarati and Marwari. It, however, also included a Muslim component.

A list I have compiled elsewhere of the major business groups operating in India in the 1931–9 period[14] does not, however, include any Muslim name, except that of the Currimbhoy group in 1931, but that list, which is based on the capital of joint-stock companies alone, is heavily biased towards large-scale industry and tends to under-estimate the importance of trading and finance, in which some Muslim businessmen accumulated significant assets.

On the other hand, basing myself on the above-mentioned sources, I have been able to compile a list of 19 important Muslim business families in pre-1947 India: they were, in Bombay, the Adam, Arag, Currimbhoy, Dada, Habib, Lallji, Tyabji, and Valika families; in Calcutta, the Adamji, Amin, Ariff, Ispahani, Salehji, and Shustari families; in Karachi, the Haroon family; in Lahore the Nasin Sheikh and Wazir Ali families; in Madras, the Badshah and Khan families. To this list of merchant dynasties could be added the names of a certain number of individuals who played a prominent role in the business world in the first half of the twentieth century: in Bombay, Sultan Chinoy, Ibrahim Rahimtoolla, and Umar Sobhani; in Calcutta, A.H. Ghuznavi; in Madras, Abdul Hakim, Yakub Hasan, and Jamal Mohamed; lastly there is the very specific case of the two ministers of the Nizam of Hyderabad, Salar Jung and Mir Laik Ali, who, thanks to the patronage of the ruler, built up significant industrial groups in the 1930s and 1940s.

Apart from the Currimbhoys, big cotton industrialists who went bankrupt in 1934, and the Adamjis who, by 1947, had large match and jute factories, the other Muslim capitalists were mostly traders and 'contractors'. The Habibs, however, were large bullion traders and financiers and founded in 1941 what was to be the first large-scale Muslim-controlled bank and insurance company. As traders, Muslims were particularly represented in the wheat and rice trade (Adam, Arag, Dada, Ispahani), and the leather and skin trade (Ispahani, Khan, Jamal Mohamed), where they occupied dominant positions, while they also figured in the jute trade (Adamji, Amin), the sugar trade (Haroon), and coastal shipping (Ghuznavi), but were weak in the essential cotton and cotton textile trades. Some Muslims were prominent as contractors: the firm of Shalebhoy Tyabji was dominant in contracting for the railways, while Wazir Ali led in military canteens in the Punjab (a huge business given the number of military garrisons in that province); Haroon was heavily involved in the building of New Delhi (he got part of the contract for the construction of the Legislative Assembly building).

Looking more closely at the composition of that elite in sectarian and regional terms, one is struck by the importance of the Shi'a element. Out of 17 families for which data are available, seven were Shi'a (Currimbhoy, Habib, Lallji, Tyabji, Valika, Ispahani, and Shustari), and Shi'as were particularly prominent in Bombay (with five of the eight biggest Muslim business families). The share of Shi'as in the business elite was thus out of proportion to their overall numbers (at most 10 per cent of India's Muslim population). Amongst Shi'as, Ismaili were not overrepresented: there were only the Tyabjis and Valikas, both Ismaili Bohra families belonging to the Mustali'an branch of Ismailism.[15] Ithna-ashari Khojas figured more prominently, with the Currimbhoys, Habibs, and Lalljis. Of ten Sunni families, five (Adam, Adamji, Arag, Dada, and Haroon) belonged to the Memon community of Kutch and Kathiawar who, like the Bohras and Khojas, were relatively recent converts to Islam from Hinduism. Therefore three groups of recent converts from Gujarat and Kutch accounted for the bulk of the Muslim business elite. Of the seven non-Gujarati families, two (Ispahani and Shustari) had Iranian origins, one (Khan) was of Afghan background, three (Amin, Nasin Sheikh, Wazir Ali) hailed from the Punjab and only the Madras-based Badshah family belonged to the group of North Indian Urdu-speaking Muslims who were culturally and politically dominant in Indian Islam.

It is noteworthy that Bengali Muslims, demographically the largest section of Indian Islam, were not represented at all in the elite, not even in Calcutta. It is clear that the composition of the Muslim business elite did not reflect that of the overall Muslim population, whether in regional or in sectarian terms.

Whatever is known of the history of these families does not reveal the existence of common features as strong as appear in the trajectory of elite Hindu business families. Although they often belonged to longstanding merchant lineages, their rise seems to have been fairly recent. One of the reasons is that the class of great Muslim maritime merchants of the Mughal era, whose most flamboyant representative was the famous Mulla Abdul Ghaffur of Surat,[16] was a direct victim of the monopolization of India's long-distance maritime trade by the East India Company. In internal trade, Muslims also seemed to be losing ground in the eighteenth century, as revealed by the pathetic tone of Shah Walliullah's (1703–80s) address to the Afghan ruler Ahmad Shah Abdali, whose invasions of the Punjab are still remembered, in which he thus described the situation of his co-religionaries: 'Wealth and prosperity are concentrated in their hands (of the Hindus) while the share of Muslims is nothing but poverty and misery.'[17] The situation got only aggravated during the second half of the eighteenth century and C.A. Bayly notes that, in Gangetic northern India, Muslim merchants, already on the decline circa 1750, had been all but wiped out by 1800.[18] The completion of British conquest brought about no reversal of trend, and a Muslim business elite re-emerged very gradually from within the colonial port-cities during the nineteenth century. By the end of the century, some Muslim businessmen were in a position to exploit some of the opportunities which opened up in the Indian colonial economy. Thus, in the 1880s, the Currimbhoys, who had made a fortune in the opium trade with China, started a successful career as industrialists in the fast developing cotton textile sector. The Ispahanis, rich Iranian merchants who landed in Bombay in 1820, moved to Madras in 1867 and finally settled in Calcutta in 1900, where they came to play a big role in the then thriving indigo export trade. When indigo declined, they shifted to leather, where they quickly occupied a strong position.[19] It was in the 1920s that the Adamjis, who had been trading in Calcutta since the late eighteenth century and were active in the Burma rice trade (they owned rice mills in Burma) started investing in the jute and match industries. They were for a while the largest match manufacturers in India. In the same decade, Abdullah Haroon, a Karachi-based Kutchi Memon who started business on a modest scale in 1896, emerged as the 'Sugar King', the biggest importer of Java sugar (which then accounted for most of

India's consumption). It seems nevertheless that in the 1930s some Muslim businessmen went through difficult times (the Currimbhoys even went bankrput), precisely at the time when some Hindu Marwari businessmen were particularly successful.[20]

While in all the main commercial centres there were Muslim businessmen, some of whom occupied important positions in certain branches of trade, is it possible to see this Muslim business elite as the embryo of a specifically Muslim capitalist class, clearly separate from the rest of the Indian capitalist class? This is a doubtful proposition. What strikes the student of the Muslim business elite is rather its fragmentation, a trait which is characteristic of Indian business in general.[21] While a certain amount of solidarity seems to have existed amongst Muslim businessmen in Calcutta and Madras from the 1920s onwards, it appears to have been largely absent in Bombay.

Prior to the late 1930s, Muslim businessmen from different regions and cities had very little to do with each other. The first enterprise created thanks to the cooperation between Muslim businessmen in Calcutta and Bombay was the Eastern Federal Insurance Co., set up in 1932 with the financial support of one of the major Muslim princely rulers, the Nawab of Bhopal, with the specific aim of allowing Muslim businessmen to insure themselves with a Muslim-controlled company. But it was only in 1946 that, at Jinnah's prompting, a Muslim air company and a Muslim shipping line were set up.[22] Till the eve of Partition, even those Muslim capitalists such as Adamji or Ispahani who were closest to Jinnah and the Muslim League, continued to co-operate with their Hindu colleagues (thus Ispahani, the main financier of the Muslim League, had joint ventures with Birla, the main financier of the Congress).

From 1932 onwards, there was nevertheless a growing trend towards the creation of separate Muslim chambers of commerce and trade associations. That same year, a Muslim Chamber of Commerce was created in Calcutta, and, from the late 1930s, such organizations mushroomed. According to the *Muslim Yearbook*, there were 88 of them in 1948 in both India and Pakistan. But it was only in 1945, following

Jinnah's vigorous intervention, that most of these chambers and associations federated themselves into a 'Federation of Muslim Chambers of Commerce and Industry' which was a Muslim response to the Federation of Indian Chambers of Commerce and Industry (FICCI), formed in 1927 and dominated by big Hindu capitalists such as Birla.[23] The belated birth of such an organization was testimony to the fact that it was not easy to link together Muslim businessmen from different regions and different backgrounds. Only politics could bring them together.

It should also be noted that, unlike their Hindu and Parsi colleagues who, in the 1944 blueprint known as the 'Bombay Plan', had set up a coherent economic programme, which was largely implemented by India after Independence, Muslim businessmen did not formulate policy guidelines relating to the future economic strategy of Pakistan. This may have had to do partly with the fact that most of them were traders, with little experience in the matter of industry. Which leads to the following interrogation: why did Muslim businessmen contribute so little to the development of large-scale industry in pre-Partition India?

## Muslim Businessmen and Industry

During the 'second colonial century' (*c.* 1850–1947), India underwent a process of industrial development, albeit limited and haltingly slow.[24] In this process, an important role was played at first by European businessmen (mostly in the jute industry of Calcutta), but gradually Indian businessmen took the lead in it. These industrialists came mostly from a merchant background. But, while numerous Parsi, Hindu, and Jain merchants transformed themselves at least partly into industrialists, there were few Muslim merchants who followed that same trajectory.

The only two Muslim merchant families which attained prominence in industry were the Currimbhoys and Adamjis (leaving aside the very specific case of the 'Nizam's capitalists' in Hyderabad State). How to account for such a low level of participation by Muslims in colonial industrial development? Is it to be explained in structural terms, as the result of socio-cultural determinations, or is the explanation more contingent, the end result being the outcome of a specific set of circumstances? Post-1947 Pakistani businessmen favour the first kind of explanation: they assert that, prior to Partition, Muslim businessmen were the victims of a real 'Hindu plot' meant to prevent them at all cost from carving for themselves a place in the manufacturing sector.[25] Unfortunately this assertion is based on scanty empirical evidence. In fact, if there was discrimination in the business world of colonial India, in particular in the lending practices of the major banks, it was in favour of European businessmen and to the detriment of Indian businessmen of whatever community.[26] One of the few authors to have considered the question, Theodore Wright puts forward a Weber-inspired sociological explanation: according to him, the 'protestant ethic' would have been present only amongst some small communities and sects, mostly Shi'a, and would account for their successes in business.[27] Apart from the fact that the implicit assimilation of Shi'a to protestants is disputable, there remains to be explained why even Bohras, Khojas, and Memons, however much endowed with a greater entrepreneurial spirit than most of their co-religionaries, still shied away from investing in industrial ventures.

In her above-quoted article, Hanna Papanek emphasized two points: firstly, the educational backwardness of Muslims, which would have made them ill-prepared for engaging in modern activities which required a certain level of technical knowledge, and secondly, the role of caste in Indian society which tended to favour monopolization of certain activities by specific groups and gave a premium to already entrenched interests in specialized branches of activity.[28] Regarding the first point, it could be shown that most Hindu industrialists had very little technical knowledge either, which tends to throw doubt on the worth of that line of reasoning. The second point is more complex, and it is necessary to disentangle the structural aspect of caste from its more conjunctural manifestations. Regarding caste itself, recent anthropological literature tends to argue that it was operational among Muslims also, although in a context which differed from the one prevailing among Hindus.[29] It cannot be said therefore that the caste system per se favoured Hindus to the detriment of Muslims. On the other hand, it is true that once a particular caste group had become entrenched in a particular branch of activity, it was difficult to dislodge it. The fact is that Hindus generally occupied dominant positions in most branches at the time when Muslims were in a position to enter them, and that it became difficult for Muslims to achieve a breakthrough. There is no clear evidence, however, of deliberate attempts at excluding Muslims as such from specific branches of industry. In all branches which do not go through a process of rapid growth (and this was the case for most branches of industry in India prior to 1947), those who are already in place tend to exclude newcomers.

Two other socio-cultural factors have been invoked at times: the structure of the family and the Koranic prohibition against interest. It is accepted that Hindu businesses derived part of their efficiency from their close identification with the Hindu joint family. Such a structure allows for an optimal utilization of limited human and financial resources and the fact that it has legal recognition facilitates the integral transmission of assets between generations. As to the situation of the Muslim family in India, it was characterized by complexity. Recent anthropological studies show the joint family to have been as widespread among Muslims as among Hindus.[30] The Muslim joint family did not, however, enjoy the same kind of legal recognition in British India as the Hindu joint family. In matters of succession, the so-called 'Anglo-Muslim' legal system, which claimed to be based on the *shari'a,* tended to favour fragmentation rather than integral transmission of assets.[31] It is interesting to note that, in matters of succession, the Khojas, as well as the Memons (till 1938) had their own law, closer to Hindu than to Muslim law: in these communities women did not inherit and a person could bequeath by will the totality of his assets to a person of his own choice, an option that, in Koranic law, is limited to one-third of a deceased's assets.[32]

How much the prescriptions of shari'a and the supposedly shari'a-based Anglo-Muslim law in matters of inheritance and succession were actually implemented among Indian Muslims is of course a moot point. Therefore the difference between Hindu and Muslim family structures should not be given too much prominence as an explanatory factor for differences in economic behaviour. The same strictures apply to the Koranic injunction against *ri'ba*: there is little congruence between Koranic prohibition and observable facts.[33] It seems established that, in the Indian countryside, moneylending was more or less a monopoly of Hindus, mostly banias, and the profits accrued to moneylending were an important source of capital accumulation for such Hindu business communities as the Marwaris. But, in urban areas, some Muslim groups such as the Pathans were important credit providers and applied rates which were as high as those demanded by their Hindu colleagues. On the whole, however, their relative weakness in the financial sector was certainly a disadvantage to Muslim businessmen.

Even if caste solidarity was not as developed among Muslims as among Hindus, the former's lower degree of participation in industry cannot be accounted for in socio-cultural terms. The most plausible explanation is in terms of a combination of conjunctural factors, which in turn are linked to the historical trajectory of the Muslim community in India.

The decisive factor is the late entry of Muslims into large-scale trade, which is due on the one hand to the losses sustained by them in the crucial eighteenth century, and on the other hand to the attitude of the colonial authorities and European businessmen who used mostly Hindu (and Parsi) merchants as brokers and intermediaries in their commercial and financial transactions from the late seventeenth century onwards. This preference, which was rooted in economic causes, might have taken on a political tinge at some point, as Muslims often appeared more hostile than Hindus to British rule. Whatever the reason, this attitude cost Muslims a lot by preventing them from accumulating capital in an intermediary role, which proved important to the overall success of Hindu (and Parsi) businessmen. When colonial policies changed, in the early 1920s, and the administration became more favourable to Muslims, who were seen as less prone to nationalism than Hindus, the latter had already started their partial reconversion towards industry, while Muslims were still struggling to carve a niche for themselves in commerce. In the 1920s, of the major Muslim business families, only the Adamjis moved significantly into the industrial sector. Why did no other follow suit? There are three possible explanations: firstly, a systematic opposition to Muslims' entry on the part of existing entrenched Hindu interests; secondly, the existence of more attractive opportunities elsewhere; and thirdly, internal factors hampering the move of Muslims into industry.

The first point, as already mentioned, is doubtful. The second one, on the other hand, does not seem devoid of validity. It appears that Muslim businessmen, in the 1920s and 1930s, found, outside industry and outside India, opportunities which were more alluring than industrial investment. It seems that, from the 1920s onwards, although empirical evidence is not abundant, it was easier for Muslims than for Hindus to get contracts from the colonial administration. Not that the British authorities systematically discriminated in favour of Muslims, but, because many Hindu businessmen were, rightly or wrongly, suspected of Congress sympathies, the British became reluctant to award them contracts, especially in sensitive areas, such as defence. Muslims who, like the Parsis, were generally deemed 'loyalist' necessarily benefited from it and the evidence from *Who's Who* and biographical dictionaries is that, among Muslim prominent businessmen, there was a growing number of people who could be described as contractors. The example of the firm of Wazir Ali in the Punjab and its acquisition of a quasi-monopoly over military canteens is one case in point. Paradoxically, the belated acquisition by Muslim businessmen of privileged linkages to the British blocked their entry in industry, because State contracts offered possibilities of profit which were higher than in the industrial sector.

Another factor which deterred Muslim businessmen from investing into industry in India was the attraction of outside investment, particularly in British territories. Among Indian merchants settled outside India, especially along the western shores of the Indian Ocean, the proportion of Muslims was high.[34] They were mostly Gujarati, in particular Ismaili Khojas, and in the inter-war period they generally expanded and maintained close links with their communities in India, socially as well as economically. Muslims from South India, in particular the Marakkayars of Tamil Nadu, also had a strong outward orientation, mostly to Southeast Asia.

The most decisive factor explaining the weak position of Muslims in industry is, however, most probably the attitude of the dominant groups of Indian Muslim society towards industry. While big Hindu landlords and princes, as well as some professionals, invested a significant share of their savings in industry, and thus powerfully supported indigenous industrial enterprise, nothing comparable occurred among Muslims. Muslim elites, whether the big landlords or the small semi-urban gentry of the *qasbahs*, were little affected by the development of a trend of economic nationalism epitomized by the Swadeshi movement, which contributed in no small way to directing a part of the savings of the Hindu middle class towards industry. Muslim grandees did not show particular interest in the few industrial ventures of their co-religionaries. Although the two richest Muslim princes, the Nizam of Hyderabad and the Nawab of Bhopal, extended some financial support to Muslim enterprises in the 1930s and 1940s, their contribution could not be compared to that of some of the Hindu princes, like Scindia of Gwalior, the Gaekwar of Baroda, or the Maharaja of Darbhanga. Lack of support from a Muslim public was a major handicap for the development of Muslim industry. The leaders of the community, whether the secular elite or the *ulama,* had little awareness of the problems of modern economic life. Jinnah was the first to have understood the long-term implications of the industrial weakness of the Muslim community. But his efforts to incite Muslim businessmen to create Muslim industrial enterprises largely fell upon deaf ears. Muslim businessmen on the whole did not think of themselves as belonging to an economically separate community and, in the way they conducted their businesses, short-term economic considerations weighed more than religious solidarity.

If the economic behaviour of Muslim businessmen is characterized by the weak role played in it by ideological factors, how does one explain the fact that in the late 1930s and in the 1940s many of them tended to support the Muslim League and accept Pakistan? We shall briefly attempt to answer that question.

## Muslim Businessmen and Partition

Hana Papanek has dealt with the question in the above-quoted article. She is careful not to overestimate the importance of economic motivations and capitalist interventions in the rise of Muslim separatism. At the same time, she draws attention to the growing links which developed from the late 1930s onwards between Jinnah and a handful of big Muslim capitalists, such as the Adamjis, Habibs, and Ispahanis. The most politically active of Muslim capitalists was undoubtedly Al Haj Mirza Abul Hassan Ispahani, who became in the late 1930s the main financier of the Muslim League. Most of his colleagues were much more prudent in supporting the League and some of them, like Husseinbhoy Lallji and the Tyabji family in Bombay, openly opposed Muslim separatism.

The attitude of big Muslim capitalists, seen as a group, appears not devoid of ambiguity. It seems that they kept their options open till the very last moment. The fact that they maintained close business links with Hindu colleagues till at least 1946 (Birla and Ispahani set up in that year a joint venture in Calcutta) shows that they had not put all their bets on a partition. They probably hoped (like Jinnah?) for a last-minute compromise between the Congress and the League which would allow a partition to be avoided while giving Muslims a real influence in the post-colonial Indian regime. If a separate state was to come into being, then the question of its exact limits was important to them. In Bengal in particular, Muslim capitalists' assets were mostly in Calcutta rather than in East Bengal, and the division of Bengal proved costly for some of the biggest Muslim capitalists, including Ispahani and Adamji. They decided that they had no option but that to migrate to the new state of Pakistan, leaving behind most of their assets. Although the exact reasons why they made that choice are not known, it is probable that they thought that in India they would have little opportunities for success. This, in spite of the fact that, in 1947, Pakistan's economic prospects did not appear very bright. So it is difficult to decide whether they rallied to the Pakistan cause out of genuine enthusiasm or because it appeared a lesser evil. The fact that the choice they made proved in the end rewarding must not lead us to think that it was the only possible one.

## Conclusion

In an article published in 1970, M.A.H. Ispahani gave his own interpretation of the factors behind India's partition. He wrote:

> The economic situation in pre-independence India was one of the factors which influenced the Muslims to seek their deliverance and security in the shape of a separate homeland and state. Business and industry were overwhelmingly the monopoly of the Hindu bania. . . . Most of the industries and almost the entire internal trade, from money-lending to the buying and selling of all types of produce—raw and finished—were in the hands of the Hindus. Muslims only subsisted on the crumbs which were swept off these monopolists' tables . . ..[35]

Although he recognized in a later passage that there were a few exceptions to the Hindu domination and a few cases of successful Muslim businessmen (including himself, one could add), his overall description of the situation of Muslims in the subcontinent in 1947 largely echoed that penned by Shah Walliullah two centuries before. On the basis of our findings here, we cannot of course subscribe to such views, which fit in a little bit too cosily with the 'black legend' that passes off in Pakistan for historical truth.

It seems reasonable to clearly differentiate between the problems faced by the broad masses of the Muslim population, including small traders and small industrialists, and those of a small elite of big merchant capitalists. The mass of Muslims had the same difficulties and suffered from the same evils as the mass of Hindus: the relative stagnation of agricultural output combined with growing demographic pressure, the growth of indebtedness, the difficulty for small traders and industrialists to get credit at reasonable rates, etc. There is no clear evidence that in the 1930s and 1940s the Muslim masses suffered more than the Hindu masses from the economic turbulences that the subcontinent was subjected to. On the basis of the data in the 1921 Census of India, we could gain an approximate idea of the place occupied by Muslims in the commercial and industrial sectors. In spite of a lack of precise data, what is known of the trend in 1921–47 does not lead to the conclusion that the position of Muslims deteriorated more than in a marginal way.

Regarding the Muslim elite, on which our attention has been focused, things appear in a clearer light. That elite, which had emerged mostly in the late nineteenth and early twentieth centuries, seemed on its way up in the 1920s but saw its rise blocked in the 1930s and 1940s, a period characterized by rapid growth for Hindu and Parsi capitalists who were in a position to increasingly challenge the domination of British capital over the 'modern' sector of the Indian economy. It is their inability to move from trade into industry, at a moment where opportunities were being increasingly restricted in the trading sector, which was the determining factor of the lag between Muslim entrepreneurs and their Hindu and Parsi colleagues. As to how to interpret these facts, our choice has been to underline conjunctural factors as well as certain general features of the Indian Muslim elites.

Turning to the situation as it is in the mid-1980s, some 40 years after Partition, it appears that those who emigrated from India after 1947 have done well for themselves in Pakistan. A list of the major Pakistani business groups in the late 1960s[36] is clear evidence of it. On that list figure most of the names of the pre-1947 all-India Muslim business elite., who account for a third of the total. If it is added that a contemporary list of big business groups in India includes only one Muslim name,[37] present facts will appear as a clear vindication of the choice of Pakistan by most of the big pre-1947 Muslim business families. It seems in retrospect that the creation of a Muslim state was a necessary and sufficient condition for the flourishing of Muslim capitalism. This statement, however, must be nuanced. Firstly, there is no proof that, had India remained united, Muslim businessmen would not have achieved the breakthrough they achieved in Pakistan. Perhaps it was only in the late 1940s that they were really ready to enter industry in a big way. Let us not forget either that these émigrés could bring with them to Pakistan part of their liquid assets, that they often received some compensation for their lost properties, that they benefitted from a state policy in Pakistan which was exceptionally favourable to private enterprise, and that the massive departure of Hindu businessmen from the Punjab and Sind left the field wide open.

As to the travails of Muslim businessmen in post-1947 India, it must be kept in mind that emigration deprived the community of some of its most dynamic elements. The few families who stayed behind rapidly sank. The reconstruction of a Muslim business elite in India will necessarily be a slow process, for moving from trade or small-scale industry to large-scale industry is even more difficult than it was before 1947, given the strongly oligopolistic structure of the Indian big business sector. However, the successes obtained by Muslims in certain fields (like the metals industry) show that they do not lack enterprise, and therefore the gradual re-emergence of a Muslim business elite in India is not ruled out. In any case, it is still too early to pronounce a final verdict on the economic balance sheet of India's Partition.

## Notes

1. See M. Rodinson, *Islam et Capitalisme*, Paris, 1966, a work which remains seminal in its conclusions which apply also to South Asia.
2. C. Geertz, *Peddlers and Princes: Social Change and Economic Modernisation in Two Indonesian Towns* (Chicago, 1963).
3. One of the few monographs bearing specifically on Muslim merchants is M. Mines, *Muslim Merchants: The Economic Behaviour of an Indian Muslim Community* (New Delhi, 1972).
4. Some figures on the urbanization rate of the Muslim population in various provinces and Indian States in 1931: Madras, 25.3 per cent, United Provinces, 28.9 per cent, Hyderabad State, 33.5 per cent, Rajputana States, 35.8 per cent, Mysore State, 42.7 per cent, Central Provinces, 45.2 per cent, Central Indian States, 47.5 per cent. *Census of India 1931*, volumes for different provinces and Indian States.

5. Highest in Punjab with Muslims accounting for 89.3 per cent of the total, significant in Madras with 54.3 per cent, and the United Provinces with 49.6 per cent, but low in Bengal, with only 22.2 per cent. Table XX, 'Distribution by religion of workers and dependents in different occupations', *Census of India 1921*, volumes for relevant provinces.

6. Over 30 per cent in Bombay, 33.9 per cent in Bengal, 47.8 per cent in the United Provinces. Ibid.

7. Between the 1921 and 1931 Census, the proportion of Muslims amongst males engaged in trade fell from 43.3 to 32.7 per cent. See *Census of India 1921, vol. IX, II, Cities of the Bombay Presidency,* City Table VII, and *Census of India 1931, vol. IX, Bombay Presidency*, City Table VII.

8. See in particular the list of Muslim industrial enterprises reproduced in S.M. Jamil (comp.), *The Muslim Yearbook and Who's Who* (Bombay, 1949).

9. H. Papanek, 'Pakistan's Big Businessmen: Muslim Separatism, Entrepreneurship and Partial Modernization', *Economic Development and Cultural Change* XXI: 1 (1972), pp. 1–32.

10. K. Macpherson, 'The Social Background and Politics of the Muslims of Tamilnadu, 1901–1937', *Indian Economic and Social History Review* VI: 4 (1969), pp. 381–402, and *The Muslim Microcosm: Calcutta 1918 to 1935* (Wiesbaden, 1974).

11. S.M. Jamil, *The Muslim Yearbook.*

12. In particular N.K. Jain (ed.), *Muslims in India: A Biographical Dictionary,* vol. I (Delhi, 1979).

13. See C. Markovits, *Indian Business and Nationalist Politics 1931–1939* (Cambridge 1985, reprint 2002).

14. Ibid., pp. 190–3.

15. See J.N. Hollister, *The Shi'a of India* (London, 1953).

16. See A. Das Gupta, *Indian Merchants and the Decline of Surat (1700–1750)* (Wiesbaden, 1979).

17. Quoted in K.B. Sayeed, *Pakistan: The Formative Phase 1857–1943* (Karachi, 1960), p. 2.

18. C.A. Bayly, *Rulers, Townsmen and Bazaars: North Indian Society during the Age of British Expansion (1770–1870)* (Cambridge, 1983), p. 31.

19. See Macpherson, *The Muslim Microcosm,* p. 121.

20. See T.A. Timberg, *The Marwaris: From Traders to Industrialists* (Delhi, 1978).

21. See Markovits, *Indian Business.*

22. Papanek, 'Pakistan's Big Businessmen', p. 12.

23. See the memoirs of M.A.H. Ispahani, *Qaid-e-Azam Jinnah as I Knew Him* (Karachi, 1976, 3rd edition), pp. 119–30.

24. See M.D. Morris, 'The Growth of Large-Scale Industry to 1947', in D. Kumar (ed.), *The Cambridge Economic History of India,* vol. 2 (Cambridge, 1983), pp. 553–676.

25. See in particular M.A.H. Ispahani, 'Factors Leading to the Partition of British India', in C.H. Philips and M.D. Wainwright (eds), *The Partition of India: Policies and Perspectives, 1935–1947* (London, 1970), p. 356.

26. On this point, see A.K. Bagchi, 'European and Indian Entrepreneurship in India 1900–30', in E. Leach and S.N. Mukherjee (eds), *Elites in South Asia* (Cambridge, 1970), pp. 223–56.

27. T.P. Wright, Jr, 'Muslim Kinship and Modernization: The Tyabji Clan of Bombay', in I. Ahmad (ed*.), Family, Kinship and Marriage among Muslims in India* (Delhi, 1976), p. 218.

28. Papanek, 'Pakistan's Big Businessmen', pp. 3–4.

29. See, for a whole set of studies, I. Ahmad (ed.), *Caste and Social Stratification among Muslims in India* (Delhi, 1978).

30. Ahmad, *Family, Kinship and Marriage.*

31. See, for an overall view on the legal aspect, N.J. Coulson, *Succession in the Muslim Family* (Cambridge, 1971).

32. See Hollister, *The Shi'a of India*, p. 400.

33. For a detailed and convincing discussion of this point, see Rodinson, *Islam et Capitalisme*, pp. 31–2, 52–65. He shows in particular that Indian Muslims were actively engaged in moneylending in Mecca in the nineteenth century at the time of the Haj, and he also quotes the work of Sir Malcolm Darling about the Punjab, in which the growing tendency of rich Muslim land-owners to advance money to their tenants is mentioned. See M. Darling, *The Punjab Peasant in Prosperity and Debt* (Oxford, 1947), p. 198, quoted in Rodinson, pp. 161–2.

34. For an update, see C. Markovits, 'Indian Merchant Networks outside India in the Nineteenth and Twentieth Centuries: A Preliminary Survey', *Modern Asian Studies* 33: 4 (October 1999), pp. 883–911. (Chapter 9 in the present volume.)

35. Ispahani, 'Factors Leading to the Partition of British India', in Philips and Wainwright (eds), *The Partition of India*, p. 356.

36. See L. White, *Industrial Concentration and Economic Power in Pakistan* (Princeton, 1974), Table 4–1.

37. List included in T.A. Timberg, *Industrial Entrepreneurship among the Trading Communities of India: How the Pattern Differs* (Cambridge, Mass., 1969).

5

# BOMBAY AS A BUSINESS CENTRE
# IN THE COLONIAL PERIOD

## A Comparison with Calcutta*

COMPARISONS BETWEEN BOMBAY AND CALCUTTA AS cities are a fairly hackneyed topic. However, a systematic comparison between those two metropolises, focusing on their role as command centres, has, to my knowledge, never been done. This chapter is a very preliminary attempt at such an exercise. It draws attention, firstly, to the existence of a pattern of dual dominance in the Indian colonial economy, which is generally taken for granted but actually calls for some explaining. Possible counterfactuals existed. By the middle of the eighteenth century, the emerging colonial economy of India had three major foci, Bombay, Calcutta, and Madras, and a tripolar structure was a distinctly possible outcome. Why Madras, which was the oldest British colonial foundation in India, could not maintain its rank, in spite of the consolidation of its hinterland brought about by the annexation of the Carnatic in 1801, need not detain us here. But we should keep in mind the fate of Madras, for, had not certain chance factors intervened, it could very well have been Bombay's: to become a backwater of Empire. Leaving aside the

*From S. Patel and A. Thorner (eds), *Bombay: Metaphor for Modern India* (Bombay: Oxford University Press, 1995), pp. 26–46.

question of possible counterfactuals, the chapter will focus on an analysis of the dominant couple formed by Bombay and Calcutta and of the changes it underwent over time.

In the first part of this chapter I shall therefore examine the unfolding of what I call 'dual dominance'. The story clearly falls into three periods: from 1830 to 1860 Bombay rose to parity with Calcutta; then, from 1860 to 1920 we have the heyday of dual dominance, with Calcutta as Number One, but Bombay as a close second; after 1920, as both cities went through the difficult interwar period, dual dominance, without being really challenged, found itself somehow eroded.

In the second part of the chapter I shall look for possible interpretations, focusing particularly on entrepreneurial responses. My hypothesis is that the better 'communal mix' of Bombay business, and in particular the lack of the kind of total European domination witnessed in Calcutta, was a major factor in Bombay's success, firstly at reaching parity with Calcutta, and then at maintaining it against heavy odds.

## The Unfolding of 'Dual Dominance'

Even once it had securely displaced Surat as the main centre of colonial maritime trade on the western seaboard of India, by the middle of the eighteenth century, Bombay was nevertheless not in a position to compete on equal terms with Calcutta as a trading and financial centre. Its commercial fortune was largely linked, since the 1770s, to the China trade, with all the political and economic uncertainties this entailed, and it suffered from the absence of a rich and easily accessible agrarian hinterland, which was one of Calcutta's major assets. The successive annexations of Gujarat in 1800–3 and of the Maratha empire in 1818 did not give it the boost which could have been expected, for they coincided with depressed conditions in the China trade and left unsolved the problem of better communications with the interior.

By 1820, even after the spate of annexations of the previous 20 years which had given it at last a proper hinterland, Bombay was still a fairly insignificant trading centre compared to Calcutta. In 1820–1 its merchandise export trade amounted in value to little more than a quarter of Calcutta's and its imports were valued at less than half of Calcutta's.[1] The surplus of exports over imports was worth only a small fraction of Calcutta's surplus. Exports consisted mainly of cotton and opium[2] for the China market, which was then depressed. This depression persisted until the late 1820s. However, from 1830 onwards Bombay's trade entered a period of rapid growth and, by, the late 1850s, the commercial importance of the city was comparable to that of Calcutta.

## Bombay's Rise to Parity with Calcutta—1830–1860

It is generally acknowledged that, prior to the railway age, there was no such thing as an 'Indian' economy; it was, rather, a congeries of regional economies loosely linked together, the major unifying factor being their growing subjection to British capital and the needs of the metropolitan economy. In this context, 'dual dominance' is obviously not a relevant concept. We have to consider western and eastern India as two more or less separate economic entities within a nascent 'imperial world system' of which the 'commanding heights' were situated in London, Liverpool, Manchester, and Glasgow. Within this global system both Bombay and Calcutta can be seen as second-rank imperial cities, each having its own sphere of influence, with a limited amount of overlapping. Having very little industrial production prior to the mid-1850s, they functioned primarily as commercial emporia, draining the agricultural produce of their hinterlands and dispatching to the interior a growing but still limited quantity of imported manufactures in the fashion of the classical colonial port-cities. The only way to evaluate their respective importance is through a look at the statistics of the foreign seaborne trade.

It is therefore not surprising to find that a lasting upswing in the trade cycle was largely responsible for Bombay's surge of prosperity which allowed it to catch up with Calcutta and even, for a short while, to overtake it.

The upswing was mainly due to a rise in the Chinese demand for opium as well as to a growing tendency to ship the opium of Malwa through Bombay rather than through the ports of Portuguese India. The abolition of the Company monopoly of the China trade in 1833 stimulated that trade further. With the 'opening' of China by British guns in 1842, a huge market was securely offered to the enterprising Bombay merchants, the 'drug barons' of the nineteenth century. Before becoming the 'Manchester' of India, Bombay thus became its 'Medellin'. It also benefited from a renewed interest of the (original) Manchester in Indian cotton as the textile industry of Lancashire went through a period of quick expansion and found American cotton prices too high.

Between 1830–1 and 1860–1, the value of merchandise exports from Bombay increased sixfold and the value of opium sales alone increased more than tenfold.'[3] The share of opium in the export trade rose from 25 per cent in 1830–1 to 42 per cent in 1860–1, that of cotton from an already high 36 per cent to 44 per cent.[4] The growing dependence of the Bombay export trade on those two commodities is striking. Although Bombay's exports in 1860 were 40 per cent higher than Calcutta's, the latter offered a more varied range with, besides opium and cotton, indigo and sugar being also significant staples. Bombay's imports increased only fourfold during the same interval, the major increases being in cotton piece goods (which accounted for 37 per cent of all imports in 1860–1) and metals, while a new item, railway plant, accounted for over 6 per cent of imports, signalling the beginning of the railway era.'[5] Thus Bombay had a considerable surplus of exports over imports, the magnitude of which clearly surpassed Calcutta's. The western Indian city seemed to be not only catching up with the capital of Bengal, but appeared on its way to displacing it as the 'Urbs Prima in Indis'. At some point in the 1840s, its population overtook that of its rival and the census taken in 1864, at the height of the cotton boom, revealed a population of more than 800,000, a fourfold increase since 1818.[6] Most of them were recent migrants from the Konkan area of Maharashtra; there was also a considerable influx of traders from Gujarat.

However, the foundations of this newfound prosperity were fragile. Both the opium and cotton trade were very speculative in nature and closely dependent on the state of the Chinese and British markets, and Bombay's communications with its opium and cotton-growing hinterland were still, in spite of some improvements in the state of the roads, both costly and subject to seasonal interruptions when the monsoon rains raged over the Western Ghats. In the absence of good communications with the interior, Bombay could not fully exploit its advantages as the natural 'Gateway of India' for European commerce, although a regular shipping service with England via Suez and Alexandria had been established in 1858.

The most promising development in the 1850s was actually the establishment of the first modern cotton textile mills, but in 1860 their future was still far from assured as they struggled to carve for themselves a share of the Indian market in the face of fierce competition from Lancashire's mills. The beginning of the cotton textile industry in Bombay in 1854 preceded only by one year the starting of the first jute mill in Calcutta, and this synchronism in the use of modern machinery was eloquent testimony to the emergence of a structure of 'dual dominance' in the Indian colonial economy.

## The Era of 'Dual Dominance'—1860–1920

In his compendium of the Indian empire written in the early 1880s, W.W. Hunter remarked that, 'Calcutta and Bombay form the two central depôts for collection and distribution, to a degree without a parallel in other countries', thus nicely articulating the thesis of 'dual dominance'.[7] However, the reversal of the trend after 1865 must be noticed. While, from the mid-1850s, Bombay seemed on the way to displacing Calcutta as the major centre, after 1865 it was never again able to clearly challenge the primacy of the capital of Bengal. The reasons for the re-establishment of Calcutta's supremacy have mainly to do with the political economy of colonial India, but conjunctural factors, such as the differential impact of famines and the financial collapse in Bombay consecutive to the sudden end of the cotton boom in 1865, have also to be taken into account.

But firstly it must be noticed that the last third of the nineteenth century saw some amount of real direct competition between the two cities. In the previous period, in the absence of an 'Indian' economy, there were very few opportunities for direct clashes of interests. With the advent of the railway age, it is generally acknowledged that the concept of an 'Indian' economy became more meaningful. Not that one should exaggerate the degree of unification of markets brought about by the construction of the railway network: in many ways both capital and labour markets remained segmented in colonial India. However, the railways eliminated the most glaring price differentials and stimulated the circulation of goods as well as men across the country.[8] For three or four decades there was a certain amount of fluidity as the spheres of influence of the various centres underwent some redefinition at the margins. The birth of Indian nationalism during the same period also stimulated inter-city competition as the elites of both cities started to think in terms of the role of their own city in an all-India context and anxiously surveyed the progress of the rival city.

In the ongoing contest for supremacy between the two metropolitan cities of India, Calcutta's advantages were many. It was the seat of the colonial government till 1911, a not unimportant consideration since, in spite of its adherence to the Manchester school economics, the Government of India played a big role in allocating resources between regions, especially through the way it gave concessions to railway companies, and was particularly susceptible to pressures from Calcutta's overwhelmingly European business community. Calcutta had the largest concentration of European population and European capital in India; its European firms enjoyed particularly close links with the city of London, the financial hub of the world till at least 1914; and it drained Indian entrepreneurial talent and capital from as far afield as Marwar. It had easy communications with a vast agrarian hinterland extending from Eastern United Province to Assam, which produced most of the two major export crops grown in India, tea and jute, cotton having for its part never regained its shine of the boom years; and it had access to an abundant supply of labour attracted from this hinterland and even from as far as the Madras Presidency. It was close to the major energy source used in the 'modern' sector of the Indian economy, coal, which Bombay had to import from far afield. On the other hand, Bombay's area of labour recruitment was largely limited to Maharashtra (in particular the Konkan) and its indigenous entrepreneurial class came almost exclusively from Gujarat. As far as its European firms were concerned, they were less capitalized than their Calcutta counterparts, having more tenuous links to the City. The major advantages of Bombay over Calcutta were its better harbour and the shorter distance to Europe once the Suez route started being extensively used, which happened only in the 1880s.

A look at the statistics of the foreign seaborne trade reveals that over the 1871–1939 period Bombay on the whole trailed behind Calcutta but maintained a lead in the import trade. Table 1 gives five-yearly averages of exports and imports from Bombay and Bengal for 1871–1931 and 1934–9.

On the basis of the data presented in Table 1, two major points need to be emphasized:

(a)  that, with the exception of the quinquennial period 1886–91, Calcutta's foreign merchandise trade was always larger than Bombay's, though not by a very big margin. The situation prevailing in the 1860s had clearly been exceptional.

(b)  that while, in the case of Bengal the curves of exports and imports were broadly similar, in the case of Bombay a certain disjunction is noticeable at various points in time, particularly in the 1890s when imports surpassed exports during one quinquennial period and after 1926 when the fall in imports was much slower than the fall in exports.

It seems useful, for the purpose of more detailed analysis, to distinguish between the trends in the export and import trade. In the export trade Calcutta's supremacy over Bombay was never challenged after 1870, a trend which reflected the increasingly crucial role played in India's export trade by tea and jute (both raw and manufactured) which were largely or exclusively grown in Calcutta's hinterland. On the other hand, Bombay's export trade suffered from the gradual disappearance of opium as an export commodity, from a fall in foreign

TABLE 1

Five-yearly Averages of Merchandise Exports and
Imports from Bengal and Bombay (Rupees, million)

| Period | Bengal | | Bombay | |
|---|---|---|---|---|
| | Exports | Imports | Exports | Imports |
| 1871–6 | 242 | 168 | 221 | 119 |
| 1876–81 | 302 | 192 | 225 | 154 |
| 1881–6 | 341 | 222 | 320 | 210 |
| 1886–91 | 375 | 257 | 370 | 275 |
| 1891–6 | 433 | 277 | 385 | 282 |
| 1896–1901 | 484 | 318 | 326 | 348 |
| 1901–6 | 589 | 375 | 438 | 332 |
| 1906–11 | 771 | 498 | 510 | 428 |
| 1911–16 | 924 | 621 | 580 | 522 |
| 1916–21 | 1,291 | 1,015 | 880 | 839 |
| 1921–6 | 1,302 | 902 | 1,027 | 908 |
| 1926–31 | 1,305 | 802 | 705 | 805 |
| 1934–9 | 735 | 427 | 332 | 583 |

*Sources: Annual Statements of the Trade and Navigation of British India, Annual Statement of the Seaborne Trade of British India*, for relevant years.

demand for the short-fibre cotton grown in the Deccan, and from an increasing diversion of the export trade of Sind and the Punjab to Karachi. The most successful new item in Bombay's export trade was cotton twist and yarn which started being shipped to China in 1873 and by 1900–1 accounted for 16 per cent of Bombay's exports in value, overtaking opium and equalling oilseeds (raw cotton accounted for 28 per cent).[9] However, after 1905 this export trade petered out and the relatively good performance of Bombay's exports in the 1916–26 decade is largely to be attributed to high prices for raw cotton and a good market for it in Japan. The value of wheat exports also increased in the late nineteenth century.

The trend in the import trade is more puzzling and therefore deserves careful analysis. What accounts for the fact that, at various points in time, and particularly in the 1886–1901 period and after 1921, Bombay's import trade surpassed Calcutta's in value? Moreover, how are we to explain that its overall share in India's import trade remained more or less constant during the period under study while that of Karachi increased mainly at its expense, without supposing that this loss, which could not have been compensated in its entirety by a gain at the expense of Madras, must have somewhat been made up for at the expense of Calcutta?

Very detailed mapping of the hinterlands of the various ports in India at different points in time has to my knowledge never been done, which is of course a limiting factor.[10] Networks for the redistribution of imported goods are much more difficult to analyse than those through which agricultural produce is exported; the latter are, so to speak, visible 'on the ground' and have also attracted a lot of attention from colonial officials. The former, which distribute a great variety of goods often in limited quantities, operate in a less obvious manner. For reasons of space, I shall limit myself to general remarks which are in the nature of informed guesses.

At a somewhat theoretical level, Bombay's capacity to increase over time its share of the import trade of India to the detriment of Calcutta has to be explained by having recourse to one of the following hypotheses: either an increase in the size of its hinterland at the expense of Calcutta's, or, if hinterlands were relatively fixed, growing income disparities between Bombay's and Calcutta's respective hinterlands making for greater consumption of imported items in the area supplied by Bombay (supposing an equal propensity to import in all regions, an assumption we shall make for convenience's sake and which is in any case not entirely unsubstantiated by available evidence), or widely divergent investment patterns reflecting much more rapid industrial growth in western than in eastern India. Let us examine each of these hypotheses in turn.

Change in the size of hinterlands could be either the result of the spatial expansion of Bombay's sphere of influence at the expense of Calcutta's or of a quicker pace of demographic growth in its existing sphere of influence. The latter hypothesis can be immediately rejected. Evidence from the population censuses between 1872 and 1941 tends

its import trade regularly surpass that of Bombay. It may be that this reversal was due to the changing fortunes in the rate war between railway companies, but I have not been able to test that hypothesis empirically. This was in any case a period of great commercial prosperity for India's two major cities, in spite of a certain amount of disruption created by the First World War.

However, since the middle of the nineteenth century, the economy of both cities had undergone some diversification as a sector of modern industry had developed and foreign trade can therefore no longer serve as the only gauge of their respective rankings. Bombay's cotton textile industry and Calcutta's jute mill industry were by 1914 largely comparable in terms of capital and output value while the labour force employed was much larger in the Calcutta jute mills than in the Bombay cotton mills (216,000 as against 110,000), reflecting the more labour-intensive character of the jute industry.[14] The two big cities then accounted for more than 50 per cent of total large-scale factory output in India.[15] In spite of the rapid development of the cotton textile industry in a certain number of inland centres (Ahmedabad, Sholapur, Kanpur) and of the location of the steel industry in Jamshedpur, the 'dual dominance' of Bombay and Calcutta over the large-scale factory sector remained basically unchallenged, especially if one takes into consideration that some of the largest factories situated outside Bombay and Calcutta had been set up and were controlled by Bombay or Calcutta-based firms (for example Tata Iron and Steel).

In the financial sector also, Bombay and Calcutta reigned supreme. They were the seats of the two major Presidency banks (the Bank of Madras operating on a much smaller scale) as well as of the exchange banks and most of the large Indian banks. By 1918, 83 per cent of the capital of all rupee joint-stock companies in India and 92 per cent of the capital of Sterling companies operating in India was controlled from Bombay and Calcutta.[16] The respective shares of Bengal and Bombay were 43 and 40 per cent for rupee companies, 73 and 19 per cent for Sterling companies, the difference being largely due to tea companies which were almost all Sterling. Calcutta's largely European firms then controlled resources which were larger than those controlled by Bombay's mostly Indian firms, a fact which is not surprising, given the overall domination of British capital over the 'modern' sector of the Indian economy. But it does not invalidate the thesis of 'dual dominance'.

## 'Dual Dominance' under Fire—1920–1947

In the post-1920 period the dual dominance of Bombay and Calcutta over foreign trade, high finance, and large-scale industry began to be somewhat eroded. At the political level, there was some shift in power and influence from coastal to interior areas, as exemplified by the rise of New Delhi as the effective capital of India in the 1920s and the emergence of the United Provinces as the main stronghold of the Indian nationalist movement. There were parallel trends in the economic domain: in a globally stagnant agricultural economy, the only region which continued to experience a significant growth in output was 'Greater Punjab'.[17] In large-scale industry, most of the growth of output occurred outside Bombay and Calcutta. After 1922, the Bombay cotton textile industry ceased to grow and the 1920s and 1930s saw the rise of inland centres such as Ahmedabad and Coimbatore. Between 1920 and 1939 Bombay's share in India's cotton textile industry fell from 43.9 to 28.3 per cent in spindles, and from 51 to 33.2 per cent in looms.[18] While Calcutta's jute industry continued to grow in the 1920s, although at a reduced rate, in the 1930s it actually contracted. The share of Bombay and Calcutta in global large-scale factory output had fallen to 30–35 per cent on the eve of the Second World War.[19] In the 1920s Calcutta did marginally better than Bombay but it was then more directly hit by the world depression which deeply affected the tea and jute sectors working almost exclusively for the export markets. In the late 1930s, however, Calcutta benefited from some investment in industry by large international firms, mainly British (Dunlop, Imperial Chemical Industries, BAT, etc.) and its industrial base started diversifying away from jute, while no comparable move was noticeable in Bombay. Calcutta's mostly Marwari firms also played an important role in the development of two of the 'growth' industries in India, sugar and paper.[20]

In foreign trade, the most striking development was, within a much reduced volume of business, the relative buoyancy of Bombay's import trade as contrasted to its collapse in Calcutta. If one agrees with Bagchi that, from 1914 onwards, there was 'relative stability of the outlines of the hinterlands of major ports',[21] how then to account for post-1921 developments? In the 1921–6 period, while Calcutta's import trade contracted, Bombay's imports continued to increase, though at a rate which was much slower than during the previous 20 years. Part of the explanation seems to lie in the exceptional figures for imports of cotton textile machinery during that quinquennial period: they accounted for 5.9 per cent of all imports (as against 2.2 per cent in 1916–21 and 2.4 per cent in 1926–31). During the same period imports of jute machinery accounted for 2 per cent of imports through Calcutta.[22] Most of the machinery imported through Bombay was destined for Ahmedabad and other inland centres. In the following period, the contrast between Bombay and Calcutta is partly explained in terms of the unequal pace of development of import substitution in cotton textiles: by 1930, eastern India was by far the greatest consumer of imported British piece goods, while in the rest of India the market had been largely captured by domestic producers. Between 1930 and 1939, Lancashire lost most of its remaining Indian market, mostly situated in the eastern region, and by 1939 piece goods represented only 7 per cent of all Calcutta imports.[23]

In 1939, although inland cities such as Ahmedabad, Kanpur, and Coimbatore had emerged as important industrial centres and were the seat of some fairly large business groups (Kasturbhai and Sarabhai in Ahmedabad, J.K. Singhania in Kanpur), while Karachi and Madras had somewhat enlarged their share of India's foreign seaborne trade (in 1938–9 the two ports accounted for one-quarter of total imports and one-third of total exports), the overall dominance of Bombay and Calcutta over industry, finance, and long-distance trade remained, though in a reduced degree. The two cities were then more or less evenly matched in terms of corporate power. A survey of the largest 57 business groups operating in India in 1939[24] shows that 24 Calcutta-based groups controlled 645 joint-stock companies with a total paid-up capital of over Rs 100 crores, while 16 Bombay-based groups controlled 131 companies with a paid-up capital of almost Rs 60 crores. In terms of actual economic power, the two cities were more evenly matched than the figures suggest, for many companies in Bombay were undercapitalized and had very large fixed assets.

The Second World War spelt doom for Calcutta's economy which suffered from the proximity of military operations and the impact of the Bengal famine. Partition was the decisive blow from which the city never really recovered. However, it retained its slight lead over Bombay in terms of corporate power till sometime in the 1950s. In that decade, the government's decision to equalize freight rates on coal took away its last advantage over Bombay. The political troubles of the late 1960s led to Calcutta's final demotion from its status as one of the two major centres of business activity in India. Bombay has clearly emerged as the winner in the two-century-long fight for supremacy. Calcutta is today struggling to maintain its second place in the face of the rapid rise of both Delhi and Bangalore.

## In Search of an Explanation: Business Cycles and Entrepreneurial Response

The economic history of India between 1830 and 1950 has been characterized by large-scale fluctuations in the business cycle, some directly linked to international conditions, others more locally determined. Between 1830 and 1865, Bombay was the great beneficiary of the upswing in the opium and cotton markets, but in the next phase, lasting till the depression of 1930, Calcutta benefited by its proximity to the major producing zones of jute, tea, and coal, which were the three major 'growth' commodities in the Indian economy. It would thus seem that Bombay's capacity to maintain global parity in the post-1865 phase was 'counter-cyclical' in nature. Why was Bombay over the long term more successful than Calcutta at capitalizing on the upswings in the trade cycle? In the absence of a clearly interventionist policy by the colonial government aimed at redressing regional imbalances, the answer has to be found in differences in the behaviour of the business communities of the two cities.

## Entrepreneurial Responses in Bombay and Calcutta: A Global Comparison

Measured by most conventional standards (capitalization, profits, value of output), the performance of business enterprise in Bombay and Calcutta does not seem to reveal major differences before the end of the colonial era. Calcutta business would even appear to have done slightly better. However, on closer examination, the achievements of Bombay businessmen over more than a century appear more impressive than those of their Calcutta colleagues, if one recalls the many advantages enjoyed by the capital of Bengal within the political economy of colonial India.

Bombay's ability to maximize its few advantages and minimize its many handicaps has obviously to do with the specific way in which its business community responded to opportunities and challenges. A very general comparison between business behaviour in Bombay and Calcutta would bring out a greater flexibility and a greater capacity for innovation on the part of Bombay businessmen.

They seem to have been better at adapting to changing trade conditions. Thus, although opium had been the mainstay of the fortunes of so many businessmen, the decline of the opium trade in the 1860–1910 period does not seem to have had a very negative impact on Bombay business. Most firms which had been prominent in the opium trade managed a successful reconversion towards the cotton trade or the cotton textile industry; the number of casualties does not appear to have been very high. By contrast, in Calcutta the collapse of the indigo market in 1833 led to the demise of the major Agency firms which never went back into business.

The story of the cotton textile industry shows the same kind of flexibility. At first the Bombay millowners tried to gain a share of the domestic market in yarn and cloth but, faced with fierce competition from Lancashire and, increasingly from other centres in India, from 1873 onwards they turned to the Chinese market in a big way. In the

1880s, 80 per cent of Bombay yarn production went to China.[25] However, faced with growing competition from Chinese and Japanese mills, they turned gradually again to the domestic market and, taking advantage of the Swadeshi movement of 1904–7, they reoriented their mills towards the production of cloth for the Indian consumer.[26] On the other hand in Calcutta the jute industry did not manage to carve a secure market for its products before the 1890s and, after a period of exceptional prosperity up to the First World War, was faced with a diminishing market due to the progress of jute substitutes.[27] While the Bombay industry constantly introduced changes in layout and organization to adapt itself to changes in market conditions, Calcutta's jute barons remained faithful to fixed methods and refused to see the writing on the wall.

More generally, Calcutta business was less successful than Bombay's at shifting its activities to the domestic market, once external trade went through a prolonged depression from 1926 onwards. Of the major industries working for the internal market and, from 1930 onwards, benefiting from a varying degree of customs protection, only two, sugar and paper, owed part of their development to Calcutta's entrepreneurs, while cotton, iron and steel, and cement were all three dominated by Bombay firms.

Apart from greater flexibility, Bombay businessmen also showed greater capacities for innovation. Most of the 'firsts' in the history of Indian finance and large-scale industry originated in Bombay: the first successful modern factory was Cowasji Davar's Oriental Spinning floated in 1854. Modern methods of financial promotion were introduced by the extraordinary financial genius, Premchand Roychand, who towered over the Bombay financial scene for 15 years.[28] The first Stock Exchange, however rudimentary, was started in Bombay in 1875, while in Calcutta the Stock Exchange was formally constituted only in 1908. Bombay entrepreneurs were responsible for most of the technological innovations in Indian industry: thus the ring spindle was first introduced and adapted to Indian conditions at Tata's Empress Mills in Nagpur, a Bombay-financed and controlled company; Portland cement production was started by the Bombay firm of Khatau; modern steel production started in 1913 in the works of Tisco at Jamshedpur, another Tata company; the first large-scale hydro-electric schemes were promoted by the Tatas in the Western Ghats; the automobile and aeronautics industries were started by the great Bombay-based pioneer, Walchand Hirachand. The contributions of Calcutta entrepreneurs were less numerous and less remarkable: George Acland started the first jute mill in 1855, using an extremely rudimentary technology; Sir P.C. Ray pioneered the chemical and pharmaceutical industries at the time of the Swadeshi movement.

Although one should beware of exaggerating the contrast between the two cities and of romanticizing Bombay entrepreneurs, among whom were included the usual contingent of crooks and failures, the fact remains that over a long period Bombay business showed more dynamism than Calcutta's.

## Race, Community and Enterprise: The Contrast between Bombay and Calcutta

Since Bagchi's pioneering study of 1970 drew attention to the contrast between the situation in western India and in the rest of India, not much work has been done on the impact of race and community on business.[29] However, I think it is in that direction that lies the most plausible explanation of the contrast between Bombay and Calcutta.

It has been often remarked that in Bombay relations between Indian and European businessmen were marked by less discrimination and less mutual antagonism than in Calcutta. To account for the difference, scholars have put forward two main explanations: firstly the fact that western India was conquered by the British at a later stage than eastern India, thus escaping the period of unabashed exploitation which cost indigenous merchants in Bengal so dearly, and secondly the exceptional role played in Bombay by the Parsi community which was Indian but had a special relationship with the British. We need not go in detail into this problem here, but the situation in Bombay in the first quarter of the century is aptly characterized by Asiya Siddiqi who writes:

there was, on the whole, little conflict between Indian merchants on the one hand and, on the other, European merchants and the Bombay Government. The Indian merchants, along with the members of a small group of European agency houses, with whom they were often intimately connected as brokers and business partners, formed a remarkably close-knit oligarchy which governed both the island and its overseas trade.[30]

The close relationship between the great Parsi entrepreneur Jamsetji Jejeebhoy and the British China merchant William Jardine exemplifies that situation. During the same period in Calcutta, the dominance of the European Agency Houses was well established and their Indian collaborators were never treated as equals. When the Agency Houses collapsed in 1833, it was precisely the group of Indian collaborators who paid the heaviest price and the story repeated itself at the time of the crisis of the Union Bank 'which shook whatever confidence wealthy Indians in Calcutta had in their ability to collaborate with Europeans on profitable terms'.[31] The contrasting fates of Dwarkanath Tagore and Jamsetji Jejeebhoy, who were near-contemporaries, highlight the different ways in which partnerships between Indians and Europeans worked in Calcutta and Bombay.

By the middle of the nineteenth century, the contrast between Bombay and Calcutta was clear: in Calcutta Indian businessmen were excluded from the upper ranks of the business hierarchy and operated only as brokers, not as partners, while in Bombay partnerships between Europeans and Indians, mostly but not exclusively Parsis, were a common feature of business life, in the opium as well as in the cotton trade. In the promotion of banks as well, between 1840 and 1860 Indians were as much involved as Europeans.[32]

In the post-1865 period, indigenous business in Bombay suffered in its turn from the increasing European domination of international shipping and trading networks, but it nevertheless managed to retain strong positions in some fields of foreign trade (in particular, China, the Middle East, and East Africa) as well as in the cotton textile industry. In spite of losing ground to Europeans (and Japanese) in the to show that the rate of growth of the population living in the zone served by Calcutta was marginally higher than that of the population living in Bombay's sphere of influence.[11] There remains therefore the possibility that Bombay's sphere of influence increased spatially at the expense of Calcutta's. Actually there is some evidence that, during the first phase of the railway era, *c.* 1860–1900, there occurred a certain redefinition in the hinterlands of the various ports and Bombay managed, thanks to the railway, to capture trade flows which were previously channelled through Calcutta. Given the fact that Bombay was closer to British and European ports than Calcutta, it could have made sense for an importer operating in interior areas which were more or less equidistant from both ports to reroute some imports to the western Indian port. One has also to take into consideration the fact that, in the 1880–1916 period, there was a sort of rate war between railway companies serving the three ports of Karachi, Bombay, and Calcutta.[12] Although its outcome is not very dear, railway statistics indicate that Bombay increased its share of the trade of the United Provinces and Hyderabad State, two areas which in the pre-railway age were largely included in Calcutta's sphere.[13] So the pattern of railway development seems to have somehow favoured Bombay at the expense of Calcutta, and it had a greater impact on imports than on exports because the former were not subject to the kind of physical constraints which largely influenced the location of export crops. A change in the size of their respective hinterlands may therefore be the major explanation for Bombay's success in enlarging its share of India's import trade at the expense of Calcutta in the 1871–1901 period. Imports of cotton textile machinery through Bombay also appear to have been always higher than imports of jute machinery through Calcutta, but the evidence of trade statistics is not enough to suggest widely divergent investment patterns in the areas respectively served by Bombay and Calcutta.

During the following 20 years, while India's overall imports increased at a very quick pace, there was a reversal of trend as Calcutta regained some of the ground lost during the previous period and saw cotton trade, Indian businessmen in Bombay maintained an overall position of equality with the Europeans. In no sector of the economy was European business in Bombay capable of establishing the kind of oligopolistic control that a few managing agencies exercised in Calcutta over jute, tea, and coal. On the eve of the Second World War, the largest business firm in Bombay was an Indian firm, Tata, with assets which were larger than those of the major European managing agencies such as Killick, Nixon & Co.; Forbes, Forbes, Campbell; Wallace Bros.; and James Finlay & Co. Out of 16 business groups included in the above-mentioned survey, ten were exclusively under Indian control, four were British-controlled, but with Indian partners, one was Indian-controlled with a British partner (Associated Cement Companies) and one was controlled by a Baghdadi Jewish family (E.D. Sassoon & Co.). By contrast, in Calcutta, out of 24 groups, 20 were under exclusive British control, one under American control (A. Yule), one under joint British and Indian control (Martin Burn), one British-managed but financially controlled by a big zamindar, the Maharaja of Darbhanga (O. Steel), and only one under exclusive Indian control (Birla).

Although most indigenous businessmen hailed from only one region, Gujarat, the ethnic and communal diversity of Bombay's business world was striking: it included merchants belonging to many communities of Gujarat, including the Parsis, the Hindu Vanis and Bhatias, the Muslim Bohras, Khojas, and Memons, as well as businessmen from other provinces of India (Sind, Marwar), Baghdadi Jews (the different branches of the famous Sassoon family), non-British Europeans (the Swiss firm of Volkarts), Japanese (Toyo Menka Kaisha), and Britishers of various origins. The contrast was clear with the increasingly polarized and oligopolistic world of Calcutta where only two communities mattered: the Scots and the Marwaris. By 1914, merchants belonging to other communities (Bengalis, North Indian Muslims, Armenians, Jews) played only a minor role.

The polarization in Calcutta between the Scots and the Marwaris, the result of a symbiotic relationship which turned more and more antagonistic in the post-1914 period, had damaging effects on the fortunes of the city. The Calcutta Scots had become, in the second half of the nineteenth century, such an entrenched business community that they had taken complete control of trade in the three commodities which were the mainstay of Calcutta's prosperity: tea, jute, and coal. During the same period, the Marwaris gradually replaced the Bengalis as brokers to the big European business houses in Calcutta.[33] The Scots behaved very arrogantly with their Marwari brokers who, in the jute trade, were an indispensable link to the rural areas, and did not form partnerships with them. The only way for the Marwaris to make a real breakthrough in the trade was therefore to resort to *fatka* (speculation) which they started doing around 1905 with a devastating effect on the spot prices of jute.[34] As the Marwaris advanced from jute trading to jute baling, from there to shipping jute directly abroad and, after 1918, to setting up jute mills, the whole sector suffered from constant price wars which led to a very unhealthy situation. The racial arrogance of the Scots, signalled by their refusal to seek a compromise with the Marwaris, was partly responsible for the long-term decline of the industry in the post-1914 period. In the complex process of collaboration-cum-competition between those two business communities, they were both transformed. To fight European domination, the Marwaris were led to maximizing their existing assets, of which the major one was their skill at speculating. On the other hand, to prevent the growing inroads of the Marwaris into what they perceived as their preserve, the Scots increasingly relied on their political clout, which was, however, diminishing in a time of growing Indian nationalism. In the bargain they largely lost whatever entrepreneurial drive they ever had. Although the Marwaris emerged as the eventual winners, since by 1950 they controlled practically the whole of the jute sector and part of the tea sector, their victory was costly: they bought at highly inflated prices mills which were full of obsolete machinery, had a bad record of industrial relations, and faced the problem of diminishing markets. They had wasted a lot of energy and money to control a declining business and in the process the whole of Calcutta's economy suffered since Marwari capitalists, too busy buying jute mills (and tea gardens), invested little in the more promising fields. There are many causes of Calcutta's post-1940 economic decline but the racial polarization of its business world is not the least of them.

Of course Bombay's business world was not the picture of harmony either. There were conflicts galore, especially in the difficult decades of the 1920s and 1930s. Racial exclusiveness and arrogance on the part of British businessmen was not unknown either, but the racial conflict did not dominate everything as in Calcutta. The conflict between the 'industrialists' and the 'marketeers' on the Bombay cotton market was not primarily along racial lines.[35] If the 'marketeers' were all Indians, the industrialists were also in their majority Indians.

Relations between Hindu and Muslim businessmen also appear to have been better in Bombay than in Calcutta. Bombay's active Gujarati Muslim business communities fully participated in the life of the various business associations, such as the Indian Merchants' Chamber, and a separate Muslim association was not created before the mid-1940s. In Calcutta, on the other hand, where Muslim participation in business was probably on the whole less important than in Bombay, but where there were a few powerful Muslim business groups (Adamji, Ispahani), a separate Muslim Chamber of Commerce was created as early as in 1932.

Less racial and communal strife in the business world meant a more rational use of capital resources. Businessmen belonging to various communities more easily formed partnerships in Bombay than elsewhere in India. Shareholding in joint-stock companies was more cross-communal in character there than in Calcutta.[36]

The conclusions I draw from this rapid study are mainly two: firstly that, within the common framework of a colonial economy, significantly different regional sub-systems can develop, depending on the specific curve of the trade cycle in different commodity markets and the varying capacity of the local business communities to capitalize on the upswings; secondly, that over the long term the particular ethos and 'communal mix' of the local business community can be more decisive than factor endowment in explaining the rise of a city. Thus, while Calcutta suffered a lot from being the sterile battleground of a racial war dividing its business community, Bombay benefited from a more dynamic atmosphere of emulation and competition. This is not to say that the kind of capitalistic development that Bombay has come to exemplify is morally appealing; it is after all the city of the scam. But, in terms of efficiency, it clearly emerged as the winner.

## Notes

1. The exact figures for Bengal were: exports, Rs 56,800,000; imports, Rs 22,500,000. See K.N. Chaudhuri, 'Foreign Trade and Balance of Payments (1757–1947)', in D. Kumar (ed.), *The Cambridge Economic History of India*, vol. 2 (Cambridge, 1983), Table 10.4, p. 828. For Bombay, they were: exports, Rs 15,500,000; imports, Rs 11,000,000. See *The Gazetteer of Bombay City and Island*, vol. 1 (Bombay, 1909), Appendix IV, pp. 514–15, and Appendix V, pp. 518–19.

2. Raw cotton exports were worth Rs 5,200,000 and exports of opium amounted to Rs 3,200,000. *Gazetteer*, ibid.

3. In 1830/31, opium exports were worth Rs 6,300,000; in 1860/61 they reached Rs 66,000,000. Ibid.

4. Calculated from figures in ibid.

5. Total imports of metals were over Rs 12,000,000, some 13 per cent of the total value of imports. Calculated from ibid.

6. M. Kosambi, *Bombay in Transition: The Growth and Social Ecology of a Colonial City, 1880–1980* (Stockholm: Almqvist & Wiksell, 1986), p. 36.

7. W.W. Hunter, *The Indian Empire: Its People, History and Products* (London: Trubner, 1886, 2nd edn.), p. 560.

8. J.M. Hurd, 'Railways', in *Cambridge Economic History of India*, vol. 2, pp. 737–61.

9. Calculated from figures in *Gazetteer* of *Bombay City*.

10. See, however, I. Banga (ed.), *Ports and their Hinterlands in India (1700–1950)* (Delhi, Manohar, 1992).

11. During the 1871–1921 period, the east zone, which largely corresponded with Calcutta's hinterland had an average annual growth rate of 0.52 per cent, which was higher than the rates of the west zone (0.14 per cent) and the central zone (0.47 per cent), which formed the bulk of Bombay's hinterland. See L. Visaria and P. Visaria, 'Population (1757–1947)', in *Cambridge Economic History of India*, vol. 2, Table 5.8, p. 490.

12. Hurd, 'Railways', pp. 753–4.

13. In 1888–9, railborne exports from Bombay to the United Provinces represented 6.5 per cent of total railborne exports from Bombay and those destined for the Nizam's territory accounted for 5 per cent of the total. In

1907–8, the respective shares of the United Provinces and the Nizam's territory in Bombay's railborne export trade were 8 and 6 per cent. (Calculated from figures in *Gazetteer of Bombay City*, p. 448.)

14. M.D. Morris, 'The Growth of Large-Scale Industry to 1947', in *Cambridge Economic History of India*, vol. 2, pp. 553–676.

15. Calculated from ibid., Table 7.22, p. 641. Jute manufactures, entirely concentrated in Calcutta, represented 15 per cent of the net output of large-scale factory production, and cotton textiles 36 per cent, of which Bombay accounted for over 40 per cent. Assuming that the two cities accounted for approximately 50 per cent of the output of all other industries, that is, around 25 per cent of total factory output, one reaches a total of 50–55 per cent.

16. O. Goswami, 'Calcutta's Economy 1918–1970: The Fall from Grace', in S. Chaudhuri (ed.), *Calcutta, The Living City*, vol. II (Calcutta: Oxford University Press, 1990), pp. 88.

17. G. Blyn, *Agricultural Trends in India 1891–1947: Output, Availability and Productivity* (Philadelphia: University of Pennsylvania Press, 1966).

18. See *Indian Textile Journal Jubilee Number*, 1940.

19. Calculated from Morris, 'Growth of Large-Scale Industry to 1947'. The share of jute manufacturers in total output had fallen to 8 per cent, that of cotton textiles to 29 per cent (of which Bombay accounted only for one third).

20. A.K. Bagchi, *Private Investment in India, 1900–1939* (Cambridge: Cambridge University Press, 1973).

21. A.K. Bagchi, 'Reflections on Patterns of Regional Growth in India During the Period of British Rule', *Bengal Past and Present*, vol. XCV (I): 180 (1976), p. 253.

22. Calculated from figures of textile machinery imports in Bagchi, *Private Investment in India*, Table 7.10, p. 258 and Table 8.1, p. 273.

23. See *Annual Statement of the Seaborne Trade of British India, 1938–39* (Calcutta, 1940).

24. C. Markovits, *Indian Business and Nationalist Politics, 1931–39* (Cambridge: Cambridge University Press, 1985), pp. 192–3.

25. D.H. Buchanan, *The Development of Capitalistic Enterprise in India* (New York: Macmillan, 1934).

26. S.D. Mehta, *The Cotton Mills of India, 1854–1954* (Bombay: The Mill-owners' Association, 1954).

27. D. Chakrabarty, *Rethinking Working-Class History, Bengal 1890–1940* (Princeton: Princeton University Press, 1989).

28. R.S. Rungta, *Rise of Business Corporations in India, 1851–1900* (Cambridge: Cambridge University Press, 1970), pp. 81–3.

29. A.K. Bagchi, 'European and Indian Entrepreneurship in India, 1900–30', in E. Leach and S.N. Mukherjee (eds), *Elites in South Asia* (Cambridge: Cambridge University Press, 1970), pp. 223–56.
30. A. Siddiqi, 'The Business World of Jamsetjee Jejeebhoy', *Indian Economic and Social History Review*, XIX: 3 & 4 (1982), p. 305.
31. A.K. Bagchi, *The Evolution of the State Bank of India: The Roots, 1806–1876. Part I: The Early Years, 1806–1860* (Bombay: Oxford University Press, 1987), pp. 147–9, 223.
32. Ibid., p. 357.
33. T.A. Timberg, *The Marwaris: From Traders to Industrialists* (Delhi: Vikas, 1978).
34. O. Goswami, 'Collaboration and Conflict: European and Indian Capitalists and the Jute Economy of Bengal, 1919–39', *Indian Economic and Social History Review* XXI: 2 (1982), p. 143.
35. A.D.D. Gordon, *Businessmen and Politics: Rising Nationalism and a Modernising Economy in Bombay, 1918–1933* (Delhi: Manohar, 1978).
36. As comes out of perusing shareholders' lists included in P. Lovett, *The Mirror of Investment* (Calcutta: Capital, 1927).

6

# THE TATA PARADOX*

BUSINESS FIRMS IN INDIA HAVE NOT RECEIVED MUCH ATTEN-
tion from economic historians. Most of the literature available
belongs to the genre of firm histories, the writing of which has
generally been commissioned by the firms themselves and is therefore
often apologetic in nature, if not hagiographical. Of modern Indian
business firms, however, the house of Tata is undoubtedly the one
which has received the most extensive coverage. One might well ask
why add a few more pages to the already abundant literature on this
best-known and most studied of all Indian firms. I cannot claim to
have discovered anything really new about the Tatas. However, I find
the existing literature, although informative and often insightful, either
too much informed by a 'heroic' conception of entrepreneurship, or
too exclusively preoccupied with microanalysis of the specific growth
process of particular companies, like the Empress Mills or Tata Iron
and Steel Co. (TISCO). It is not my intention to belittle the extraordinary feat of entrepreneurship represented by the emergence of such a
firm in the specific context of colonial India. But I think one has to
go beyond that kind of statement. Some synthetic survey of the firm
across a time span of over a century, aiming at situating it within the
general context of Indian entrepreneurial history and attempting to
link it to macroeconomic trends appears to be needed.

*From B. Stein and S. Subrahmanyam (eds), *Institutions and Economic Change
in South Asia* (Delhi: Oxford University Press, 1996), pp. 237–48.

I must therefore clearly state at the outset that the 'Tata paradox', or rather paradoxes which are the theme of this chapter, have a meaning only within a political economy framework which has become largely dominant in historical studies of Indian capitalism, without however having acquired the status of a 'paradigm', since no global consensus can be claimed for it. This framework owes a lot to the work of economists such as A.K. Sen and Amiya Bagchi. A crucial element in this approach is the distinction made between indigenous and expatriate firms operating in colonial India. Bagchi has mainly stressed the institutional disadvantage of the former in relation to the latter in terms of access to the state and participation in worldwide trading and financial networks, ultimately tracing its origins in the racial bond of affinity between British rulers and British businessmen.[1] On the other hand, Tomlinson has drawn attention to some advantages Indian firms had over their British competitors, particularly in the jute market, in relation to supply factors, due to the existence of 'informal' credit networks, largely caste- and kinship-based, which allowed them more direct access to rural producers.[2] In spite of their widely divergent views, it seems to me that both authors would agree that to differentiate between indigenous and expatriate firms in the Indian colonial context is meaningful, a view that 'pure' economists would certainly find strange. It is doubtful in any case whether such 'pure' economists would find in India many 'firms', British or Indian, which would fit in with the often-quoted definition of the firm as a profit-maximizing agent, endowed with a known and given technology and operating subject to a well-defined market constraint.

This definition of the firm posits as universal characteristics certain features of modern Western industrial firms. Leaving aside the question of technology, when applied to Indian firms it raises two different sets of questions. The first one pertains to profit-maximization. In a well-known analysis of North Indian merchant firms in the eighteenth century, C.A. Bayly has argued in favour of a 'Chayanovian' model, stressing the similarities between merchant and peasant families, in particular the emphasis on reproduction of the family.[3] He sees Indian merchant firms as informed by a logic of kinship which does not necessarily enhance profit-maximization, but makes credit, identified with family prestige, the crucial notion. According to him, this specific logic can run contrary to the logic of profit maximization in dictating, for instance, marriage alliances which do not necessarily contribute to an enlargement of the firm's assets. It is interesting to note that this kind of behaviour can be found in modern Indian industrial firms. Thus the great Ahmedabad industrialist Kasturbhai Lalbhai is known to have created companies with the stated purpose of endowing nephews of his, without very definite calculations about expected profits.[4] Of course it remains a moot point whether one can validly generalize from all this and put forward a theory of the 'Indian' firm as non-profit-maximizing. However, serious doubts are in order regarding a definition of the firm as a profit-maximizing agency in the Indian context. Serious reservations have also been expressed by students of Indian firms regarding the nature of the market constraints. Morris D. Morris in particular has stressed the high degree of un-certainty regarding the market due to lack of infrastructure and paucity of reliable information.[5] In India, therefore, the market constraint does not appear to have been 'well defined' but in a state of constant flux which hindered rational calculations of cost.

Of all firms operating in colonial India, the firm of Tatas is probably the one which would come closer to that definition, since it was less informed than most Indian firms by a logic of the family and kinship and operated under market constraints which tended to be better defined than for most firms (the steel market is not dependent on the vagaries of the monsoon as is the market for cheap cotton cloth, and the parameters which regulate it are somewhat open to rational types of calculations). But I am not here going to examine Tatas in the light of different 'theories of the firm', an exercise for which in any case I am not competent. Rather, I am interested in exploring what I perceive as a paradox in relation to the above-mentioned 'political economy framework' and its possible wider implications, treating 'paradox' as a sort of heuristic device.

My point of departure is what I call the Tata paradox, basically that of a firm which displayed characteristics of both the indigenous and expatriate ones, in addition to some which appear largely unique, and which therefore tended to straddle the boundary between those two types of firms.

If the Tatas are compared with other large Indian firms, the following features will be noticeable. First, the character of the firm was strictly 'non-family', as manifested in particular in the employment of professional managers on a scale unknown in most other large Indian firms, but more common in expatriate firms. Thus the role of Sir Bezonji Dadabhai Mehta, who had started his career in the railways, in the success of the Empress Mills in Nagpur is well known.[6] Though a Parsi, he was not a direct relation of the founder of the firm, J.N. Tata, and yet the latter trusted him with the management of his first major venture, a fairly rare occurrence in the mostly Hindu Indian business world, where family connections were of such crucial importance; Burjorji J. Padshah, another Parsi, who was not a relation, played a very similar role in the development of TISCO and the electric companies.[7] How much of this was due to differences in family structure between Parsis and Hindus is not a point I shall consider here. Secondly, the firms' financial structure was characterized by a greater degree of reliance on the stock market than in most other large Indian firms; and by a marked divorce between ownership and control, the former being widely diffused among individuals and companies,[8] while the latter was clearly concentrated in the hands of a few members of the Tata family (rather than in the family as a corporate entity). Moreover, from 1914 onwards, the Tatas enjoyed a close and almost institutionalized relationship to the colonial state such as no other Indian firm ever matched, reinforced by the constant hiring of retired ICS officers as board members or managers,[9] a practice which was not widespread amongst other big Indian firms. (Of course the latter could not offer such attractive conditions as the Tatas, not only in terms of salaries but also of work environment.) Thus the Tatas almost overcame the 'racial' barrier which prevented most Indian capitalists from gaining social acceptance by the British rulers.

This does not mean that the Tatas did not also display some traits which were characteristic of other big Indian firms. For instance their approach to labour problems was not, in spite of well-publicized welfare measures,[10] fundamentally different from that of other big Indian employers of labour. It is true that the success of the Empress Mills in Nagpur is often attributed in part to a particularly enlightened policy of wooing labour in a region where Tatas were the first large-scale industrial employers.[11] But gradually the Tatas seem to have aligned their labour policy with that of most industrial firms operating in India. TISCO in particular is known for its bad record of labour relations,[12] and the anti-union bias in Jamshedpur was strong. It should be noted that in this field the line between Indian and British firms was rather blurred: labour practices in India were largely shaped by the structural characteristics of the labour force and employers' strategies did not play such a large role as is often assumed.[13] In their financial practices as well, in spite of a reputation of honesty, the Tatas were not above resorting to methods which one associates more with Marwaris, if one is to believe the widely diffused rumour about the existence of a private firm through which much of the profits of their companies was siphoned off without the knowledge and approval of the shareholders. This is not meant to suggest that British businessmen in India were more honest than Indian businessmen: it is just that their ways of dealing with shareholders were different. The Tatas' marketing network appears also to have been built according to 'Indian' rather than 'British' principles, although I have not come across a detailed study of Tata dealerships.

However, in some other ways Tatas were a unique firm in the context of colonial India, particularly in their approach to technological innovation and in their pattern of diversification. They tended as a rule to adopt the latest technology available, and not to follow British practices slavishly, as most Indian firms did. Their knowledge of world conditions was unparalleled in Indian industrial circles which still looked to Manchester and Birmingham as the Meccas of textile and iron technology. In cotton textiles it is true that, to look after the technical side of the Empress Mills, they hired Lancashire men, such as James Brooksby and Robert Roscoe, thus following the general trend among Indian millowners.[14] However, those two technical men proved to be exceptionally capable and innovative. They were largely responsible for the adoption of the ring frame,[15] a pioneering experiment at the time, since Lancashire mills did not yet use it on a significant scale. They adapted this new technology to the specific needs of the Indian textile industry, particularly the spinning of the coarser counts of cotton which were grown in India and which the throstle could not spin. In striving for technical innovation and excellence, the two Britons always had the full support of J.N. Tata. When setting up the TISCO steelworks, the Tatas also gave preference to state-of-the-art technology while striving to adapt it to local conditions, and this attitude was a key factor in the technical success of the venture. It compares favourably not only with that of most Indian cotton mill-owners, but also with that of the Scottish managing agents of the Calcutta jute mills. Most of the technical personnel who helped start the Jamshedpur steelworks had been recruited at high cost in America and Germany.[16] Britons formed only a small part of the staff, and that kind of cosmopolitan approach was unknown in India at the time.

Other unique features of Tatas were their almost exclusive concentration on industrial activities, as well as the pattern of diversification of the latter. Regarding the first point, one should beware of simplifications. The Tatas never eschewed finance and trade, on principle. The founder of the firm, J.N. Tata, used to lend monies for many years, but then found investment in real estate in Bombay a more profitable proposition,[17] and the firm seems never to have returned to money-lending on a significant scale. In the same way, the Tatas' large venture in the China trade, which played a significant role in the primary accumulation of capital by the firm, was entrusted to a cousin of J.N. Tata, R.D. Tata,[18] and although a success in financial terms, became something of a side-show in relation to the firm's manufacturing ventures. In any case, the success of TISCO and its continuous expansion stretched the managerial resources of the firm to the utmost and prevented it from expanding much in other fields.

However, the pattern of diversification of the activities of the firm was not totally opportunistic like that of most large Indian firms, but followed a certain industrial logic. The product mix of the Tata conglomerate prior to 1947 was wide-ranging, since, apart from the two core activities of cotton textiles and steel, it encompassed real estate, hotel management, electricity production, construction (Tata Construction which was ceded to Walchand in the 1930s), cement production (the three Tata cement factories were amalgamated with others to form the Associated Cement Companies in 1936), tinplate (as a minority partner in a joint venture with Burmah Shell operating in Jamshedpur next to TISCO), oil, and soap. If the link between cotton textiles and steel is not obvious, since the major linkage of textile machinery production was not represented, nevertheless it is clear that steel in its turn led to tinplate and at a later stage to trucks, and electricity production in the Ghats was geared to the needs of the cotton mills of Bombay. Actually the pattern of diversification went even beyond a simple logic of the firm to become the first attempt at some kind of systematic economic planning in the Indian context. The firm of Tatas thus came to fill a vacuum and to take upon itself some of the economic functions which were those of the state in a Listian conception which was, before 1914, still anathema to the British rulers of India.

However, this did not lead to a direct clash with the colonial state but rather resulted in a process by which the firm of Tatas and the colonial state became closely enmeshed. This is perhaps the most paradoxical aspect of the whole Tata saga, the fact that an Indian firm was capable of manipulating the colonial state to ensure its growth even before the adoption of a policy of 'discriminating protection' which at a later stage was a significant boost to the growth of many Indian firms. How crucial the help of the colonial state was at different stages to the growth of TISCO is well known. Let us simply recall here Lord Curzon's decision of 1899 to change the rules regarding the granting of mining concessions,[19] Lord George Hamilton's constant encouragement to J.N. Tata's scheme which played such a role in overcoming bureaucratic obstacles,[20] the manifold help given by the government at the time of the setting up of the steelworks, the guaranteed purchase by the Indian Railways of part of the production,[21] and the role of various technical departments of the government in the successful advancement of the project.

How to account for the attitude of the colonial state, keeping in mind the political economy framework within which I have situated myself? Why did the colonial state go out of its way to support an industrial venture in which there was no direct British participation? The question has often been asked but no really satisfactory answer given. The rise of Indian nationalism has often been quoted as one of the factors which influenced the attitude of the government, but in the pre-1917 phase it cannot have been of great significance. A search for more plausible reasons brings to mind firstly a certain amount of strategic foresight on the part of the British rulers of India: having an iron and steel industry could help in the event of war, as it eventually did. There may also have been reasons of a more psychological nature, related to a certain conception of 'fair play'. J.N. Tata was perceived as a risk-taking entrepreneur, conforming to a certain normative ideal, and not subject to the strictures which the British rulers applied to most Indian businessmen, whom they viewed as 'greedy banias'. Helping such a man reinforced the self-image the British had of themselves as fair and liberal; it was also a way of silencing the critics of the Raj without endangering any existing British interests.

The Tatas were always very good at getting government support without tarnishing their image as a true 'swadeshi' firm inspired by an exclusive consideration for the interests of India. J.N. Tata himself, though at heart deeply loyalist, was never a 'toady'; he did not hesitate to criticize the government at several junctures, for instance, over the countervailing excise duty on Indian textiles in 1894.[22] The fact that he was always refused the knighthood he so much desired, and which his services easily deserved (he did not even live to see his son Dorab knighted in 1910), is testimony to a perception by the British that his sympathies were too much on the side of Indian nationalism. His firm reaped the benefit of it when in 1907 the TISCO shares were subscribed in three weeks by the Indian public in the great wave of patriotic enthusiasm generated by the Swadeshi movement in Bengal.[23] The link with Indian nationalist aspirations remained an essential source of strength for the Tatas and the adoption by the Indian Legislature in 1924 of the Steel Protection Bill which saved TISCO from incoming bankruptcy owed as much to the support of the Swaraj Party as to the sympathetic attitude of the government.[24]

Thus the Tatas appear to have had the best of both worlds, enjoying on the one hand the support of the colonial state at different crucial moments in their history, and on the other, benefiting by the growth of Indian economic and political nationalism. A unique position which was threatened when India became independent.

If one relates the Tata story to macroeconomic developments, some disjunctions will become apparent. Thus the firm grew fastest in the 1907–39 period when overall industrial development in India was fairly sluggish. The great problem here is how to account for the successful development of an iron and steel industry at a time when the railway network had already been completed while there was not yet a mechanical engineering industry in India. Between 1913 and 1939, when TISCO enjoyed a position of quasi-monopoly in steel production in India,[25] the market for steel products did not expand significantly, although the market for some types of steel expanded (steel for constructional engineering) while that for steel rails declined dramatically after 1927–8.[26] The expansion of TISCO occurred almost exclusively on the basis of import-substitution and mainly at the expense of non-British exporters of steel products (Belgium in particular). Tatas were therefore exceptionally well placed to benefit by a policy of protection combined with preference for British products, since their main competitors were non-British producers. The Steel Industry Protection Act of 1924 was the first instance of the introduction in India of differential duties on imports from the UK and from other countries, a policy of 'imperial preference' which was generalized in 1932 with the signing of the Ottawa agreement. Although the impact of protection was not very great in direct terms, the tariffs were instrumental in bringing about a fall in production costs which made TISCO better able to weather foreign competition.[27]

The same trend was noticeable in cotton textiles: the Tata cotton mills, like most Bombay mills, were more threatened by Japanese competition in the lower segments of the market than by Lancashire competition in finer goods, and the Tatas were largely behind the Lees-Mody pact of 1933, an alliance between Bombay and Lancashire millowners against the threat of cheap Japanese textiles flooding the Indian market.[28] The pact led to the conclusion of an Indo-Japanese trade agreement which imposed a ceiling on the sales of Japanese cotton piece goods to India. The specific 'political economy mix' of the 1917–47 period, characterized by a limited conjunction of interest between some British and some Indian groups, suited the Tatas particularly well. However, it did not survive the Second World War and the coming of independence.

When British rule came to an end, other big Indian firms had a more intimate connection to the Indian state as a result of the support they had given the Congress during the independence struggle. This was particularly true of the Birlas and some of the Ahmedabad textile magnates. As for the Tatas, as I have shown elsewhere,[29] their attitude remained ambiguous at least till 1942; it is only after this date that they can be said to have openly supported Indian national aspirations (although making big profits thanks to government orders during the war). While they had joined hands with other representatives of Indian big business in framing the Bombay Plan, their political influence was never very great in post-1947 India. They did not take very kindly even to the mild form of 'socialism' associated with Nehru, not, I think, mainly because of a strong ideological commitment to economic liberalism, but because, being mostly steel producers, they were not allowed to expand in an unrestricted manner in that branch, as steel was, par excellence, the kind of basic industry which the state sought to control directly. The extent of their clash with the Indian state should not, however, be exaggerated: they were allowed an expansion of their Jamshedpur installations, new opportunities opened up in the automobile industry (TELCO) as well as in other branches, and they collaborated with the state in the running of Air India, which developed from Tata Airlines. But their position of dominance in the Indian private sector was gradually eroded in the 1950s and 1960s by the rise of their arch-rivals, the house of Birla.[30] Resentment at alleged government preference for other firms probably explains the role they played in the setting up of the Forum of Free Enterprise, an anti-socialist think-tank, in 1955, and their alleged support to the creation of the Swatantra Party in 1959.[31] Though this support was short-lived and the 1960s saw a rapprochement between big business in general and the government,[32] the Tatas were never as close to the Congress as the Birlas. Given the role of the state in the Indian economy and the emergence of the 'licence Raj' in the 1960s, it is tempting to relate their relative decline to the influence of political factors. For there was no clear decrease in entrepreneurial ability, no Marshallian generational cycle at work: if the sons of the founder, Dorab and Ratan, mainly completed and consolidated what their father had initiated, the third generation represented by Naval and J.R.D. Tata showed a renewed capacity for initiative, with further diversification moves into such fields as chemicals, automobiles, and electronics. They also benefited from the help of exceptional managers such as S. Moolgaokar, for many years the chairman and managing director of TELCO,[33] probably the most successful Tata firm in the post-1947 period.

The Tata paradox is thus also that of one of the few big Indian firms which did not benefit by the coming of independence as much as could have been expected, because it lost the almost unique position, akin to a sort of niche, it had carved for itself during the colonial period. Having lost their privileged relationship to the state, the Tatas had actually lost their main competitive advantage over their big business rivals and found themselves somewhat at odds with the new logic presiding over the relationship between the state and the private sector. In the new dispensation, the private sector was expected to occupy the interstices left open by the growth of the public sector, an opportunistic model of diversification which perfectly suited operators such as Birla. It was a new kind of niche into which the Tatas found it somewhat difficult to insert themselves successfully. With the new liberal policy initiated by the Government of India in 1991, they may again find the right niche. This concept of specific niches occupied by firms in relation to particular configurations in the political economy might be helpful in closing the gap between macro and micro levels which is so evident in the existing literature on the history of Indian capitalism and Indian industry.

'Niche' conveys the idea of insulation, of a protected space, of a specific kind of adaptation to an environment. In a political economy perspective it could refer to the capacity of a firm to grow counter-cyclically by exploiting very specific opportunities in very specific markets over a specific period of time, defined by a particular conjunction of political and economic factors. In the case of the Tatas during the interwar period, the crucial political factor was the weakening hold of the British over India which led the colonial rulers to contemplate concessions to Indian interests in order to ensure at least their neutrality; the crucial economic factor was the position of the British steel industry: faced with dwindling markets worldwide, the British steelmakers were content with maintaining more or less their market share in India by squeezing out their major competitors, the European steelmakers, particularly those of Belgium and Luxembourg, and they saw the Tatas as potential allies in that fight. However, it is only because the Tatas had established a close connection with the colonial government that the British steelmakers perceived them in that light. The colonial government was the indispensable broker of the de facto alliance which emerged between the Tatas and the British steelmakers against the more dynamic European producers. Thus, in an ironically paradoxical way, the already eroded imperial relationship between Britain and India nurtured and then protected the most 'national' of all Indian industries, the one which was identified with power and independence. The imperial connection thus acted as a kind of substitute for a thriving industrial environment.

## Notes

1. A.K. Bagchi, 'European and Indian entrepreneursip in India, 1900–30', in E. Leach and S.N. Mukherjee (eds), *Elites in South Asia* (Cambridge, 1970), pp. 223–56.
2. B.R. Tomlinson, 'Colonial Firms and the Decline of Colonialism in Eastern India 1914–1947', *Modern Asian Studies* 15: 3 (1981), pp. 455–86.
3. C.A. Bayly, *Rulers, Townsmen and Bazaars* (Cambridge, 1983), p. 376.
4. See D. Tripathi, *The Dynamics of a Tradition: Kasturbhai Lalbhai and His Entrepreneurship* (Delhi, 1981), p. 76.

5. See D. Kumar (ed.), *The Cambridge Economic History of India,* vol. 2 (Cambridge, 1983), p. 556.

6. F.R. Harris, *Jamsetji Nusserwanji Tata: A Chronicle of His Life* (Bombay, 1958, 2nd edition).

7. Ibid., p. 189.

8. When TISCO was formed in 1907, the total Tata stake was Rs 25 lakhs, about 21 per cent of the total capital subscribed. See C.M. Lala, *The Creation of Wealth: A Tata Story* (Bombay, 1981), p. 24. There was a total of 8,000 investors in the company.

9. Such as John Peterson who was Director-in-Charge of TISCO in the mid-1920s, or Sir Ardeshir Dalal who joined the Tata board in 1931. Lala, *The Creation of Wealth,* pp. 97 and 196.

10. See a list of 'firsts' in labour welfare in ibid., Appendix A, p. 203. The eight-hour working day was introduced in TISCO as early as 1912, while it was enforced by law only in 1948.

11. Harris, *Jamsetji Nusserwanji Tata,* p. 44.

12. There were strikes at TISCO in 1920, 1922, and 1928.

13. R. Chandavarkar, *The Origins of Industrial Capitalism in India: Business Strategies and the Working Classes in Bombay, 1900–1940* (Cambridge, 1993).

14. On the role played by Lancashire men in the birth and development of the Indian cotton textile industry, see my 'Transfert de technologie de Grande-Bretagne en Inde: le cas de l'industrie cotonnière (1854–1920)', in *Cahiers du Centre de Recherches Historiques,* 4 (1989), pp. 43–58.

15. Harris, *Jamsetji Nusserwanji Tata,* pp. 30–1.

16. The following description of the TISCO works in 1911 shows this: 'At the time of Mr. Fraser's visit Sakchi was an extremely cosmopolitan place. Mr Wells was general manager, and his chief assistants in the management, as well as the blast furnace superintendent and his staff, were all Americans. The crew of the steelworks and their superintendent were Germans. The superintendent and crew of the rolling mills were English There were a certain number of Austrians, Italians and Swiss, while Chinese were working as carpenters and in the pattern-shops'; ibid., p. 202.

17. Ibid., p. 67.

18. Ibid., p. 93.

19. Ibid., p. 153.

20. In 1900, on a visit to London, J.N. Tata had a long interview with Lord George Hamilton, who was then the Secretary of State for India. Lord George assured him that 'his great desire . . . was to see Indian industries developed with Indian capital'. The Secretary of State 'promised to authorize the Government of India to give him all possible help. The promise was faithfully fulfilled. Lord George wrote to India expressing the warmest

interest in the project and signifying that any steps the Government of India might take to assist it would receive his ready endorsement. From that time onward Mr. Tata and his successors never had much reason to complain of any lack of official support'. See ibid., pp. 155–6.

21. Lala, *The Creation of Wealth*, p. 25.

22. Harris, *Jamsetji Nusserwanji Tata*, pp. 57–8.

23. Ibid., p. 190.

24. 'Swarajist politicians . . . proved extremely helpful in prodding the government into granting protection to Tata's steel industry in 1924'; S. Sarkar, *Modern India 1885–1947* (Delhi, 1983), p. 232.

25. Apart from TISCO, only Mysore Iron and Steel produced small quantities of steel from 1936 onwards. W.A. Johnson, *The Steel Industry of India* (Cambridge, Mass., 1966), pp. 14–15. The year 1939 saw the launching of the Steel Corporation of Bengal by Martin Burn.

26. Rail orders received by TISCO from the Indian Railways increased regularly between 1923–4 and 1927–8, reaching a maximum of 182,800 tons in the latter year, but afterwards they declined precipitously, falling to a low of 36,500 tons in 1932–3. Indian Tariff Board, *Statutory Enquiry* 1933: *Steel*, vol. I: *Written Evidence Given by the Tata Iron and Steel Company Limited* (Delhi, 1934), p. 74, quoted in A.K. Bagchi, *Private Investment in India 1900–1939* (Cambridge, 1972), p. 315.

27. 'In a way, the credit for a large part of the fall in the cost of production must be given to the successive Tariff Boards appointed by the Government of India: TISCO was compelled to reduce costs because at every stage the tariffs or bounties proposed were just enough to cover the prime costs of production plus given percentages of the replacement value of capital and the working capital the Tariff Board considered necessary'; Bagchi, *Private Investment*, p. 319.

28. B. Chatterji, *Trade, Tariffs and Empire: Lancashire and British Policy in India 1919–1939* (Delhi, 1992).

29. C. Markovits, 'Les hommes d'affaires Indiens et le mouvement nationaliste de 1931 à1947', unpublished doctoral thesis, Paris, 1987.

30. In 1965, according to the findings of the Monopolies Inquiry Commission set up by the Government of India, the Tatas were still number one in terms of both assets and sales, but the Birlas' sales were almost as large as the Tatas'. See *Report of the Monopolies Inquiry Commission, 1965*: vols. I and II (New Delhi, 1965). By 1976, the respective turnovers of the two business houses were grossly equal, the Tatas' being still marginally higher than the Birlas'. See N.K. Chandra, 'Monopoly Capital, Private Corporate Sector and the Indian Economy: A Study in Relative Growth, 1931–76', *Economic and Political Weekly*, XIV: 30–2 (August 1979), Table 2, p. 1245. The latest estimate I have come across, for 1985, puts the Birlas slightly

ahead of the Tatas in terms of turnover, and even more in terms of assets. See Economist Intelligence Unit, *Country Profile India, 1988/89* (London, 1988).

31. H.L. Erdman, *The Swatantra Party and Indian Conservatism* (Cambridge, 1967).

32. S.A. Kochanek, *Business and Politics in India* (Berkeley, 1974).

33. Lala, *The Creation of Wealth*, p. 80.

7

# MERCHANTS, ENTREPRENEURS, AND THE MIDDLE CLASSES IN TWENTIETH-CENTURY INDIA*

THE NOTION OF A UNIFIED AND LARGE INDIAN MIDDLE class is a fairly recent construct, the product of the ongoing liberalization, and of the unreasonable expectations of market analysts and multinational firms regarding the size of the Indian market. A recent author underlines that, even understood solely in terms of consumption, the Indian middle class 'cuts a rather pathetic figure'.[1] This is, however, a view which has been formed by a comparison with the developed West. In relation to other developing countries, and even more so the mass of the poor and the ordinary working population in India itself, the figure it cuts is not that pathetic. But there remains the problem of where to locate this vast and fairly undifferentiated group on the social map of India. Prior to the 1990s, social scientists generally preferred to talk of the middle classes to take into account the extreme diversity of the middle strata of Indian society. Whether singular or plural, the two dominant narratives of the rise and growth of this group in India have been a 'Macaulayan' one and a 'Kaleckian' one. In the former, pride of place was undoubtedly given to the English-educated professionals as forming the core group in the Indian middle class, while in the latter, merchants and

*From I. Ahmad and H. Reifeld (eds), *Middle Class Values in India and Western Europe* (Delhi: Social Science Press, 2003), pp. 42–55.

entrepreneurs occupied a more central position. In this chapter, I seek to present an alternative narrative, in which Macaulay and his kind play no role, but which also takes some distance *vis-à-vis* the Kaleckian model, a narrative of the slow emergence, from within a merchant world, of a strata of entrepreneurs who have become an important component of the Indian middle classes. In the first part, I take a quick look at these two dominant narratives.

## A Critique of Two Dominant Narratives

The rise of an Indian middle class is generally traced to the colonial period, in particular to the middle decades of the nineteenth century, when Macaulay's programme—outlined in his famous 'Minute on Indian education' of creating a 'class of persons, Indian in blood and colour, but English in taste, in opinions, in morals and in intellect'[2]—started being implemented by the colonial state with the creation of universities and more generally the encouragement given to the expansion of Western education in the major cities of India. However, it should be noted that neither Macaulay nor other colonial luminaries used the term 'middle class' in conjunction with the emerging new social group of Indian English-educated literati. Actually it could be argued that the use of the term 'middle class' in the Indian context was fundamentally anathema to them. It was a basic assumption of Western 'Orientalism' that one of the major differences between European and 'Oriental' societies was precisely the absence in the latter of a 'middle estate', of an intermediate class between the tiny dominant elite and the mass of the subject population. Recognizing the existence of an Indian 'middle class' would have amounted to acknowledging a certain degree of similarity between the English and Indian societies, which would have endangered the colonial project itself. Macaulay himself thought in terms of a class of intermediaries, of cultural brokers, who were basically clerks, but not 'middle class', with the connotations of respectability and affluence which the term had in the nineteenth century. As Indian nationalism emerged in the late nineteenth century, British colonial administrators were careful not to define it as a 'middle class' movement, but tended to dismiss it as reflecting the views of a 'microscopic minority' of elite individuals totally cut off from the masses of India. The early Indian nationalists in their turn, in spite of the fact that they undoubtedly belonged to the middle strata of society (they were mostly lawyers and professionals) were wary of defining their movement and aspirations as 'middle class' and preferred to present themselves either as an aspiring elite or, in a more populist fashion, as the vanguard of the people.

The theme of the rise of an Indian middle class or rather a petty bourgeoisie was first elaborated upon only in the 1930s, mostly by Marxist authors such as Rajani Palme Dutt,[3] but in 'orthodox' Marxist fashion (although there is some ambiguity as to Marx's own position on the question), they saw this class as doomed to be squeezed by the growing polarization between a big bourgeoisie and an emerging proletariat. A slightly modified form of the classical Marxist position was articulated by D.D. Kosambi in the introduction to his celebrated book, *Culture and Civilization of Ancient India*.[4] He viewed the Indian bourgeoisie as divided into two sections: the 'real capitalist bourgeoisie' which dominated finance and mechanized factory production, and the 'petty-bourgeois class of shopkeepers', which dominated distribution, and was 'formidable by reason of their large number'. He tended, therefore, to view the petty bourgeoisie not as an 'intermediate class' but as a section of the bourgeoisie.

The first academic author to deal in a systematic way with the question of the Indian middle class, B.B. Misra, however, came from a completely  different ideological horizon.[5] He offered a broad-ranging historical survey in which he put forward a decidedly 'Whiggish' view[6] of the rise and growth of the middle class in India which he equated with a phenomenon of modernization induced by colonialism and the impact of the West. This kind of approach sounds rather obsolete forty years later, but one of Misra's merits was his alertness to the great empirical diversity of the Indian middle classes. In particular he was careful to distinguish between a commercial middle class, an industrial middle class, a landed middle class, and an educated middle class, in which he gave particular attention to the practitioners of what he called 'the learned professions', and not to reify any of these categories as constituting the Indian middle class. In spite of his empirical caution, in the 1960s the dominant narrative of the Indian middle class was nevertheless undoubtedly 'Macaulayan', inasmuch as it put at the centre of the stage those who were English-educated, and directly linked the Indian middle class to the modernization theory which was then the fashionable paradigm. This view was challenged in the late 1960s and early 1970s by the rise of the so-called 'Cambridge school', which tended to dismiss the link between Western education and political consciousness, especially in accounting for the emergence of the Indian nationalist movement, but did not come forward with an alternative sociological formulation.

In the following decades, the burgeoning sociological literature about India paid relatively little detailed attention to the middle class, preoccupied as it was with grander questions regarding caste and class, and discussions of the Dumontian and other paradigms. It was left to economists and historians operating within a broad Marxist framework to put forward an alternative view which I call 'Kaleckian' because it derived its original inspiration from a short article on 'intermediate regimes' by the famous Polish economist.[7] It had been written in the 1950s but was translated into English in the early 1970s and attracted the attention of K.N. Raj, who applied Kalecki's insight to the Indian case in a well-known article.[8] Later users of the notion included Asok Mitra, Prem Shankar Jha, and Richard Fox.[9] In an attempt at synthesis, the historian Burton Stein elaborated on Kalecki's and Raj's contributions to put forward a *longue durée* view of India as an 'intermediate regime' centred on a characterization of the 'petty bourgeoisie' as a particularly significant category in both economic and political terms.[10] The rise of this petty bourgeoisie was related to a particular form of the transition to capitalism which started in the eighteenth century before colonization but remained largely unrealized till the late twentieth century. Far from being a sign of triumphant modernity, the rise of this class was perceived by Stein as emblematic of an arrested transition and the kind of populist politics that it bred. This class was seen by Stein and others as a class in itself and not as a section of the bourgeoisie: it often frontally opposed the latter, but it was also in an exploitative relationship *vis-à-vis* the mass of the people. Stein's view, which was couched in a somewhat dogmatic language, never gained wide acceptance in an academic community which was increasingly steeped in culturalism and postmodernism, and the 'Kaleckian' paradigm, with its clear Marxist connotations, largely fell into disuse during the 1990s. It is interesting to note that a recent widely-celebrated essay on the Indian middle class ignores Kalecki altogether, and basically goes back to a Macaulayan narrative of the origins of the middle class.[11]

These two narratives, while addressing different concerns and adopting different angles of vision, attempt to locate the middle class in some broad historical scheme, but give little detailed attention to the historical process of formation of a class of merchants and entrepreneurs. In this chapter I shall focus exclusively on the latter group and shall not preoccupy myself primarily with definitional problems. I leave it to the sociologists to present us with neat classifications. For the purpose of this chapter, I shall adopt a largely pragmatic and empirical definition. The section I shall be looking at will be those merchants, traders, and entrepreneurs who are not strictly speaking shopkeepers (the latter constituting a very large category on which there exists practically no empirical work in the Indian context), but do not belong to the very top echelons of the business world either. I will thus deliberately exclude from my area of inquiry the Birlas, the Tatas, and other big capitalists, who are certainly not 'middle class' and about whom I have written at length elsewhere.[12] The people I am going to talk about are 'middle' in terms of their incomes, in the sense that they do not belong to the low-income majority or to the tiny elite of the really rich, but range from the moderately well-off to the conspicuously affluent, although, given the lack of reliable income tax statistics, nothing very detailed can be said about their actual income. They are merchants, traders, and medium- or small-scale industrialists. They obviously account for a significant chunk of the overall middle classes in terms of numbers, but there remains a big question as to whether they constitute a separate social group or can be seen as part of a broader sociological category. My approach to them will be decidedly historical because there is a certain lack of readily available historical literature on the subject.

## The Mercantile and Entrepreneurial Sector of Indian Society since the Middle of the Nineteenth Century

Although the chapter is supposed to address specifically the twentieth century, I feel it would be totally artificial to start the narrative around 1900, since there was a large amount of direct continuity between the developments in the second half of the nineteenth century and those in the first two decades of the twentieth century, the first significant break occurring only around 1920.

The middle decades of the nineteenth century saw a series of concomitant developments which concurred to reshape to a significant extent the profile of the mercantile world of India, although they did not amount to a complete revolution. These developments were on the one hand of an economic nature: the beginning of a transport revolution with the building of the first railways, the birth of a mechanized textile industry (cotton in Bombay, jute in Calcutta), and the reorganization of banks (with the passing of the Presidency Banks Act of 1876) and financial markets (with the gradual emergence of stock markets in Calcutta and Bombay) along 'modern' lines. On the other hand these developments were of a political and legal nature: the completion of the British conquest of India and the political reorganization following the end of the 1857 Revolt, with the introduction of British company law and more generally a British-inspired legal system into India. The mercantile world felt the impact of those developments only gradually but they reinforced trends which were already at work from the 1830s. One of the main outcomes of these decades of reorganization was the definitive eclipse of the elite indigenous merchant bankers who still dominated the scene in most of northern India in the first half of the nineteenth century. As British power sought to reorganize itself along modern financial principles,

Indian bankers were totally deprived of their functions as state bankers, which survived only in the princely states, and the 'new men' who emerged had a different kind of link with the British. The collapse, in the 1880s, of the last great house of traditional north Indian bankers, the Mathura Seths, was emblematic of the new dispensation. It should also be noted that the 1857 Revolt itself had a significant impact on the map of wealth in India, as many landowners who had supported the Revolt or had been perceived as too lukewarm in their support to the British saw their estates confiscated, while those who had been conspicuously loyal were rewarded. An important transfer of wealth occurred in the wake of the Revolt and it helped to propel forward a new type of merchants and men of business. The increasing commodification of agriculture linked to the growth of exports produced by the limited transport revolution provided this set of operators with new opportunities. They were mostly 'upcountry merchants' who migrated from some of the princely states to the colonial port-cities. In Calcutta, they came mostly from Bikaner, Marwar, and the Shekhawat area of Jaipur State, the so-called 'Marwaris'.[13] They displaced the Bengali traders, the Gandhavaniks and the Suvarnavaniks, who had become the intermediaries of the British in the eighteenth century. In Bombay, there was a similar influx of traders from Kutch (Memons, Khojas, and Bhatias) and from the Kathiawar states, and a decline of the 'indigenous' Konkani Muslims who had played a significant role in the first half of the nineteenth century. These new men were pushed out by the poverty prevalent in the princely states of the 'dry zone' of north-western India (Gujarat, Rajasthan), and the decreased opportunities linked to the decline of old trade routes caused by the domination of colonial capital. They were also, more positively, drawn by the beckoning opportunities in the port-cities and were adept at exploiting residual political differences between British India and the Indian states, particularly in the matter of taxation law. The absence of income tax in the princely states made it advantageous to regularly remit there a part of the profits earned in British India. There thus began a regular stream of remittances from Bengal and the Bombay Presidency to the princely states of Rajputana, Kutch, and Kathiawar, and many great *havelis* were built in small towns and villages of these areas thanks to the profits earned from the sweat labour of the peasantry of Mymensingh and other areas of jute and cotton cultivation in eastern and central India. The 'new men', some of whom also hailed from the Punjab, Sind, and other semi-arid areas of British India, were mostly traders, moneylenders, and brokers of different kinds, who played the role of intermediaries between the mass of peasant cultivators and the mostly British export firms operating from a few colonial port-cities. The chain of intermediation found its concrete translation in the rise of merchant networks which linked the brokers in the port-cities (known as the *banians* to the big British firms), with the traders in the market towns and the moneylenders in the rural areas through a web of family, caste, and community relationships. Some of these men of business also played a major role in the growth of the new mechanized industries, in particular of the cotton textile industry. While the original entrepreneurs had often been people from outside the world of trading (such as Ranchhodlal Chhotalal, a Nagar Brahmin who created the first cotton mill in Ahmedabad), merchants very quickly seized the new opportunities and, through the managing agency system, established their domination over much of industry. While an upper stratum of big merchants accumulated significant fortunes, the majority of these traders definitely remained in the middle-income brackets. Altogether this mercantile wealth probably accounted for only a small share of the landed wealth of the big zamindars and maharajas, even if the latter were often heavily in debt.

The growth of an entrepreneurial group was further accelerated after 1920, by the granting of fiscal autonomy to India and the adoption of a limited policy of discriminative protection which de facto reserved for local entrepreneurs a share of the domestic market in steel, cotton textiles, sugar, and other basic industrial commodities.[14] The coming of independence and the rise of the 'licence raj' from 1960 onwards gave further impetus to the growth of this section, which came to occupy an important position in the political economy of India. As the industrial sector grew in both size and complexity, small- and medium-scale industrialists exploited specific niches, especially after the banning of imports of manufactured consumer goods in 1957.[15] They came from various backgrounds, but many were importers who converted themselves into industrialists and therefore, had a trading background. In spite of the rise of a significant industrial sector in India from 1920 onwards, it would still be difficult to argue for the emergence of a class of industrialists separate from the vast mercantile world which spawned it in the first place. Marketing and financial skills were always at a premium in Indian industry as compared to 'technical' skills, a situation which has perhaps started to change only very recently.

The mercantile world of India in the pre-Independence period, in spite of its own great internal diversity, remained largely separate from the world of the English-educated middle classes which were more conspicuous and influential, politically and culturally. Merchant communities, with the notable exception of the Bombay Parsis, did not pay great attention to English education, which was of limited interest to them. Its main use was in the legal arena, and there were enough competent English-educated lawyers available for hire by mercantile interests, Gandhi being only one case in point. They remained steeped in vernacular regional cultures, to which they often contributed significantly through patronage of writers, journalists, and musicians. Another factor responsible for separateness was ethnic differences. In eastern India for instance and particularly in Bengal, the commercial middle class was overwhelmingly dominated, from the late nineteenth century onwards, by the Marwaris and other North Indian elements. The Bengali commercial element was largely displaced or confined to the lower rungs of mercantile activity and the separation between the educated Bengali middle class and the 'new' commercial middle class was complete. In Maharashtra likewise there was a wide gulf between the Marathi-speaking, largely Pune-based, educated middle class and the Gujarati-speaking commercial middle class based in Bombay. Even in south India, particularly in Tamil Nadu, where such ethnic differences were absent as both the Nattukottai Chettiars, who dominated the world of financial, mercantile, and industrial enterprise, as well as the educated Brahmin and non-Brahmin middle class were

Tamil speaking, there remained a certain amount of social distance, in particular between Chettiars and Brahmins. With the coming of independence and the economic development it helped nurture, there occurred a limited rapprochement between the mercantile world and that of the educated middle classes through the medium of the state and the role it played in furthering industrialization. But it is only with the advent of consumerism as a dominant ideology in the 1990s that these two universes can be said to have engaged in a process of fusion which, however, remains far from complete. I shall now focus more specifically on the problem of values.

## Merchants' Values and Middle-class Values

Do middle classes have values? It would be easy to give this question a cynical answer, which one could couch in the language of the Frankfurt school ('minima moralia') and stress that the central value for middle-class people is making money, while their mode of thinking favours social conformism ('keeping up with the Joneses'). In India, it has become fashionable to deplore the 'moral vacuum' of the present day middle class and its lack of social responsibility, as it remains apparently unconcerned by the persistence of mass poverty on an enormous scale. Such moral condemnations are facile, especially when they come from middle-class Westerners who do not face the same kind of ethical dilemmas as their Indian counterparts. In a different vein, it should be noted that sociologists of the Bourdieu school have emphasized the importance of cultural assets, the so-called 'symbolic capital' to the constitution of social elites, and the area of values deserves an exploration. The merchant world of India, particularly the dominant Hindu and Jain merchant communities of northern and north-western India, was characterized by the existence of a set of values which amounted to a 'moral economy', and could be seen as a well-constituted 'habitus' already by the eighteenth century. On the other hand, the 'new' educated middle classes which developed in India in the second half of the nineteenth century were more uncertain as to what constituted their core values. Although strongly influenced by the kind of Victorian values which were then dominant in Britain, they sought at the same time to preserve a domain of 'indigenous values' which, as has been often pointed out, they located largely in the sphere of 'domesticity'. On the contradictions this dichotomy between public sphere and domestic sphere could entail, Satyajit Ray provides an illuminating and ironical commentary in *Charulata*. Merchants precisely did not have to contend to the same extent with a contradiction between two spheres, since the world of business, thanks to the dominance of the family firm, was largely coeval with the world of domesticity and did not entail entering into a 'public sphere'. Most businessmen raised capital from within their own family, kin, caste, or community and did not go 'public'. If they operated in the marketplace, the latter was so segmented as not to constitute a 'public arena' in any significant sense. Even nowadays, it is only a minority of large-scale firms which raise capital from the public at large. Most small- and medium-scale firms rely on family and kin resources for their managerial staff and permanent capital and on borrowings from state banks for their working capital. This gives the business sector a wide measure of autonomy *vis-à-vis* other sections of the middle class, such as professionals, who tend to invest only in the big publicly quoted companies.

One difficulty in pursuing a comparative exercise regarding value systems is the existence of a certain degree of asymmetry in terms of information. While members of the educated middle classes were prone to express themselves orally and in writing and to leave traces of their views, merchants were a more inward-looking group, which rarely expressed itself in public. For the modern and contemporary period, there is no equivalent of the *Ardhakathanak*, the autobiography of the seventeenth-century north Indian Jain merchant Banarsidas which is a precious source of information on the mentality of late medieval or early modern merchants.[16] We are left to deduce merchant values from an examination of the behaviour of the merchants rather than from texts written by them. This behaviourist approach has its limitations of course, but, in the absence of direct expressions, it is the only course open to the researcher.

As a point of departure, we can take the view of the late-eighteenth-century north Indian merchant world presented by the historian Christopher Bayly in his well-known *Rulers, Townsmen and Bazaars*, a world which appears to have remained largely unchanged till the twentieth century.[17] It is a broadly 'Chayanovian' view which stresses the similarities between the merchant family and the peasant family inasmuch as it makes reproduction of the family rather than enlargement of its assets, its primary goal, leading to behaviour which could be 'anti-accumulationist'. The central notion for merchants was that of credit which was largely equated with honour and social prestige: its preservation was deemed more precious than any aggrandizement. Great store was set on austerity and conspicuous consumption was looked down upon as unworthy as well as economically counterproductive. Whether merchants actually conformed to this set of norms is of course open to question and it would be only too easy to find instances of non-conforming behaviour. It appears nevertheless also fatuous to totally dismiss norms to which there was undoubtedly deeply felt adherence, in spite of lapses in actual conduct. Were these norms very different from those which guided the 'English-educated' section of the middle classes? Some common features would be immediately apparent, such as the devaluation of conspicuous consumption and the emphasis put on thrift and self-denial. In matters of sexual morality, there would also be a lot of common ground, a markedly 'puritanical' ethic, although on the question of female education, merchants would for a long period be characterized by a very cautious attitude, which would leave them open to accusations of 'backwardness'. An area of both difference and commonality would be that of 'service', the typical Indian middle-class notion of *seva* which was popularized by organizations such as the 'Servants of India Society' and given central place by Gandhi who made it the basis of his teachings. Seva implied a certain distancing *vis-à-vis* family and community to encompass a notion of society at large, and that is where the ways of the merchants and some members of the educated classes tended to diverge. While the latter often aspired to make 'service' the central vocation of their lives, merchants were too embedded in the universe of family and caste to conceive of such a devotion. They often financed liberally these 'service' activities but rarely engaged in them very deeply. Their sociability remained bound by notions of caste and family, which prevented them from interacting with society at large. This is one factor of explanation for the support given to Gandhian movements by many merchants. By financing these movements, often on a generous scale, the merchants could assuage their consciences without having to engage too openly with a public arena. Gandhi imported into the sphere of public action notions of honour *(abru)* and trust which were directly borrowed from the world of the Gujarati banias to which his family belonged.[18] However, the Gandhian attempt at a synthesis between the values of the merchant world and the more 'Victorian' values of the educated classes did not succeed in completely bridging the gap between those two sections of the middle classes and its long-term impact remains a matter for speculation.

Independence and the increased role played by the state in the economy tended to result in some measure of further rapprochement between different middle-class sections. In the heydays of the 'licence Raj', aspiring capitalists had to develop a rapport with bureaucrats if they wanted to enjoy the bounties of the state, and a certain closeness ensued, although one would need detailed empirical data on topics such as matrimonial alliances to know how far it all went. Prior to the recent reforms, there was nevertheless no clear trend of integration between different middle-class sections and the idea of one 'great Indian middle class' remained largely a fantasy. Since 1991, the exponential growth of consumerism (though it already existed) has tended to provide a unifying ideological cement to the diverse components of the middle class. However, it is not certain as to whether the growth of consumerism is sufficient to keep together such an unstable conglomeration of groups.

Merchants and entrepreneurs constitute a numerically important section of the Indian middle class, but their place in its overall configuration remains uncertain. One durable characteristic which sets them apart from other middle-class sections is their fairly narrow base of recruitment in terms of caste. While the middle-class intelligentsia is drawn from a fairly large conspect of caste and regional groups, albeit mostly from upper castes, most merchants and entrepreneurs still belong to a limited number of castes, the bania and assimilated castes, and are drawn disproportionately from specific areas of the subcontinent, mostly the north-west (Gujarat, Sind, Rajasthan, Punjab). This situation has its roots in certain specific historical developments going back at least to the sixteenth century, which I have analysed elsewhere,[19] and which I shall not evoke here. Pan-Indian merchant networks such as those of the Marwaris have entrenched themselves in many areas and are not perceived any more as forming 'immigrant communities'. It is even said that in Assam it was the Marwari merchants, whose presence in the region goes back to the beginning of the nineteenth century, who were partly behind the anti-Bengali agitation of the 1970s and 1980s. They continue to give preference in employment in their firms to members of their family, kin, caste, and community, even if they are less competent than 'outsiders' (although probably to a lesser extent now than in earlier periods). Whether the ongoing 'liberalization' will result in breaking the hold of the bania castes on the mercantile and industrial sector is an open question. A new breed of entrepreneurs, not belonging to these castes, is undoubtedly present on the one hand in the agro-industrial sector (where they often come from peasant castes), and on the other hand in the so-called 'new economy' such as the computer software sector (where there are many Brahmins and members of other upper castes), but the overall importance of these high-tech activities should not be exaggerated. The 'old economy', where the merchant castes are still solidly entrenched, weighs more in the balance in terms of assets (once the present-day bubble bursts, as it has already started doing) as well as of employment. Notice should, however, be taken of significant changes in the way the members of the 'traditional' merchant castes relate to education and politics. They have taken to English education to a greater extent than before, often have MBAs from American universities, and some of them have developed more permanent links with political parties, particularly, in northern and western India, to the BJP. In view of the recent rise of the Sangh Parivar, it is sometimes suggested that, through their privileged links to the Hindu right, the merchant castes have been able to acquire a kind of hegemonic position and that they have imposed their values on the middle class at large. This raises two kinds of questions: first, that of the exact type of relationship which the merchant castes have with the Hindu nationalists, about which little serious empirical work has been done and second, that of the 'hegemonic' nature of Hindutva ideology, which seems to be very much open to debate.[20]

To conclude, it is not obvious to me that the merchant and entrepreneurial classes are as yet getting subsumed into an ensemble which could be called 'the great Indian middle class'. In spite of a rapprochement between this group and the professional and technical intelligentsia at the level of education and lifestyle, there remain significant differences. The universe of the merchants and small- and medium-scale entrepreneurs is still centred more around the family, which remains the basic economic unit, than that of other sections of the middle class which are more dependent either on the state or on the market at large. This might partly explain the apparent paradox that while, in theory, the entrepreneurs should be the driving force behind the ongoing liberalization process, in fact large sections of this group have various reservations *vis-à-vis* the process and tend to act as a brake rather than as an accelerator. Many of its members are still too deeply steeped in the structure of entitlements linked to the old economy to fully embrace a liberalization which could result in a complete reshuffle and redistribution of cards. As a result, they cannot be expected to give a clear direction to the process, and it will be left largely to the bureaucrats and politicians, constrained as they are by the compulsions of populist politics, to define its pace.

## Notes


1.  D. Gupta, 2000, 'India's Unmodern Modernity', in R. Thapar (ed.), *India: Another Millennium?* (Delhi: Viking, 2000), p. 95.
2.  Macaulay, 1835, quoted in P. Varma, *The Great Indian Middle Class* (Delhi: Penguin, 1998), p. 2.
3.  R.P. Dutt, *India Today* (London: Victor Gollancz, 1940).
4.  D.D. Kosambi, *The Culture and Civilisation of Ancient India in Historical Outline* (London: Routledge and Kegan Paul, 1964), p. 2.

5. B.B. Misra, *The Indian Middle Classes: Their Growth in Modern Times* (London, New York, Bombay: Oxford University Press, 1961).

6. Typical is the following passage, p. 69: 'The growth of the Indian middle classes in modern times proceeded from certain new conditions which developed under the rule of the East India Company, especially after the abolition of its trading monopoly in 1833. These new conditions were, for example, the mild and constitutional character of Government and the rule of law, the security of private property and the defined rights of agricultural classes, a national system of education and a period of continued peace, an economy of *laissez-faire* and a liberal policy of employment and social reform.'

7. M. Kalecki, 'Social and Economic Aspects of "Intermediate Regimes" ', in *Selected Essays on the Economic Growth of the Socialist and Mixed Economy* (Cambridge: Cambridge University Press, 1972).

8. K.N. Raj, 'The Politics and Economics of "Intermediate Regimes" ', *Economic and Political Weekly* VIII: 27 (July 1973), pp. 1189–98.

9. A. Mitra, *Terms of Trade and Class Relations: An Essay in Political Economy* (London: Macmillan, 1977); P.S. Jha, *India: A Political Economy of Stagnation* (Bombay: Oxford University Press, 1980); R.G. Fox, 'Urban Class and Communal Consciousness in Colonial Punjab: The Genesis of India's Intermediate Regime', *Modern Asian Studies* 18: 3 (1984), pp. 459–89.

10. B. Stein, 'Towards an Indian Petty Bourgeoisie: Outline of an Approach', *Economic and Political Weekly* XXVI: 4 (January 1991), pp. PE 9–20.

11. Varma, *The Great Indian Middle Class.*

12. *Indian Business and Nationalist Politics 1931–1939: The Indigenous Capitalist Class and the Rise of the Congress Party* (Cambridge: Cambridge University Press, 1985) and 'The Tata Paradox' in B. Stein and S. Subrahmanyam (eds), *Institutions and Economic Change in South Asia* (Delhi: Oxford University Press, 1996), pp. 237–48. [Chapter 6 of this volume.]

13. T.A. Timberg, *The Marwaris: From Traders to Industrialists* (Delhi: Vikas, 1978).

14. R.K. Ray, *Industrialization in India 1914–1947: Growth and Conflict in the Private Corporate Sector* (Delhi: Manohar, 1979).

15. Jha, *India: A Political Economy of Stagnation.*

16. R.C. Sharma, 'The Ardha-Kathanak: A Neglected Source of Mughal History', *Indica*, VII: 1 (1970), pp. 49–73, 106–20.

17. C.A. Bayly, *Rulers, Townsmen and Bazaars: North Indian Society in the Age of British Expansion, 1770–1870* (Cambridge: Cambridge University Press, 1983).

18. D. Haynes, *Rhetoric and Ritual in Colonial India: The Shaping of a Public Culture in Surat City: 1852–1928* (Berkeley: University of California Press, 1991).

19.  C. Markovits, 'Merchant Circulation in South Asia (Eighteenth to Twentieth Centuries): The Rise of Pan-Indian Merchant Networks', in Markovits, C.J. Pouchepadass, and S. Subrahmanyam (eds), *Society and Circulation: Mobile People and Itinerant Cultures in South Asia 1750–1950* (Delhi: Permanent Black, 2003), pp. 131–62. [Chapter 8 in this volume.]

20.  T. Hansen, *The Saffron Wave: Democracy and Hindu Nationalism in Modern India* (Princeton: Princeton University Press, 1999).

# PART III
# Merchant Networks

8

# MERCHANT CIRCULATION IN SOUTH ASIA (EIGHTEENTH TO TWENTIETH CENTURIES)

## The Rise of Pan-Indian Merchant Networks*

IN CONTEMPORARY SOUTH ASIA, PARTICULARLY IN INDIA, large-scale trade, finance, and industry tended, at least in the era prior to the liberalizing reforms of the 1990s (it remains to be seen to what extent the reforms have actually changed the situation), to be activities dominated by businessmen belonging to a limited number of communities, such as Marwaris, Gujaratis, Parsis, Sindhis, Chettiars, etc. This situation is not unique to South Asia: in many countries of Asia, Africa, and Latin America, specific 'ethnic' or regional groups often have a kind of monopoly over trade and finance. In the Indian case, this pattern of specialization is not primarily the 'natural' outcome of some deeply entrenched division of labour between commercially oriented and non-commercially oriented groups (although such a division of labour existed to a certain extent), but rather the result of longstanding processes of circulation, by which a

*From C. Markovits, J. Pouchepadass, and S. Subrahmanyam (eds), *Society and Circulation: Mobile People and Itinerant Cultures in South Asia 1750–1950* (Delhi: Permanent Black, 2003), pp. 131–62.

small number of merchant communities or networks originating from one part of the subcontinent gradually managed to establish a pattern of dominance over trading and financial activities across the entire subcontinent and even beyond.

This chapter focuses on the history of such a process of circulation and seeks to unravel the dynamics at work behind episodes like the large-scale migration of Marwari businessmen from Rajasthan to central and northern India. Given the fact that most pan-Indian merchant networks originated from the northwest of the subcontinent, in particular from Rajasthan, the Punjab, Sind, and Gujarat, a hypothesis will be put forward that the expansion of such networks was part of a wider process of circulation of skilled personnel between a 'dry zone', characterized by a partly pastoral economy, and areas of more reliable precipitations devoted to riverine agriculture. This attempt to link merchant expansion with a wider 'ecological' theme draws its original inspiration from an insight of Burton Stein, who showed how, in the context of medieval South India, environmental differences between dry zones and areas of permanent moisture could translate into differences in societal forms.[1]

I focus first on some of the comparative advantages in terms of market and financial skills enjoyed by the merchant communities of the 'dry zone', and then chart the process of expansion by which they were gradually able to penetrate most areas of the subcontinent. While some attention will be paid to an earlier phase, the main emphasis will be on the more recent period, from the middle of the eighteenth century onwards, and, apart from secondary literature bearing on Marwari and Gujarati expansion, some use will also be made of personal research on little-known merchant networks from Sind.

## Merchant Communities of the Dry Zone and their Pre-nineteenth-century Spread

The vast 'dry zone' which occupies most of the northwest of the subcontinent and includes parts of the Punjab, Sind, Rajasthan, and Gujarat—all areas characterized by scanty and unreliable rainfall—is the cradle of many specialized communities of merchants, traders, and bankers, forming a kind of cluster which makes it into one of the great breeding centres of merchant skill and enterprise in Asia. Suffice it to name Khatris, Aroras, Multanis, Marwaris, Bhatias, Khojas, Lohanas, Bohras, and Memons to form an idea of the disproportionate contribution of merchant groups with their roots in this part of the subcontinent to the ranks of the pan-Indian elite of trade and finance. This is not a new development, but can be traced back at least to the sixteenth century, if not to an even earlier period. Nor has it remained unnoticed by travellers, administrators, and social scientists. However, since D.R. Gadgil's pioneering and in many ways preliminary studies of the 1950s,[2] the subject has attracted only a limited amount of interest, from sociologists and historians. The question as to why merchant communities from this dry zone were better able to fulfil certain functions at a pan-Indian level than merchant groups from other, climatically more favoured areas, remains something of a mystery.

A fairly obvious type of explanation immediately comes to mind, connected to Ravenstein's well-known 'push factor':[3] it points towards a direct correlation between the relative poverty of these dry areas and the fact that their merchant communities sought better opportunities in more prosperous regions of riverine agriculture. More specifically, one is drawn to emphasize that merchants in the dry zone, in spite of playing a particularly important role in the system of revenue collection of the different states of the area, appear to have found it difficult to acquire land on a significant scale, and that, in the absence of any other local outlet for investment of capital, this might have been an incentive to move outside the region. In his study of Jaipur state in the 1650–1750 period, S.P. Gupta remarks that the local trading classes, in spite of having enlarged their income and wealth at the expense of the state and the peasantry, 'did not apparently convert their money claims into land rights'[4] and rarely appeared in the ranks of the *bhomias*, the local equivalent of the zamindars, which continued to be dominated by the Rajputs and the superior agrarian castes. Similar phenomena are reported for Sind in the pre-annexation era:

the Hindu banias who controlled local trade and finance rarely owned land, which generally belonged to big Muslim landowners, the *waderos*. Identifying some of the 'push' factors at work, however, gives only a partial answer to the questions regarding the actual movement of merchants. Three basic puzzles are still left unanswered, relating in the first place to the specific context which made possible this long-term movement, secondly to the reasons for the remarkable success obtained by the dry zone merchants in their endeavours, and thirdly to the particular time sequence of their movements, which appears staggered, characterized by numerous fits and starts, resulting only in the 1930s in a kind of stabilization which further events (except those directly linked to the 1947 Partition) did not significantly alter.

To address the first point, some general picture is needed of the comparative advantages that the mercantile groups of the dry zone enjoyed over mercantile groups in other regions which became the destinations of their movements. They have to do firstly with a possibly small difference in the relative degree of commercialization of agriculture between different areas in Mughal times. Even if we assume (an assumption which is, however, openly questioned by the editors of a recent volume devoted to the historiography of the Mughal state[5]) that a fairly uniform revenue demand tended to produce a certain homogeneity in this regard across the entire Mughal domain, the great internal diversity of the dry zone, where pockets of irrigated and rain-fed agriculture alternated with vast tracts devoted to a semi-nomadic form of pastoralism, stimulated exchange and the early development of commercial expertise in a particular way. Active marts dotted the area, where the grain of the oases and areas of rain-fed agriculture was exchanged for the wool and ghee of the pastoral areas. These marts sometimes developed into nodal points within a wider system of exchange. For in the long term, the main advantage the marts in the dry zone had over those situated in areas of riverine agriculture in the Ganges basin and the Deccan was situational: they lay astride the main land and sea routes which linked Central Asia and the Middle East with northern India, routes through which a large share of India's foreign trade was carried on until the nineteenth century. It is partly thanks to the profits they made in that trade that the merchants of the dry zone were able to accumulate capital on a scale sufficient to allow them to progressively expand outside their region. However their ability to keep to themselves the bulk of the profits accruing from that kind of trade was in its turn related to the specific skills they deployed not only in trading but also in finance. The honing of their financial skills was certainly helped by the uncertainties of agriculture in an area of weak and irregular precipitations, which led to the early development of a futures market in grain crops, the existence of which is documented at least for Rajasthan, as well as by the important role assigned to them in the revenue-collection apparatus of the state in the entire region at an early period. It seems also, and some causal relationship can be inferred there, that it was in that part of the subcontinent that the *hundi* (bill of exchange) first evolved as a relatively sophisticated financial instrument. Although its use became generalized only in the eighteenth century in northern India, it appears to have been already known by some merchants of the north-west at an earlier period. Merchants trading with Central Asia, known as Multanis, probably made use of it in the seventeenth century.[6] Its increasing use to transfer revenue within the Mughal empire in the seventeenth century (although its exact extent is a matter of controversy) seems directly linked to the rise of firms of merchant bankers originating in the north-west. In the eighteenth century, when it became well established as a means to transfer large sums of money, it helped solve the problem of the circulation of specie over long distances in disturbed political conditions, and, as significantly, had a kind of multiplier effect by allowing merchant groups with relatively limited capital resources to control trade over large areas. Their mastery of the hundi system and of fairly sophisticated double entry bookkeeping practices not unlike those developed by the merchants of medieval Italy allowed some of the merchant groups of the north-western 'dry zone' to steal a march at an early stage on other groups in the rest of the subcontinent, although many of the empirical details in this story are probably irretrievably lost.

However, as crucial to the gradual emergence of a kind of dominance over pan-Indian trade and finance were other factors of a more political nature. They were a direct consequence of the forging of close bonds between Rajput polities and specific merchant groups in some areas, in particular Rajasthan and Saurashtra. It could be objected that Rajput polities did not exist only in the dry zone, but, for reasons which are not entirely elucidated, in some of the Rajput principalities of the dry zone, merchants came at an early stage to occupy important political positions and to exercise a measure of control over state finances and revenue collection. Thus G.D. Sharma, in his study of the Marwaris,[7] mentions that the Rajput rulers of Rajasthan followed the practice of appointing moneylenders in the office dealing with the revenue both at the *pargana* and the state levels, a practice which became more widespread during the eighteenth century.

After the Mughals had established their dominance over the whole of northern India, the existence of this link with Rajput princes facilitated the commercial penetration of merchant networks from the north-west into the whole of northern India. It is thus said that leading merchant houses of Benares in the early twentieth century claimed descent from merchants having arrived from Rajasthan in the sixteenth century as commissary officers to Rajput units attached to the Mughal armies.[8] The ease with which, under the Mughals, merchants from the north-west travelled to the Gangetic area is illustrated by the case of Hiranand Saha, the ancestor of the house of Jagat Seth, who, in 1652, during the reign of Shahjahan, moved to Patna from his hometown of Nagore.[9] It is not known what his connections in Patna were, and whether his move was purely individual or part of a wider trend, but the fact is that he managed to quickly develop a profitable banking business, which set the foundations for the future fortune of the house of Jagat Seth. The ability of Hindu and Jain merchants of the 'dry zone' to use their links with Rajputs to establish some connection to Mughal grandees and rulers is probably one of the keys to the apparent paradox of an unparalleled expansion of 'Hindu' merchant networks under a Muslim regime. Not that some Muslim merchant networks such as those of the Bohras, Khojas and Memons did not also expand during the Mughal period, but these predominantly Shi'a groups did not benefit by any particularly close connection to rulers who were often (but not always) staunch Sunnis. There were also active Sunni Muslim merchant networks, such as those of the 'Pathans' who played an important role in south-eastern India in the second half of the seventeenth century,[10] particularly in Masulipatnam, but they do not appear to have consolidated durably and, by the nineteenth century, they had faded away.

By the end of the seventeenth century, European accounts as well as indigenous sources reveal a picture characterized by the existence of powerful all-India networks dominating large-scale trade and finance across most of the north Indian ecumene, and making some, albeit still limited, inroads into south India. For instance Dutch sources about the important centre of Kasimbazar, in Bengal, in the late seventeenth century mention a list of eighteen big traders, none of whom was Bengali, the majority being apparently Gujarati.[11] Some of these 'outside' merchants, particularly those from Gujarat, made early connections to European traders, first the Dutch, then the English and the French, but, with the exception of the Parsis at Surat, they do not appear to have developed into a class of privileged brokers to the Europeans in general. They kept closer links with various indigenous rulers. It is quite possible, although this would require to be supported by a lot more empirical data, that these all-India networks suffered in some ways from the weakening of Mughal power. There are indications in C.A. Bayly's work that in the Gangetic region in the eighteenth century, Gujarati merchants, who had been a powerful group at the beginning of the century, especially in the western part of the region, suffered a significant decline around 1750.[12] On the other hand the consolidation of post-Mughal regional regimes benefited some merchant-bankers from the north-west who had forged close links to emerging dynasties: the case of the Jagat Seths who, having settled first in Patna, then moved to Dacca under Manik Chand, Hiranand's son, and ultimately to Murshidabad where they rose to become the financiers of the Nawabs-Nazims of Bengal is of course the most well known, but there were others as well.

By the time of the British conquest of Bengal, the situation appears to have been in a state of flux. Political instability over large tracts of northern and central India, the growing inroads of the British themselves into the internal trade of India, disrupted the pattern of long-distance inter-regional trade and this often allowed local merchants to reassert a measure of control over local economies at the expense of pan-Indian networks. However, the consolidation of British rule across most of the subcontinent by 1818 seems to have coincided with a new wave of expansion of the pan-Indian networks originating from the 'dry zone' of the north-west, especially the so-called 'Marwaris' from Rajasthan. Before taking up this story in more detail, it seems worth having a closer look at some of the most active merchant groups of this north-western dry zone.

Although the majority of these groups can be somehow placed within the vast cluster of castes known as bania castes, sometimes also figuring in the colonial literature as Mahajans, their origins could actually be quite diverse. The Khatris, a group which tended to dominate trade in the Punjab area,[13] as well as the Lohanas, who were the leading trading group both in Sind (where they were subdivided into the non-trading Amil segment and the trading Bhaibands) and in Kutch, and the Bhatias of Sind and Kutch, all claimed some kind of Rajput ancestry, often far-fetched, and did not advertise a bania identity for themselves. The principal Muslim trading groups, such as the Bohras, Khojas, and Memons, in spite of being relatively recent Hindu converts, also did not claim a bania—preferring a Rajput—ancestry. This left only two major groups of merchants of strictly bania caste, those from Gujarat known as the Gujarati Vanis, and those from Rajasthan, increasingly known to outsiders as Marwaris, although the majority of them actually originated from the Bikaner and Jaipur states, in particular from the Shekhawat area of the latter, and only a minority from the Marwar state. The distinction between these two broad regional groupings was not always clear-cut, as some so-called Gujarati banias were descendants of immigrants from Rajasthan of an earlier generation. Most of these banias in their turn belonged to a small number of castes, in Gujarat the generic Vanis (with a division into several subcastes) and the Shravaks, in Rajasthan the Agarwals, Maheshwaris, Oswals, Khandelwals, and Porwals which generally had both a Hindu and a Jain segment; these segments tended to remain separate but Hindu and Jain banias of the same caste intermarried to a certain extent. In the Punjab, Khatris and Aroras, which were the two dominant trading groups, tended to straddle the boundary between Hinduism and Sikhism; although few of them claimed to be Khalsa Sikhs after 1699, it was the Khatris who had provided the Sikh community with its gurus; this religious liminality was true also of the majority of the Sind Lohanas, who called themselves Nanakpanthis. In the dry zone therefore, although the merchant world was predominantly Hindu, Hinduism engaged in various forms of interaction with Jainism, Sikhism, and Shi'a Islam (as well as with various Sufi practices which had a big impact on Hindu traders in Sind and the Punjab, many of whom were *murids* of various sufi *pirs*).

The paucity of in-depth studies makes it difficult to ascertain whether there was a specific merchant culture and ethic in the dry zone as distinct from a more general north Indian merchant culture and ethic on which C.A. Bayly has written so persuasively.[14] There is, however, one area in which merchants of the dry zone appear to have enjoyed a clear advantage over most of their colleagues in the vast North Indian ecumene: because of their already-mentioned long-standing connections with Rajput clans, particularly in Gujarat and Rajasthan, they appear to have developed at an early stage political skills which were more finely tuned. Sustained interaction with Rajputs may have also led them to develop particular ideas about mercantile honour, in spite of the obvious opposition between warrior and Jain ethics.

A greater degree of political skill might help explain why these banias of the dry zone were, at least from the seventeenth century onwards, capable of significantly encroaching on the turf of the banias of the core Gangetic area, who often belonged to the same castes. Thus in Gangetic northern India, one finds a large segment of the Agarwals who did not hail from Rajasthan but had strong local roots. They appear nevertheless to have lost ground to their caste brethren from Rajasthan in the seventeenth and eighteenth centuries. One possible line of explanation is that Muslim rulers, first the Mughals and then their successors, preferred to deal with 'outsiders', especially when they had close connections to their Rajput feudatories, thinking them politically safer than the local Hindu bankers and merchants.

In other areas, such as the Deccan and parts of Central India, there do not seem to have existed local trading castes, and, although Brahmins and other members of the local upper castes often engaged successfully in trade, successive waves of migrant traders from the dry zone gradually carved for themselves a significant, although not necessarily dominant, position in the commercial and financial sector.[15] These migrants often responded to deliberate policies on the part of the rulers meant at attracting merchants from other areas in India. This was in particular the case with Maratha chiefs in the second half of the eigtheenth century. They are known to have made great efforts at attracting merchant capital to their states, and many Gujarati and Marwari merchant families moved to the Deccan during that period.

In the next section, I concentrate more specifically on the renewed expansion of pan-Indian networks in the nineteenth century under British rule, which largely laid the foundation for the present-day situation.

## The Renewed Expansion of Pan-Indian Merchant Networks from the 'Dry Zone' under British Rule, *c.* 1810–1930

Some attention has been paid in the existing literature to the large-scale migration of merchants in the nineteenth and twentieth centuries, in particular to the spectacular spread of the so-called Marwaris across the entire subcontinent (with the exception of the extreme south). In a well-known paper,[16] Rajat Ray has analysed these migrations, in which he distinguishes three major streams, in relation to the growth of a specific indigenous sector in the colonial economy of India, which he calls the 'bazaar'. One major problem with his model is that it assumes a kind of dualistic shape with the clear-cut distinction it introduces between indigenous and European sectors. The rise of the Marwaris in colonial India has precisely to be partly understood in terms of the connection between these two sectors and it is therefore doubtful that a 'dualistic' model is the best way of looking at it. Besides,

Ray seems to ignore the existence of all-India business networks prior to the nineteenth-century phase of expansion.

During the nineteenth and twentieth centuries, traders from the 'dry zone' of the north-west considerably extended the range and depth of their networks. Some of these networks were already well entrenched by 1800, while entirely new ones also came into being after that date. Although assigning an exact 'beginning' to this renewed surge might seems hazardous, there is some evidence that it started around 1810–20, thus coinciding with the final thrust of British conquest in the third Maratha War. Whether this was more than a simple 'coincidence' remains a moot point. At least two different kinds of argument could be built around it. One could argue, in keeping with the apologetic tradition of imperial history, that the advent of Pax Britannica, by ushering a new kind of security on the trading routes, was the key factor in facilitating the circulation of merchants across long distances. Or one could take the opposite view that it was precisely the general disruption of existing patterns brought about by the extension of British rule to vast new areas which eased the entry of newcomers. Most probably, the truth lies somewhere in between, but some of the ways in which British conquest facilitated the renewed spread of the merchants of the dry zone can be briefly outlined. One significant connection was with the military aspect of conquest: provisioning and supplying the huge armies of the Company as they moved to close in on the Pindaris and the Marathas offered a vast field of endeavour to various contractors and merchants, among whom men from the dry zone, like many so-called 'Marwaris', appear to have figured prominently. It was during these final campaigns that the new system of regimental bazaars was established,[17] and although, to my knowledge, no empirical study of its functioning exists, it undoubtedly offered opportunities for a more stable relationship between the merchants and the army, of which many traders from the dry zone availed themselves. As the network of army garrisons gradually spread over most of the subcontinent, this system also offered a prospect of aggrandisement to enterprising contractors who could build up supply chains. In a survey of Marwari firms,[18] it is thus mentioned that a large group of Oswals, many hailing from Belundu, a locality in Jodhpur, were settled in Jalna, a military cantonment in the north of Hyderabad, as military contractors, in the first decades of the nineteenth century and that many of them moved to Madras in the last quarter of the century, perhaps following the regiments to which they were attached when the latter were transferred. 'Regimental bankers' are also often mentioned in accounts of Marwari families.

A second way in which the British conquest significantly affected the spatial range of trading networks was even more unintentional: new opportunities opened up at the time for smuggling opium on a big scale to China, using the ports of Portuguese India, in open defiance of the East India Company's monopoly. It is remarkable that the heyday of smuggling in 'Malwa opium', grown in the princely states of Central India, which competed on the Chinese market with 'Bengal opium', mostly grown in Bihar, over which the Company had kept a tight monopoly (abolished only in 1833), coincided with the 1819–39 period.[19] The Malwa opium trade is known to have played a particularly important role in the 'primitive accumulation' of capital in western India in the first decades of the nineteenth century,[20] and many Indian fortunes derived their origins from it. Among the merchant groups which played a significant role in it, were, besides the Parsis, the Ahmedabad merchants, merchants from Kutch and Kathiawar, many Marwari traders, as well as the merchants of Shikarpur and Hyderabad in Sind, all belonging, except for the Bombay Parsis, to the 'dry zone'. By the time the British occupation of Karachi in 1839 closed the main Ujjain-Pahli-Hyderabad-Karachi-Daman smuggling route, many traders of the 'dry zone' had accumulated capital on a significant scale and forged useful political connections with the rulers of various native states of Central India, in whose territories most of the poppy cultivation took place, connections which they put to good use to turn to other branches of trade, in particular cotton and grain.

Banking, in particular state banking, and the opium trade were two fields in which Marwaris and Gujaratis were already prominent in the early nineteenth century in vast areas of western, northern, and central India and the Deccan. One banking house of 'migrant' origin which rose to prominence in the first half of the nineteenth century in northern and central India was that of the famous 'Mathura Seths'.[21] The founder was a Gujarati Brahmin, Gokul Das, who was known under the name of Parikhji, which he had acquired in his capacity as treasurer to the Gwalior darbar. He settled in Mathura in the late eighteenth century and, at the time of his death in 1826, he had accumulated an immense fortune. His heirs (who were not his direct descendants, as he died childless) continued to play a major role in northern Indian finance till the late nineteenth century. The very large profits accumulated in banking and opium fed further expansion. The Marwaris became particularly conspicuous because of the extended spatial range of their operations which took on an all-India character.

Their spectacular spread during the 1810–1910 period, which transformed them from a relatively scattered diaspora dominated by a few prominent banking families such as the Jagat Seths into a much 'thicker' network of traders, merchants, and moneylenders controlling a significant chunk of trade and finance across a large swathe of the subcontinent, has been extensively documented in a study by Timberg,[22] which is, however, inadequate as a synthesis. That author estimates that by 1920, there were between 200,000 and 400,000 Marwaris outside Rajputana, mostly traders. This estimate is to be treated with some caution, as there are many problems with the use of census data to evaluate the size of the trading migration from the Marwari area. A more limited, but probably more reliable estimate, also based on census data, bearing on the number of male emigrants from the three states of Bikaner, Jaipur, and Marwar in eastern India in 1921, is presented here. It gives a more precise idea of the size of the Marwari migration in the area where it had the greatest impact.

The exclusive focus on male migrants is justified by the fact that, prior to the 1920s the Marwari migration was indeed overwhelmingly a male one. Very few Marwari women accompanied their husbands on their voyages, and those who did rarely participated in trade.

Actually there is no mention of Marwari women managing shops or firms. Some may, however, have given a helping hand to their husbands, but did not work full time in the shop.

This table shows the total number of male emigrants from the three states of Rajputana which supplied most of the so-called Marwari migrants to have been less than 50,000. Assuming, on the basis of data in the 1911 Calcutta census,[23] that half of them were traders, this would indicate the presence of some 25,000 traders from the 'Marwari' area in eastern India. There were also certainly a few thousand locally born Marwari traders, descendants of earlier generations of immigrants. Non-trading Marwaris included both Rajputs who offered some kind of protection to the traders as bodyguards and helped them in the process of debt collection, and low-caste servants and other menials generally employed by the traders in their homes and shops. The overall numbers are not very impressive but the importance of the migration was not directly related to its demographic size. What is remarkable is that a community of a few tens of thousands of traders could exercise an overall domination over the trade and finance of an area which had over 90 million inhabitants.[24] This was possible only because the Marwari traders in eastern India belonged to an all-India network and could draw sustenance from a constant supply of capital and personnel from other areas of the subcontinent. The circulatory pattern of their movements was an essential element of strength, as close links could thus be maintained with their localities of origin. In the case of the Marwaris, the direct connection between

TABLE 1

Male Emigrants from Bikaner, Jaipur, and
Marwar in Eastern India in 1921

| Province | Male emigrants from Bikaner | Male emigrants from Jaipur | Male emigrants from Marwar |
|---|---|---|---|
| Assam | 4,464 | 3,855 | 1,489 |
| Bengal | 14,532 | 11,345 | 3,491 |
| Bihar and Orissa | 1,257 | 7,475 | 986 |
| Eastern India | 20,253 | 22,675 | 5,966 |

*Source*: *Census of India 1931, vol. xxvii, Rajputana Agency* (Meerut, 1932), p. 32.

moneylending and trading was also one of the keys to dominance. Control of rural credit channels allowed Marwaris, who tended often to work in collusion to keep prices as low as possible, to achieve a strong position in the market for some commodities like jute or rice, which ensured high profits and permitted gradual diversification into processing of agricultural products (rice milling, jute baling) and secondary industry (jute mills, sugar mills). Advances to producers were systematically used as a device to procure produce cheaply, as peasants were rarely able to repay their debts in cash, and moneylenders in their turn rarely chose to foreclose on unpaid mortgages, the acquisition of land generally not being a major aim for them.

Leaving aside the purely demographic aspect, which is not the most important, I have attempted to form a clearer picture of the process of Marwari expansion, by using Timberg's own findings, and supplementing them with data collected from various census reports and gazetteers, in which however there remain significant gaps.

There would appear to have been two stages in the process: in the 1810–60 period, Marwari traders and moneylenders were able to extend their operations to the whole of India, except the extreme south, from Bombay on the west coast to Cuttack in Orissa on the east coast and to the Brahmaputra valley in Assam in the north-eastern corner of the subcontinent. This movement, which occurred in the pre-census era, cannot be quantified even approximately, but the many family and caste histories collected by Timberg and others show that most Marwari migrants made the initial move from Rajasthan during that period. By 1860, although they were present all across northern and central India, they rarely exercised a complete dominance over trading and financial activities, except in a few pockets.

The Deccan Riots Commission Report,[25] compiled after the relatively mild disturbances which affected two districts in the Deccan, Poona and Ahmednagar in 1875, offers some interesting indications about the role of the Marwaris in the economic life of the area, although it is a document which is not devoid of ambiguity. On the one hand it describes the disturbances as 'anti-Marwari' riots, stressing the ethnic aspect, but on the other hand, in the detail it offers a more nuanced analysis. From the report we learn that although the Marwaris were the dominant moneylending community in those two districts, they were far from having a monopoly over that activity. The situation could vary a lot between one *taluka* and another within the same district. In the same way, the report is not very clear as to the role of the 'ethnic' factor in triggering the disturbances. Sometimes, it tends to emphasize the role played by members of the local elites, mostly Brahmins, in inciting the local peasantry to launch attacks against the Marwari moneylenders, in a manner reminiscent of the Polish gentry's attempts in seventeenth-century Ukraine, at the time of the Bogdan Khmelnistky revolt, at diverting the anger of their tenants towards their Jewish estate managers. In other passages, it tends on the contrary to minimize the role of these elites in inciting the peasantry. What comes out most conspicuously from the report, however, is the way in which Marwaris, by the 1870s, had managed to entrench themselves deeply in many villages of this area of the Deccan which was the old Maratha heartland.

In the second phase, that is, roughly 1860–1914, Marwari expansion occurred mostly in eastern India. In northern, western, and central India and the Deccan, Marwari traders and moneylenders remained an essential component of the moneylending and commercial classes but they occupied only certain specific niches in trade and finance, and had to contend with the presence of other merchants, belonging either to local communities or to other diasporic networks, especially the Muslim networks of the Bohras and Kutchi Memons, as well as those of the Parsis and the Gujarati Hindu banias. Whether this relative stabilization of their position had anything to do with the outcome of the Deccan disturbances themselves remains a moot point. Although some legislative measures were taken, which aimed at limiting land transfers to moneylenders, the exact impact they had on the Marwaris, who in any case were reluctant to foreclose on mortgages when loans were not repaid, is not clear. In eastern India, on the other hand, comprising Bengal proper, Bihar, and Assam, Marwaris established a clear dominance over regional trade and finance, often in close conjunction with the operations of British businessmen.

The broad contrast between these two areas is to be explained primarily in terms of the different functions they fulfilled in the colonial economy. In eastern India, large-scale production of export commodities such as indigo, jute, and tea, either through the commodification of peasant production or directly through the development of plantations, attracted British capital on a significant scale and the Marwaris gradually emerged as the privileged intermediaries between the British exporting firms in the ports and the peasant proprietors or salaried employees in the regions of production. The story of their rise in the jute belt of Bengal and the export trade of Calcutta, partly at the expense of Bengali traders, is well known,[26] and does not need retelling, although the exact causes of their success still somewhat elude us. They also acquired a prominent position in the import trade in cotton textiles from Lancashire and dominated the distribution network of Manchester cloth all over eastern India, which was the major market in India for UK textiles. Anand Yang gives some details on the rise of the Marwaris in Saran district in north Bihar. In the district centre of Chapra, the Marwaris, who had established themselves in the 1830s and 1840s, 'had by the late nineteenth century taken over the cloth and cotton trade'.[27] They imported cloth from Calcutta and Benares, cotton from Agra, Kanpur, and Mirzapur and supplied dealers as far as in Gorakhpur and Nepal. They were described in an 1891 report as 'the principal dealers in cloth in the district, found almost at all big markets, and generally wealthy'. It is worth noting that their role was even greater in the tea-producing areas of Assam and north Bengal where they provided tea-garden labour with the necessities of life, through the shops they had in the tea estates. They extended credit to the labourers at often exorbitant rates, allowing the planters to concentrate exclusively on the production of tea.

In other areas of the subcontinent where British capital was less directly present, and where locally produced goods like cotton cloth from the Bombay and Ahmedabad mills commanded a greater share of the market, the Marwaris could not play the same role of privileged intermediaries, and they had to work their way up more gradually, always having to contend with other trading communities, local or pan-Indian, which were often well entrenched.

Other networks from the north-west which expanded significantly under British rule, but tended to occupy more specific 'niches' than the Marwaris, were those of the Parsis, who were specialized in the liquor trade and more generally in the trade in 'European' articles, the Sindworkies of Hyderabad (Sind), who dealt in silk and 'curios' for a mostly European clientele,[28] the Bohras, who specialized in hardware, and the Kutchi Memons, who dealt in cloth, spices, rice, and other commodities. The dominance of the Kutchi Memons in the interprovincial trade in rice (including the considerable Burma rice trade) deserves particular notice. The rise of the Memons, who hailed from the princely state of Kutch (Kutchi Memons) and from several Kathiawar states (Halai Memons), illustrates one subsidiary theme, that of the growing role played in British India by traders who had migrated there from the princely states, mostly those of the dry north-western zone. The Marwaris, hailing from Bikaner, Jaipur, and Marwar states, were a prominent case in point of course, but there were many others. In Bombay, the Memons as well as the Khojas hailing from Kutch and Kathiawar tended to displace the 'indigenous' Konkani Muslims who had played a prominent role in trade in the first half of the nineteenth century. Being legally domiciled in a princely state gave traders of the dry zone a further competitive advantage inasmuch as they could repatriate to their native states, where there existed no income tax, some of the profits made in British India, where income tax became a permanent fixture from the 1880s onwards. In south India, it should be similarly noted that the Nattukottai Chettiars, the dominant banking and trading community, were mostly domiciled in the princely state of Puddukottai, which also enhanced their comparative advantage over other trading communities.

Even if none of these diasporas was comparable in sheer size and financial worth to the Marwari diaspora, note should be taken of the Multani (Shikarpuri) bankers from Sind who, after having played a major role in financing Central Asian trade,[29] relocated in India after the Russian Revolution and by 1930 had acquired a prominent position in the financing of agriculture and small industries across the Bombay and Madras Presidencies.[30]

Regarding the spread of pan-Indian networks, India (outside the north-west) around 1930 could be divided into three broad zones: a zone of Marwari dominance, corresponding to most of eastern India (although some other traders of the north-west like the Khatris were also active, particularly in Calcutta), a zone of co-dominance of different networks from the northwest, covering western, northern, and Central India and the Deccan, and a zone of weak penetration of the pan-Indian networks, including most of South India (in spite of the strong position occupied by the Marwaris and Multanis in indigenous banking in parts of the Madras Presidency).

The pattern of expansion of merchant networks could vary according to the area and the period. The *Gazetteer* of Nasik district compiled in the early 1880s describes the spread of the Marwaris in the area as follows:

> A Marwar Vani when he first comes is generally poor. If he has capital, he brings with him a string of camels loaded with soft white blankets from Ajmir by Khandva to Khanajaon in Berar or some trade centre in the Central Provinces, he disposes of the camels, as there is little demand for them further west, and makes a tour by rail or on foot to sell his blankets. After selling his blankets, he sends the proceeds to Marwar or buys a fresh stock. When he reaches Nasik, he either takes service in the shop of a friend or acquaintance, or goes from one place to another dealing in haberdashery. When, chiefly by extreme thrift, he has made some money, he establishes himself in some village under an agreement with the headman. He opens a grain and grocery shop and begins to lend money and advance seed. The interest on money or grain advances varies from 25 to 50 per cent in good seasons, and in bad years rises to 100 per cent or even more. . . . Men of this class, after they have established themselves in a business, sometimes return to Marwar, but more often settle in the district, marrying with families of their own class, building or buying a home, and sending a relation to look after their affairs in their native land where they send a large share of their earnings.[31]

In this case, expansion appears to be a fairly anarchic process, largely left to individual initiative. This might be due to the point of view of the observer, the colonial administrator, who perceives only the surface of events and is liable to miss the internal logic of the process. What is lacking in particular is the sense of the continuity of the network, through which the various individual merchants were interlocked. Other sources point out that newcomers to a district among Marwari merchants generally benefited from credit advanced by their already established caste-fellows.

The dispersed merchants hailing from different areas of the dry zone of north-western India, maintained close connections with their regions of origin in various ways. One of these was through the development of large all-India multi-branch firms. Such firms had their headquarters in Rajputana or Bombay and branches in various scattered localities: capital and personnel moved constantly from headquarters to branches, while profits were regularly remitted in the other direction. Big firms and smaller merchants could also be linked through credit and supply chains. Some small merchants started in a relationship of dependency *vis-à-vis* these big firms, but eventually managed to establish themselves as independent operators. Their ties to the community of merchants from the same region were 'social', in particular through the marriage network, rather than economic, but it was a rare occurrence that a merchant who had 'migrated' from a specific region had no relationship at all, even a very informal one, to merchants from the same region residing in the same locality. Merchant networks defined by a common regional origin in one area of the 'dry zone' were thus fairly ubiquitous in colonial India, but not necessarily very conspicuous. Contrary to what happened in other colonial societies in Asia or Africa, they did not have a strong 'ethnic' flavour, and those who belonged to them were not easily distinguishable from the bulk of the 'native' population. For instance in Assam the Marwaris, locally known as Kayias, had, by the late nineteenth century, become very much part of the landscape of riverine Assam. Although their presence attracted some resentment on the part of the locals and there were occasional anti-Marwari riots in Assam, the inevitable grudges brought about by their sharp lending practices remained generally directed at specific individuals rather than their community at large. It is mostly in Bengal, and more specifically in Calcutta, that the presence of an articulate 'indigenous' Bengali middle class did create an ambience of hostility which remained, however, generally muted and rarely erupted into open violence. Attacks on Marwari moneylenders in Calcutta took place mostly during episodes of 'communal' violence, such as the disturbances of 1918 and 1926, in which Marwaris were targeted by Muslim mobs. The reasons for the particular hostility of lower-class Muslims towards the Marwaris were complex: besides general resentment at their high-handed practices, were more specific grievances relating to the clearance of Muslim-inhabited slums to make way for Marwari mansions and to frequent interference with Muslim rituals and festivals.[32]

'Expatriate' Marwari traders for several generations kept a strong sense of their separate identity, including at the political level: they generally remained attached to their status as British-protected subjects of different native states of Rajputana, and not only for the sake of the advantages they enjoyed in matters of taxation. Thus it was reported in the *Rajputana Gazetteer* in 1879 that, on the death of the Maharaja of Jodhpur, all Marwaris in Calcutta and Bombay had shaved their heads and faces as a mark of mourning.[33] By the 1930s, however, most Marwari traders in Bengal were balancing loyalty to their native states with the prospect of being discriminated against as subjects of 'foreign' rulers, within an evolving federal India, and their spokesmen took the line that they had become *de facto* British Indian subjects.[34] They could argue, in support of their claims, that they were perfectly cognizant of the local language and did not live in ghettoes separated from the local population. In Assam and, to a lesser extent in Bihar, some of them married local women and they often became totally integrated. In Bengal, where there was less integration, they nevertheless interacted with the locals in various ways. Even the most heavily Marwari areas of Calcutta like Burra Bazar always retained a majority of non-Marwari population. Although they had their own temples and their own favourite goddesses, such as Rani Sati,[35] and brought priests from Rajasthan, Marwaris also took part in the religious life of the localities where they settled and their religious charities were never exclusively directed at their own community. On the whole, in eastern India Marwaris managed to retain a separate identity while at the same time reaching a certain level of integration with local society. In spite of having generally, by the 1930s, become permanent residents in their places of business, and having brought their families to live with them, they remained attached to their native land and, when a son was born to a Marwari family in Calcutta or elsewhere, he was brought back to Rajasthan for his first haircut so that his locks could be offered to the goddess in the temple of his ancestral village.[36] One is tempted to explain the success of the Marwaris in achieving such a balance by the fact that they were a Hindu (and Jain) group living in the midst of a predominantly Hindu society. But even Muslim 'expatriate' traders do not seem to have had problems in being accepted locally, including in such a predominantly Hindu setting as that of Orissa, and when there were communal riots, they were rarely a target. The undramatic and unconspicuous character of most trading migration in colonial India should lead us to recognize that it was viewed by society at large as a phenomenon of 'circulation' much more than of migration, that it was considered fairly 'normal' and did not generate widespread reactions. No discourse on ethnicity seems to have been strongly adhered to either by the migrants themselves or their hosts. Popular attitudes focused much more on the rates of interest charged and on the kind of sharp practices characteristic of some of the moneylenders than on their specific ethnic background.

Coming back to the question of the reasons for the success of merchant networks of the 'dry' zone, one has to be wary of a certain kind of conventional wisdom about 'ethnic' merchant networks and the specific kind of solidarity a common ethnicity entailed. My own work on merchant networks from Sind which expanded both into Central Asia and into the world at large has convinced me that too much is often made of such 'ethnic' solidarity. Two points in particular need to be underlined: firstly, that what appears as 'ethnic' solidarity to outside observers is often a misnomer for much more local solidarities based on a specific caste, locality, or micro-region or some combination of these. Among 'Marwari' merchants, localities of origin played a particularly important role in nurturing solidarities. Timberg has identified a certain number of localities from where most of the Marwaris originated.[37] Caste distinctions were also important, inasmuch as merchants belonging to different castes often followed different lines of trade and went to different areas. Agarwals were more prominent in banking, Maheshwaris in the opium trade, Oswals in military contracting. The former were particularly represented in northern and eastern India, the latter in the Deccan and central India, while Maheshwaris were more equally spread out. Among Marwaris, it appears that communal institutions such as the *basa*, or communal kitchen, or the *dharamshala*, or communal hostel, were managed on the basis of specific castes or regions: there were thus Agarwal Shekhawati basas or dharamshalas rather than 'Marwari' ones, and it is only at a later stage, in the 1920s and 1930s, that all-Marwari institutions took root, mostly due to political reasons.

The second point to note is that trust within merchant networks was not automatically a function of the fact of belonging to the same caste, kin, or regional group, but depended a lot on reputation: the only real advantage regional merchant networks offered in terms of trust-building was that, as information circulated widely through their channel, it was easier to check on the reputation of someone belonging to the same regional group: one did not have to rely purely on bazaar gossip to know whether one could trust so-and-so, but one could easily check a record of his transactions. So the specific strength and resilience of the merchant networks of the dry zone could not be explained by the exceptional level of trust fostered by a common ethnicity. Nor could it be ascribed to the particular solidity of such institutions as the joint family or the caste or to the role of the marriage network, which characterized all merchant groups in India. It had probably more to do with the cumulative impact of such differences as a small initial superiority in knowledge and skills. The 'social economy' of merchant networks is as much an information- and know-ledge-based economy as it is a 'moral' economy, a point often missed in the existing literature, and it was generally a superior degree of knowledge and skills, built over the years, rather than a greater degree of 'ethnic' solidarity which allowed some merchant networks to have the better of others.

Basically, those merchant groups which managed to create pan-Indian networks had no 'essential' characteristics differentiating them from other merchant groups which did not achieve similar success. Their achievements were largely due to the way in which they managed to take advantage of the opportunities which history presented them with. Thus some of the so-called 'Marwaris' made use of the experience accumulated by their ancestors in serving the needs of the Mughal empire and the successor states to establish an early rapport with the British and at a later stage emerge as their privileged intermediaries in eastern India, where no 'indigenous' groups had a similar kind of experience. But, over a long period of time, advantages thus acquired, which are an outcome of specific historical conjunctures, become cumulative and are perceived as given.

There remains the more general question as to why practically all the groups which were successful at an all-India level had their roots in the' dry zone' of the north-west. A possible hypothesis is that, given the particular accumulation of specific merchant skills and knowledge over the centuries in that relatively compact area, they were easier to acquire there than in other merchant milieux. Merchants from the north-west operating in other regions also took great care to preserve the secrets of their trade and not to leak them to local mer-chants. This secrecy was facilitated by the widespread use of special scripts, alphabets, and codes which were very difficult to break into for the uninitiated. The superior control over information and know-ledge channels that the merchant groups of the north-west managed to establish and maintain over the centuries was the main reason for their being able to dominate some of the most lucrative fields of trade and finance across the entire subcontinent.

Mercantile organization was also an important asset. Widely spread merchant networks had to evolve specific organizational forms to be able to function efficiently and keep transaction costs low, especially in a weakly integrated economy where there were obstacles to the smooth physical circulation of persons and goods. Merchant networks of the north-western dry zone proved particularly adept at using and adapting such organizational forms which were sometimes borrowed from the Islamic world, sometimes more 'indigenous' in their origins. They showed particular ingenuity in creating systems of partnership which were extremely flexible and adapted to a changing and uncertain political and economic environment.[38] Prior to the advent of the telegraph, these networks were also characterized by the speed with which information circulated through special couriers, who provided channels of communication sometimes more efficient than those of the rulers. How the bankers of Poona were the first to know about the Maratha disaster at Panipat in 1761 and thus managed to limit their losses, in a manner reminiscent of the Rothschilds at the time of Waterloo, is a well-known instance of how speedily information could circulate within India even before the advent of modern means of communication. After the telegraph—apparently a great leveller in terms of circulation of information—had been introduced, the net-works of the dry zone nevertheless managed to retain an edge thanks to the depth of their knowledge of economic conditions and the state of the market.

It should be noted that mobility in itself was not necessarily a key to long-term success. The story of two groups of itinerant traders, the Banjaras and the Gosains, which at one moment played a very impor-tant role in the trade of northern India and eventually sank into obli-vion is a case in point. Regarding the former, it is well known that their armed caravans of bullock carts played a major role in the trans-port of merchandise across India by land prior to the advent of the railways in the mid-nineteenth century. Why they were not able to accumulate capital on a significant scale at any stage during this period of several centuries remains somewhat puzzling, but has probably to do mostly with their low social status and weaknesses in their social organization. In spite of their crucial role in trade, they were never recognized as a trading caste and always had to live on the fringes of caste society as a sort of 'tribal' group. Their characterization by the

British as a kind of 'criminal tribe', assimilated to the gypsies of Europe, did not help in ensuring their social and economic advancement. The Gosains, bands of armed 'ascetics' which controlled very large caravans in the Gangetic area during part of the eighteenth century and at some point achieved a kind of domination over trade in some regions, were even more directly victims of Pax Britannica which put their brand of warrior-traders out of business for good. In the new set-up created by British conquest, in which the colonial state arrogated to itself a kind of monopoly over armed violence, those merchant groups which had completely eschewed military skills, especially those which had been heavily influenced by Jainism, were better placed to take advantage of beckoning opportunities than groups which had combined fighting with trading.

Political skills, as distinguished from military skills, were, however, as much at a premium during the colonial era as they had been during earlier periods. Those merchant groups which were able to forge close connections with important actors in the colonial political system, whether British or Indian, were generally more successful than those which were not. Given their long experience at dealing with Rajputs, Mughals, and other rulers, some of the groups from the dry zone proved particularly adept at dealing with the British. For instance those groups which most conspicuously sided with the British at the time of the 1857 Revolt reaped rich rewards from their political posture. Stories of successful business families in India in the late nineteenth and early twentieth centuries generally include references to 'loyalism' during the Revolt, and the boost it gave business in the form of access to confiscated properties and government contracts. It would appear that Marwari merchants, benefiting by their close links to the Rajput princes, who on the whole remained steadfastly loyal to the British, were particularly conspicuous for their loyalty in 1857, and gained handsomely by it. On the whole, merchant communities like the Marwaris, the Sindhis, the Bohras, Khojas, and Memons remained amongst the most staunchly 'loyalist' elements of the Indian middle classes till 1920 when many shifted their allegiance to Gandhi and the Congress. The Parsis remained predominantly 'loyalist' till the late 1930s or early 1940s. In the case of the Marwaris, this loyalism combined somewhat uneasily from the 1890s onwards with the strong support given to the cow protection agitation and other 'Hindu' causes such as the promotion of the Hindi language. The close links forged with the colonial state were nevertheless particularly useful in procuring government contracts, including army contracts, and this helped in establishing all-India supply chains.

## The Impact of Pan-Indian Merchant Networks on the Economy of Colonial and Independent India

What effect did the domination exercised by the merchant networks of the dry zone over some of the major financial and trading circuits have on the overall course of the Indian economy in colonial and postcolonial times? A first question relates to their role in the rise of the colonial economy. It is a familiar argument that colonial capitalism has some kind of structural link with the existence of so-called 'middleman minorities'. The role of the Chinese in Malaya, in the Dutch East Indies, and in French Indochina, that of the Indians in British East Africa and Burma, of the Greeks and Armenians in Egypt, etc. are all cases in point. In these cases, however, the so-called 'middleman minorities' were ethnically, religiously and linguistically distinct from the majority of the population, and this separateness could fit in many ways the objectives of the colonial powers. But in the case of colonial India, the middleman minorities did not differ all that significantly in terms of ethnicity and religion from the majority population (leaving aside some specific cases of Hindu traders in Muslim-majority areas and of Muslim traders in Hindu-majority regions) and their use did not necessarily present the same advantages to the colonizers. In any case, there is no evidence that the British systematically encouraged the migration of Marwaris or other traders of the north-west to the Gangetic area and the Deccan. These migrations were largely 'spontaneous', building on the strength of already existing networks and received only an extra boost from the consolidation of British rule across the subcontinent. It was more a matter of existing networks taking advantage of specific opportunities linked to the advent of British rule rather than of the British themselves encouraging traders to migrate from their home regions to other areas. Actually, at the time of the Deccan riots of 1875, the British even explicitly, although rather belatedly, expressed some dismay at the expansion of the range of the Marwari moneylenders into the heart of the Deccan.

There is no denying that the existence of powerful all-India merchant networks pre-dating the colonial conquest was generally a boon to the British who could rely on their intermediation to gain easier access to commodities and markets in the Indian hinterlands, outside the area of direct operation of most British firms, which were based in the colonial port-cities, but the migratory nature of these networks was not the crucial point for the British. Their functional utility in relation to British needs came from their specific knowledge of markets and financial skills, as well as their lack of military clout, not from the fact that they were 'strangers' to the regions where they operated. Once more, we come back to the same theme, that of the central role of skill and knowledge in differentiating between various merchant groups. Thanks to their possession of unrivalled knowledge and skills, the merchant networks from the north-west were in their turn able to determine to some extent the shape and content of colonial economic penetration. Had not the Marwaris and other 'diasporic' merchants been already well entrenched in the cotton-producing zones of the Deccan at the time of the cotton boom of the American Civil War, it is possible that the British would have been forced to develop a plantation system, which would have resulted in a very different political economy in colonial India.

One important related question is whether the existence of a kind of monopoly exercised by some specific communities over certain types of activities retarded economic growth in colonial India. It has been sometimes suggested that the predominance acquired by communities whose skills were mostly financial exercised a negative influence over the mode of industrialization. For, with the possible exception of the Parsis, few communities combined technical or engineering skills with financial ones. Most technicians and engineers in India came from non-bania castes, mostly from the ranks of the Brahmins, and as a result they were rarely able to evolve into industrial entrepreneurs because of their lack of resources and financial skills. So that the 'modern' industry which developed during the colonial period became dominated by banias who knew little about technology and tended to favour an attitude of slavish imitation of British techniques. This attitude somewhat survived after Independence and could partly explain the low input into R&D by most Indian private firms, which in turn tended to hamper industrial growth.

Such strictures on merchant networks are, however, largely misdirected: the merchants did not create the structures of the economy but merely adapted themselves to those that were there.[39] In colonial and postcolonial India, at least prior to 1991, the greatest rewards went to entrepreneurs who were 'opportunistic' rather than to those who pursued well-defined long-term objectives. For one single house of Tatas, which pursued a coherent long-term strategy of industrial diversification from steel into trucks and other engineering goods,[40] there were many business houses of the Birla type which diversified according to a financial rather than to an industrial logic.

On the other hand it could be plausibly argued that the existence of pan-Indian merchant networks contributed in its own way to the unification of markets in India and therefore to the rise of Indian nationalism. In the absence of a developed system of modern banking and efficient capital markets, which played a major role in the emergence of national economic systems in Europe, it is tempting to see in the existence of pan-Indian trading and financial networks a kind of substitute and to ascribe to them a role in the emergence of an Indian national economy which accompanied the movement towards political independence. It has also been noticed that pan-Indian networks such as that of the Marwaris played a significant role in supplying Gandhi and the Congress with funds to pursue their political and social activities.[41] The existence of such widespread communities facilitated the circulation of funds and made it more difficult for the British to control financial flows towards the nationalist movement.

More complex is the question whether, after Independence, the monopoly exercised over trade, finance and most of industry by businessmen belonging to a limited number of communities has tended to discourage talent and innovation and therefore limit economic growth. Did these networks continue to dominate because of their superior level of knowledge or skills, or did the institutionalization of their position lead them to resort to Malthusian practices to maintain their dominance? No easy answer can be given to this question, in the absence of sufficiently detailed and focused surveys. One can only hazard the guess that such practices were not unknown, but one can also point to a certain number of counter-examples which suggest that they were not universal. The overwhelming domination of family firms over the modern sector of the economy[42] would in any case have been an obstacle to the free flow of entrepreneurial talent. Whether the fact that most family firms belonged to a small group of community-based networks was an additional restrictive factor is open to question. To the counterfactual question whether the Indian economy would have done better if the field had been more open to talent, no convincing answer is possible. Widespread migration of talent from India to greener pastures outside tends to suggest a positive answer, but some caution has to be exercised in using such an argument. Another strand of counterfactual reasoning would point to the fact that private enterprise remained strong in India in spite of the domination of a kind of socialist ideology, and that part of the credit should at least go to the much decried 'business communities'.

In post-Reforms India, the circulation of talent is supposed to be regulated by market factors rather than by the pull of community. The rise of such hubs of technology-driven activity as Bangalore and Hyderabad, in which talent drawn from all over India mixes in a fairly undifferentiated way, appears to suggest that time is running out for the business networks from the dry zone. They continue nevertheless to occupy dominant positions in cities such as Bombay and Calcutta, which still have a big role in India's economy. It is perhaps too early to write an obituary for the Gujaratis, Sindhis, Parsis, and Marwaris. They remain solidly entrenched in many sectors of the 'old' economy, which still account for the bulk of India's economic activity. Besides, some entrepreneurs belonging to these communities have also taken the turn towards the 'new' technology-driven economy. But their traditional dominance is for the first time under attack and they face their biggest challenge ever since the beginning of the nineteenth century.

## Notes

1. For an elaboration of this theme, and detailed references to Stein's writings, see the Introduction in Markovits, Pouchepadass, and Subrahmanyam (eds), *Society and Circulation*, pp. 1–22.

2. D.R. Gadgil, *Business Communities in India* (New York, 1951) mimeographed; and idem, *Origins of the Modem Indian Business Class: An Interim Report* (New York, 1959) (also mimeographed).

3. E.G. Ravenstein, 'The Laws of Migration', *Journal of the Statistical Society*, 48 (1885), pp. 167–227 and ibid., 52 (1889), pp. 214–301.

4. S.P. Gupta, *The Agrarian System of Eastern Rajasthan (c. 1650–c. 1750)* (Delhi, 1986), p. 143.

5. See M. Alam and S. Subrahmanyam, 'Introduction', in Alam and Subrahmanyam (eds), *The Mughal State 1526–1750* (Delhi, 1998), p. 15.

6. This is suggested, although not too explicitly, in S.F. Dale, *Indian Merchants and Eurasian Trade, 1600–1750* (Cambridge, 1994), p. 126.

7. G.D. Sharma, 'The Marwaris: Economic Foundations of an Indian Capitalist Class', in D. Tripathi (ed.), *Business Communities of India: A Historical Perspective* (Delhi, 1984), pp. 185–207.

8. T.A. Timberg, *The Marwaris: From Traders to Industrialists* (Delhi, 1978), p. 42.

9. See J.H. Little, *House of Jagat Seth* (Calcutta, 1967), pp. 6–7.

10. See S. Arasaratnam, *Merchants, Companies and Commerce on the Coromandel Coast, 1650–1740* (Delhi, 1986), pp. 166, 169–71. Some of these Pathans are also likely, however, to have been Mahdawis.

11. Mentioned in P. Curtin, *Cross-cultural Trade in World History* (Cambridge, 1984), p. 174.

12. C.A. Bayly, *Rulers, Townsmen, and Bazaars: North Indian Society in the Age of British Expansion, 1770–1870* (Cambridge, 1983), p. 161: '. . . the main feature of the eighteenth century in the Ganges valley was the decline of their trading power of the Gujerati Bania and Gujerati Brahmin merchants who had dominated the great cross-country trade routes between Surat . . . and Murshidabad . . . during the days of the Mughals and their immediate predecessors.'

13. See J.S. Grewal, 'Business Communities of Punjab', in Tripathi (ed.), *Business Communities*, p. 214.

14. See Bayly, *Rulers, Townsmen and Bazaars*, pp. 369–426.

15. See V.D. Divekar, 'Business Elements and Business Class in Maharashtra: A Historical Analysis', in Tripathi (ed.), *Business Communities*, pp. 83–108.

16. R.K. Ray, 'The *Bazaar:* Indigenous Sector of the Indian Economy', in ibid., pp. 241–67.

17. See Oriental and India Office Collections of the British Library, London, India Office Records, Board's Collections 1796–1858, part 111, 1820–30, File 18 127, 'Establishment of Regimental Bazars for the Better Provisioning of the Troops, June 1816–June 1820' and File 19 356, 'Successful Introduction of the Bazar System in the Military Cantonments in Central India, October 1820–January 1823'.

18. Timberg, *Marwaris*, pp. 224–5.

19. See C. Markovits, *The Global World of Indian Merchants 1750–1947: Traders of Sind from Bukhara to Panama* (Cambridge, 2000), pp. 39–43.

20. See A. Farooqi, *Smuggling as Subversion: Colonialism, Indian Merchants and the Politics of Opium* (Delhi, 1998).

21. See, for a brief history of the family, D.L. Drake-Brockman (comp.), *U.P. Gazetteers, vol. vii, Muttra* (Allahabad, 1911), pp. 121–2.

22. Timberg, *Marwaris*.

23. *Census of India, 1911, vol. vi, City of Calcutta, part ii, Tables* (Calcutta, 1913), Appendix A to Table XI, 'Age and Occupation of Immigrants from Selected Areas', showing that 1481 out of a total of 2757 male immigrants from Bikaner and 1787 out of a total of 4024 male immigrants from Jaipur were traders.

24. At the 1921 census, the population of the east zone was 93.54 million. See L. Visaria and P. Visaria. 'Population (1757–1947)', in D. Kumar (ed.), *The Cambridge Economic History of India*, vol. 2 (Cambridge, 1983), Table 5.8, p. 490.

25. *Report of the Committee on the Riots in Poona and Ahmednagar 1875* (Bombay, 1876).

26. See Timberg, *Marwaris*, pp. 56–64.

27. Anand A. Yang, *Bazaar India: Markets, Society and the Colonial State in Bihar* (Berkeley, 1998), p. 257.

28. These merchants operated worldwide, and the bulk of their operations was outside India. But, within India, they tended to corner part of the trade in luxuries and curios for the European population. They had shops in the main cities and hill stations which did a brisk business. See Markovits, *The Global World*, pp. 110–55.

29. See ibid., pp. 57–109.

30. See Ray, 'The *Bazaar*', in Tripathi, *Business Communities*, pp. 253–4.

31. *Gazetteer of the Bombay Presidency, vol. xvi, Nasik* (Bombay, 1883), p. 116.

32. On the context of the 1918 riots, see S. Das, *Communal Riots in Bengal 1905–1947* (Delhi, 1991), pp. 61–2.

33. *The Rajputana Gazetteer, vol. ii* (Calcutta, 1879), p. 250.

34. The big Marwari businessman Rai Badridas Goenka wrote in a letter to Sir Charles Teggart dated 17 December 1934: 'We feel that to class us as subjects of Indian States is to do us a great injustice. True that about a century ago our forefathers came to British India from some Indian states of Rajputana, but, as you know, we have since permanently settled and have invested our wealth in trade, commerce, industry and immovable property in British India and to most of our people now resident in British India, it is also the country of their birth. The Marwaris are thus within the alliegance of the Crown and are as much British subjects as the indigenous population'. Enclosed in Political (Internal) Department Collection, no. 11, File 73, 'Reforms', OIOC, India Office Records, Political and Secret Department Records, L/P& S/13/681.

35. On the cult of Rani Sati, see A. Hardgrove, 'Sati Worship and Marwari Public Identity in India', *Journal of Asian Studies*, 58: 3 (August 1999), pp. 723–52. The main temple of this goddess was in Jhunjhunu in Rajasthan, where a new, imposing structure was completed in 1936, but she had temples all over India, in every locality where there existed a sizeable Marwari community. A temple to Rani Sati was built near Calcutta in 1837, only eight years after the official abolition of sati by the colonial government. However sati puja, as practised by Marwari women, should be distinguished from the actual practice of sati.

36. Mentioned in ibid.

37. Timberg, *Marwaris*, pp. 107–14.

38. For a case study based on material from Sind, see Markovits, *The Global World*, pp. 157–66.

39. For an elaboration of this argument, see A.K. Bagchi, *Private Investment in India 1900–1939* (Cambridge, 1972).

40. See C. Markovits, 'The Tata Paradox', in B. Stein and S. Subrahmanyam (eds), *Institutions and Economic Change in South Asia* (Delhi, 1996), pp. 237–48. [Chapter 6 of this volume.]

41. See C. Markovits, *Indian Business and Nationalist Politics 1931–39: The Indigenous Capitalist Class and the Rise of the Congress Party* (Cambridge, 1985).

42. On the role of family firms in the economy of contemporary India, see S. Dutta, *Family Business in India* (Delhi, 1997).

9

# INDIAN MERCHANT NETWORKS OUTSIDE INDIA IN THE NINETEENTH AND TWENTIETH CENTURIES

## A Preliminary Survey*

IN SPITE OF THE RECENT FLOWERING OF STUDIES ON THE South Asian diaspora,[1] we are nevertheless left with many gaps in our knowledge and many unanswered questions. The bulk of existing work is still focused on the migration of agricultural labour and the 'Little Indias' it spawned in various corners of the world. The recent migrations of educated professionals to the countries of the 'First World', particularly the USA, are also attracting increasing attention. The whole field of migration and diaspora studies remains, however, dominated by a host country perspective which tends to obliterate the general picture from the point of view of South Asian history.

One particularly under-researched area is that of the movements of merchants between India and the rest of the world. There are various reasons for this neglect. Some are of a definitional nature; when merchants travel abroad for purposes of business, they are not generally considered migrants, even if their trip results in prolonged residence

*From *Modern Asian Studies* 33: 4 (1999), pp. 883–912.

abroad, which can become in some cases permanent. Others have to do with the sources: since the colonial authorities did not keep any systematic record of the movements of merchants, government archives, which are such a mine of information on labour migrations, have little to say on the former. Given the understandable tendency of scholars to rely heavily on official sources, the paucity of official documents on the movements of merchants is in itself a powerful factor of oblivion.

However, in the Indian case, these movements resulted in some cases in a fairly massive relocation, not only of traders, but also of people who were employed by them, such as shop assistants or servants. As a result, the neglect of merchant migrations has also led to the obliteration of some specific kinds of labour migrations from the records. Apart from its sheer numerical importance, which, as I shall show, was far from negligible, merchant migration has been important economically, even if, in the absence of any kind of reliable data regarding capital movements, a global appraisal of its impact on the Indian economy is a difficult task.

## Indian Merchant Migrations: A General View

Movements of Indian merchants between India and the rest of the world have a very long history. Merchants from the coastal regions of the subcontinent have been crisscrossing the sea routes of the Indian Ocean for many centuries. Merchants from inland northern India and the north-western borderlands have been active in the trade of Central Asia for as long as recorded history goes. However, with the incorporation of India into a British-dominated worldwide network of trade and finance which occurred at the end of the eighteenth and the beginning of the nineteenth centuries, Indian merchant migrations accelerated and took new forms. The first aim of this chapter is therefore to draw attention to the size and geographical spread of these migrations, which touched most of the world, well beyond the few areas of well-known Indian involvement. The second point I wish to make concerns the chronology of those migrations, which accelerated considerably at the end of the nineteenth century. The third fact which deserves emphasis is the need for a disaggregated picture of this vast diaspora, in which various separate networks have to be clearly distinguished from one another.

A serious quantitative study of Indian merchant migrations is a practically impossible task. Movements of passengers from Indian ports can be reconstructed thanks to the lists of ships' passengers which have been kept, but some statistical assumptions have to be made regarding the proportion of passengers who were 'merchants'. Besides, one supplementary difficulty is that some people who pursued a merchant career outside India were not 'merchants' when they left the subcontinent. They departed as indentured or some other kind of labour migrants and, either because they were able to bring some savings with them or because they led a particularly frugal life in their place of migration, they could at some juncture shift from agriculture or some other kind of manual occupation to small-scale trading. For all these reasons, only some very general estimates of the size of these movements can be presented.

As a point of departure, I present here an estimate of the number of Indians engaged in trade and finance in countries outside India around 1930, based primarily on the fairly detailed censuses of the Indian population settled in the major colonial territories of the British Empire (including Burma and Aden, which were still administratively part of British India) which are available. Some very gross estimates of the number of Indians engaged in trade in other British and non-British territories are also appended.

According to my calculations, there were approximately a quarter of a million Indians engaged in trading and finance outside India around 1930. Of course the censuses taken in the colonies at that time cannot be considered a very reliable source. The definition of occupations was often hazy. Thus, under 'commercial' were sometimes included occupations such as motor transport, or other ill-defined ones. However, as a gross approximation, they seem acceptable.

The total number of Indians outside India must have then been in the neighbourhood of 2.5 million, of whom at least 1.5 million were gainfully occupied. Trading and finance would thus have been the occupation of approximately one out of six Indians outside India, that is, a higher proportion than in India itself (although the censuses are notoriously unreliable in their estimates of the trading population in India). There were of course wide variations in the percentage of the working Indian population engaged in trade and finance. It was particularly low in colonies of massive labour migration: thus in Fiji only a little over 3 per cent of active Indian males were in commercial occupations.[2] In colonies like Burma and Malaya, where both labour and commercial migrations had taken place on a fairly massive scale, the share of trade ranged between 5 per cent and 6 per cent (Malaya)[3] and close to 20 per cent (Burma)[4] of the working Indian population. Then there were the territories where trading and finance were the major occupation of the Indian population, like Uganda—where over 50 per cent of Indian adult males were in commerce and finance[5]— Nyasaland, or Zanzibar.

TABLE 1

Indians in Commercial Occupations in Selected Countries
of the British Empire, 1931

| Country | Indians engaged in trade and finance | | |
| --- | --- | --- | --- |
|  | Males | Females | Total |
| Burma | 90,657 | 5,554 | 96,211 |
| Malaya | 29,592 | 622 | 30,214 |
| Ceylon (1921) | 23,704 | 1,119 | 24,823 |
| South Africa (1921) | 11,849 | 525 | 12,374 |
| British Guiana | 6,316 | 1,182 | 7,498 |
| Tanganyika | n.a. | n.a. | 6,124 |
| Mauritius (1921) | 5,059 | 888 | 5,947 |
| Kenya (1926) | 5,176 | 28 | 5,204 |
| Zanzibar (1921) | 4,980 | n.a. | 4,980 |
| Trinidad (late 1930s) | 2,629 | 946 | 3,575 |
| Uganda | 3,305 | 14 | 3,319 |
| Hong Kong | n.a. | n.a. | 1,294 |
| Nyasaland | 1,256 | n.a. | 1,256 |

Table 1 (*contd.*)

| | | | |
|---|---|---|---|
| Fiji (1921) | 812 | 42 | 854 |
| Southern Rhodesia | 343 | 4 | 347 |
| New Zealand (1926) | n.a. | n.a. | 179 |
| Total | | | 204,199 |

*Sources*: Burma: *Census of India, 1931, vol. XI, Burma, Part II, Tables,* by J.J. Bennison (Rangoon, 1933), Imperial Table XI, Part II, pp. 192–3. I have added up the numbers for 'Indians born in Burma' and 'Indians born outside Burma'. The table covers earners and working dependants.

Malaya: *British Malaya: A Report on the* 1931 *Census and on Certain Problems of Vital Statistics,* by C.A. Vlieband, s.d., s.i., Tables 127, pp. 273–6, 135, pp. 298–301, 143, pp. 322–4.

Ceylon: *Census Publications, Ceylon,* 1921, *vol. IV, General Tables,* by L.J.B. Turner (Colombo, 1926), Table XVII, pp. 280–321. I have added up the numbers for 'Indian Tamils', 'Indian Moors', and 'Others' (who were almost exclusively other Indians). Only earners are covered.

South Africa: *Official Yearbook of the Union of South Africa . . . 1920–1930, no. 12* (Pretoria, 1931), p. 851.

British Guiana: *British Guiana: Report on the Results of the Census of the Population, 1931,* by C.H. Norton (Georgetown, 1932), p. XLI.

Tanganyika: *Report by Sir Sydney Armilage-Smith, on a Financial Mission to Tanganyika, 26 September 1932, cmd 4182,* p. 6.

Mauritius: *Final Report on the Census Enumeration Made in the Colony of Mauritius and its Dependencies on the Night of the 21st of May* 1921, by A. Waiter (Port-Louis, 1926), Appendix I, Table VII, pp. CX and CXI. I have added up the numbers for the 'Indo-Mauritian population' and the 'Indian population'.

Kenya: *Report on the Non-native Census Enumeration Made in the Colony and Protectorate of Kenya on the Night of the 21st February 1926,* by A.G. Baker, ed. by A. Waiter (Nairobi, 1927), Table XXIII, p. 69.

Zanzibar: *Demographic Survey of the British Colonial Empire, vol. II, East Africa . . .* by D.R. Kuczynski (London, 1949), p. 654, 'non-native population of Zanzibar, 1921 Census'. The number is that of British Indian adult males, most of whom were in trading occupations. It is therefore an overestimate.

Trinidad: J.D. Tyson, *Memorandum of Evidence for the Royal Commission to the West Indies* (New Delhi, 1939), p. 44.

Uganda: *Uganda Protectorate: Census Returns, 1931* (Entebbe, 1933), Table XXI, p. 27.

Hong Kong: K.N. Vaid, *The Overseas Indian Community in Hong Kong* (Hong Kong), 1972, p. 23.

Nyasaland: F. and L. Dotson, *The Indian Minority of Zambia, Rhodesia and Malawi* (New Haven, London, 1968), p. 47, note 41. The number is that of economically active males. Practically all of them were in trade.

Fiji: *Legislative Council, Fiji, 1922, Council Paper no. 2. Fiji Census,* 1921 (Suva, 1922), Table 28, pp. 164–5.

Southern Rhodesia: *South African Indian Who's Who and Commercial Directory, 1940, Incorporating Southern and Northern Rhodesia, Nyasaland and Portuguese East Africa* (Pietermaritzburg), 1939, p. 34.

New Zealand: *Indians Abroad Directory* (Bombay, 1934), pp. 174–5.

Those Indians engaged in trade and finance were overwhelmingly male, generally 95 per cent or more (Mauritius and British Guiana being the only territories where females accounted for more than 10 per cent of the trading Indian population). This reflects partly a reality, but also a statistical bias: wives and daughters of shopkeepers who gave a helping hand in the shop were generally not recognized as being gainfully employed. However, Indian trading communities outside India, especially the non-Muslim ones, were characterized by a markedly unbalanced sex ratio. Thus in Uganda, among Hindus (amongst whom were also many non-traders), the sex ratio was 47 women to 100 men in 1931.[6] In Kenya in 1926 it was even less favourable, being only 39.[7] Indian traders who went abroad often tended to leave their womenfolk and children in India, bringing them over only when they had been away for many years and presumably successful enough. An unbalanced sex ratio is of course a characteristic of most migrations, especially those from India, but it did not generate among merchants the same degree of hardship as among labourers, since very often the traders had a wife in India whom they visited at regular intervals. A peculiarity of trading communities was that some merchants, especially those who lived in 'isolated' locations, had a tendency to make local arrangements of a quasi-matrimonial nature, a possibility which was rarely open to labourers.

As regards the religious composition of the merchant population outside India, the available data do not confirm the widely held belief that Muslims were in a great majority. For Ceylon, data from the 1921 Census suggest that the number of Hindus was more or less equal to that of Muslims.[8] For Burma, data from the 1921 Census give the following ratio: 55 per cent of Muslims and 45 per cent of Hindus.[9] Muslims appear to have been in a clear majority only in places like Portuguese East Africa, Malagasy, or Zanzibar. Many Hindu traders obviously had no qualms about crossing the *kala pani,* or if they had any (which we do not necessarily know about), they overcame them for the sake of profit (or at least the lure of it).

TABLE 2

Estimates of Number of Indians in Trade and Finance
in Selected Countries in the Early 1930s

| Country | Estimated number of Indians in trade |
| --- | --- |
| **Asia** | |
| China | A few hundreds |
| Japan | 200 |
| Philippines | 200–300 |
| Dutch East Indies | A few thousands |
| Thailand | A few thousands |
| French Indochina | A few thousands |
| Tibet | A few hundreds |
| Afghanistan | A few thousands |
| Persia | A few hundreds |
| Iraq | 100 |
| Bahrain | 200–300 |
| Trucial Oman and Qatar | A few hundreds |
| Oman and Muscat | 400–500 |
| Yemen | A few hundreds |
| Aden | 3,000 |
| **Africa** | |
| Egypt | 200 |
| Sudan | 200 |
| British Somaliland | 100 |
| Ethiopia | 2,000 |
| Italian Somalia | A few hundreds |
| Portuguese East Africa | 3,000–4,000 |
| Malagasy | 2,661 |
| Reunion | 710 |
| Seychelles | 100–200 |

Table 2 (*contd.*)

Table 2 (*contd.*)

| | |
|---|---|
| Morocco (incl. Spanish Morocco and Tangier) | 500–1,000 |
| Algeria | A few hundreds |
| **Europe** | |
| Gibraltar | 100 |
| Spain | A few hundreds |
| UK | 1,000–2,000 |
| **America** | |
| Panama | 300 |
| Jamaica | A few hundreds |
| Surinam | A few hundreds |
| Total (including others) | 30,000–40,000 |

*Sources*: The estimates are mine, based on a variety of sources, mostly *Indians Abroad Directory*, passim. The numbers for Malagasy and Reunion are those of British Indian adult males (who were practically all in trade). For Aden, the estimate is derived from *Census of India, 1931, vol. VIII, Part III, Aden, Report and Tables*, by M.S. Johnson (Bombay, 1933), Table X, p. 25, which gives the total number employed in trade in Aden as 3,320 males and 156 females. I have assumed that 85 per cent of them were Indian, which might be an overestimate.

The idea that Hindus were reluctant to engage in maritime trade for fear of breaking a religious taboo on overseas voyages is one of the most enduring legends bequeathed to us by the Portuguese. When the latter made their appearance in the Indian Ocean, there were already important colonies of Hindu banias in many ports of the ocean, such as Muscat.[10] It could be, of course, that this kind of religious taboo was enforced more strictly at later periods. There is evidence that in the eighteenth century north Indian banias considered the crossing, not only of the seas, but even of the Indus at Attock, a violation of religious norms[11] necessitating, on the return, the undergoing of purification rituals. These rules were still enforced in the late nineteenth century in Porbandar, a port in Kathiawar which had intense commercial relations with the Middle East and Africa, judging from Gandhi's own testimony. However, all this did not prevent Hindu merchants in coastal regions as well as in the north-western borderlands from travelling extensively all over the world and establishing residence for many years in faraway lands. The most adventurous of all Indian merchants in modern times, the Sindworkies of Hyderabad (Sind) who went as far as Japan, South Africa, and the Straits of Magallanes, were Hindus, albeit of a peculiar persuasion (being generally Shaivite as well as Nanakpanthis, that is, non-Khalsa Sikhs), and there is no evidence that they underwent purification rituals when they returned to Hyderabad.

Religion does not seem to have been the determining factor in the more or less inward or outward orientation of Indian merchant communities. Some of these communities, Hindu as well as Muslim, seem to have been outward-oriented for centuries, and the advent of steam navigation and the telegraph in the second half of the nineteenth century only further accentuated this trend. Other communities, such as the Marwaris, remained India-bound. It is doubtful that religious orthodoxy was their main motivation in forsaking opportunities outside India. The truth is that they established such a powerful domination over most of India's internal trade in the late nineteenth and early twentieth centuries that there was no need for them to seek outlets outside the country. Conversely, those communities which were in a more precarious position in regard to internal trade and already had a foothold in trade outside India tended to develop their interests abroad. Of course this leaves unanswered the question as to why some communities, like the Bengali traders, who were largely squeezed out by the Marwaris on their home ground, did not seek compensations elsewhere. The answer is probably that they did not have the connections and the 'knowhow' which would have allowed them such a breakthrough.

Indian traders abroad originated mainly from a few regions of the subcontinent. Gujarat and Tamil Nadu are clearly the two regions from where the largest number of merchants migrated. Other regions which supplied a fair amount of migrants are Sind, the Punjab, and Kerala. On the other hand, few merchants from the Hindi heartland went abroad. The leading role played by the coastal regions of the subcontinent comes as no surprise, since those regions, and in particular Gujarat and Coromandel, were those through which most of India's foreign sea trade had been conducted. However, it has already been mentioned that few traders from Bengal, another coastal region active in maritime trade, left India. In the same way, relatively few traders from the Konkan emigrated. Therefore no strict correlation can be derived between coastal location and size of merchant migration. If one looks more closely at the data on Sind, one will notice that most Sindhi merchant migrants originated from two inland towns in the province, Hyderabad and Shikarpur, and that few hailed from its main seaport, Karachi. In the same way, more merchants migrated from Kutch, an area with only one proper seaport (Mandvi), than from Kathiawar, which had many. Surat continued to be the focus of large merchant diasporas long after it ceased to be an active seaport.

## Indian Trading Migrations: The Time Sequence

Although merchant migrations from India have had a very long history, they undoubtedly took a new dimension in the nineteenth century. Reconstructing a detailed chronology of these migrations is impossible, due to the lack of official statistics. The most one can do is to draw a very impressionistic picture, based on scattered evidence. Looking at the situation one century earlier than 1930, that is, around 1830, one is aware of the existence of small communities of Indian merchants in practically all the ports of the Indian Ocean, from the Persian Gulf to the Straits of Malacca. Among ports where sizeable communities of Indian merchants resided, were, in the western Indian Ocean and the Red Sea, Aden (even before its annexation by the British in 1839), Mocha in Yemen,[12] Berbera, and Massawa. In the Persian Gulf, Hindu banias had been operating at Bahrein since the beginning of the eighteenth century.[13] The largest Indian merchant community was probably that in Muscat, which numbered around 2,000 in 1840.[14] Around the same date, when Sultan Sayid moved his headquarters from Muscat to Zanzibar, there were already at least 300 or 400 Indian merchants in the latter port.[15] The first Indian traders reached Mauritius in 1829,[16] even before indentured labour migration to the island started. East of India, there were Indian traders and moneylenders in Burma, where Chettiars started going from 1826 onwards,[17] and in the Straits Settlements, which were a dependency of India till 1867.

Although no precise estimate is possible, the Indian merchant diaspora in the Indian Ocean by the 1830s was several thousand-strong, of whom a majority appear to have been Hindus. In one century its growth was therefore spectacular and its composition underwent some change, with the emergence of a sizeable Muslim element. The demographic history of these migrations, impossible to reconstruct in any detail, appears to fall into two distinct periods, with 1880 as an important cut-off point. Between 1830 and 1880, the growth of the Indian merchant diaspora was slow and haphazard. The greatest expansion occurred in East Africa, where by 1860 there were 5000 to 6000 Indian traders in the dominions of the Sultan of Zanzibar.[18] The Indian merchant presence became also more noticeable in Burma, following the British annexation of Lower Burma in 1852, and in the Straits Settlements. It is also around 1860 that the Hindu merchants hailing from Hyderabad (Sind), the Sindworkies, started their voyages to Egypt and further west.[19] The opening of China after the First Opium War resulted in some Indian merchants, particularly Bombay Parsis who had been active in the China trade since the late eighteenth century, taking up residence in the Treaty Ports. The range of Indian merchant migrations thus increased as did their size, as Indian merchants started travelling and residing in the Mediterranean and China seas.

From the early 1880s, there was a sudden acceleration in the pace and volume of Indian merchant migrations. Indian merchants started appearing in localities where they had never been seen, often in the wake of the indentured labour migrants. Thus in Durban, where in 1880 there were only seven 'Arab' (local name for the Gujarati Muslims) shopkeepers, the 1891 Census listed 598 Indian storekeepers and 172 'designated traders'.[20] Fairly detailed statistical evidence on migration from India to Malaya from the late 1870s tends to show that 'non-labour' migration, which was largely (although not exclusively) a commercial migration, suddenly accelerated around the mid-1880s.[21] The 1880s were also a decade of very fast growth in the Indian population of Burma[22] and presumably in the numbers of Indian traders. These 'free' migrations of mostly trading people, as opposed to indentured or *kangani* labour migrations, became fairly massive in the first decade of the twentieth century. During 1906–8, more than 12,000 'free' migrants left Bombay for East Africa.[23] In 1907 and 1908, 30,000 'non-labour' immigrants landed in Malaya.[24] 'Free' migration to several destinations remained at a high level till 1914, and, after slowing down considerably during the First World War and its immediate aftermath, started with renewed vigour in the 1920s. It continued to be high in the 1930s, in spite of the world depression and was durably interrupted only by the Second World War.

The sudden acceleration in the pace of merchant migrations after 1880 is not easy to explain. It is true that the 1880s and 1890s were not a period of great commercial prosperity in India, while many colonial territories, such as Burma and Malaya, went through a phase of rapid development. However, with the return of relative prosperity in India from the late 1890s onwards, the trend was not reversed, on the contrary. By then, merchant migration appeared to have acquired a dynamics of its own, which made it relatively independent of the fluctuations of the economic conjuncture in India. Economic prospects and conditions in the various countries of destination seem to have exercised greater influence on the process than the state of the Indian economy. This implies that information on conditions abroad was widely available in India and that Indian businessmen, at least in some areas, had become widely mobile and responsive to opportunities in foreign countries.

Was the spurt in merchant migration directly related to the growth of large Indian communities in some territories as a result of decades of labour migrations on a fairly large scale? Some correlation obviously existed between the two migration streams, but it was probably less than has been sometimes assumed. There is no clear evidence that most Indian traders abroad specialized in the sale of Indian goods to Indian labourers. Given the low purchasing power of the labourers, that market in any case could not have sustained over time the expansion of Indian business. Supplying the Indian labourers was often only the first step in a process. Thus in South Africa Indian traders increasingly specialized in selling goods to the natives, a field in which their low operating costs and knowledge of the market allowed them to make rapid inroads to the detriment of European competitors, mostly Jewish merchants. The same was true of East Africa, where the *dukawalla*, the Indian general country merchant, became the backbone of the local Indian trading community. However, some Indian trading communities specialized in the sale of 'European' goods mostly to European customers. This was the case in particular of the Parsis, who were often specialized in the liquor trade, and the Sindworkies who traded in silk and curios.

One essential feature of this migration is that it was generally of a non-permanent nature. Rarely did commercial migrants leave India with the avowed intention of settling abroad for good. Those who left as employees of commercial firms had contracts for a period of two or three years at most. Others who went on their own just hoped to make good in a few years so as to be able to come back to India in a better economic position. However, many of those who left never came back, either, one can presume, because their business prospered so much that India held no more attraction for them, or, on the contrary, because they were complete failures and did not dare show their face again in their native place. Others returned to India after a few years, or only to retire, often, but not always, wealthier than when they had departed. There is of course no way of knowing even approximately the number of migrants who belonged to those various categories. However, one can draw a distinction between two kinds of destinations: those which were easily accessible from India, because ship passage was relatively cheap, and those which were not. In the first category were in particular Burma, Ceylon, and Malaya. It was possible for a small trader to try his luck there and come back if prospects proved disappointing. Therefore migration to these countries was characterized by a very high rate of turnover. The only complete series available concerns Malaya, where, from 1844 onwards, it is possible to differentiate between labour and non-labour migration. In the 1844–1931 period, the total number of non-labour migrants who reached Malaya from India was 643,000.[25] Assuming that half of these arrivals were 'commercial' migrants, one could conclude that more than 300,000 traders migrated from India to Malaya during that period. Similarly high figures could be derived for Ceylon and Burma, which were even more easily accessible than Malaya from the Indian ports. It is therefore possible to estimate the volume of gross Indian trading migration to those three territories where more than 60 per cent of all Indians engaged in trade resided around 1930, to have been in the neighbourhood of 1 million or more between 1840 and 1930. In other territories, which were less easily accessible from India, the turnover was much lower. In South Africa, the 12,000 to 13,000-strong Indian trading population counted by the 1921 Census was the result of the migration of 14,000 'free' migrants between 1860 and 1911,[26] most of which took place between 1880 and 1900. Comparable ratios between the actual number of Indians in trade around 1930 and trading migrations can be inferred for most other territories. Therefore, outside Burma, Ceylon, and Malaya, a total of 200,000 or 300,000 trading migrants in the 1840–1930 period seems a reasonable estimate. This would put the total number of commercial migrants from India during this period at 1.5 million. This represents over 5 per cent of the total of approximately 27 million migrants computed by Kingsley Davis for the same period.[27] However, since most of this migration took place between 1880 and 1930, it accounted for a slightly higher percentage of the overall migrant flows during that period.

The difference between the percentage of commercial people among migrants, that is, around 6 or 7 per cent, and that of people engaged in trade among Indians residing abroad, i.e. around 15 or 16 per cent, can be explained (apart from inevitable statistical inaccuracies) by a combination of two factors. Firstly, the turnover was probably even higher among labourers than among traders, and this point is supported by much of the statistical evidence available on labour migrations to Burma, Ceylon, and Malaya. Secondly, the shift in occupation, from labour to small-scale trading, may have occurred on a fairly important scale.

By 1930, the vast majority of Indians engaged in trade outside India were immigrants from India. Only in Mauritius[28] and South

Africa were the majority of Indian traders locally born. In Burma, Indians born in the country were less than 10 per cent of the total of Indians engaged in trade.[29]

It has already been mentioned that, contrary to the case of labour migration, the state took no part in organizing or even regulating movements of traders. Provided they obtained a passport, which does not appear to have been particularly difficult (and which was not even necessary for Burma), British Indian merchants and subjects of the Indian States could freely leave India. However, it is well known that they faced many obstacles when it came to disembarking. An increasing number of countries, both within and outside the British Empire, took exclusion measures against 'Asiatic' immigrants, amongst whom Indians were as much a target as the Chinese. Many countries passed discriminatory legislation against foreign merchants, and often specifically targeted the Indian traders. In the first three decades of the twentieth century, such laws were passed by countries as diverse as South Africa, Kenya, Gibraltar, the Philippines, Panama, and protests by Indian trading interests forced the India Office to intervene on their behalf, although with little effect. Doing business abroad was becoming increasingly tricky for Indian merchants. Paradoxically, they enjoyed better protection from being British subjects in foreign countries than in many countries of the British Empire where anti-Indian hysteria was often raging and the imperial government unable or unwilling to do anything against it.

In spite of all these obstacles, Indian merchants succeeded in gaining a foothold in trade in many countries of the world. This they could achieve mainly thanks to the strength of various networks. For, in spite of being generally labelled 'free' or even 'spontaneous' migration, to distinguish it from indentured labour migration, the migration of commercial people was a highly organized process.

## South Asian Trading Networks

A crucial concept for analysing merchant migrations is that of network. It seems preferable to the concept of trading diaspora popularized by

Africanists.[30] A trading network can be defined as a spatially discontinuous structure, linking with each other several nodal points, across which different kinds of 'objects' circulate: capital, credit, goods, information, men, women. Two of these 'objects' have a tendency to circulate exclusively within the network: information and women. As a rule, a particular trading network does not trade inside information and does not exchange women with another trading network. Inversely, all members of a specific trading network are sharers of certain kinds of information ('the secrets of the trade') and, within certain limits prescribed by religious law and social custom, potential partners in marriage alliances. As regards the circulation of capital, the general rule is that members of the network are preferred partners in business and get preferential rates and conditions as regards repayment of loans (longer delays, less collateral, etc.). However, many traders borrow capital at least partly outside the network, generally from specialized banking communities. Some trading communities include both bankers and traders but this is the exception rather than the rule. Preference in employment as managers, brokers, shop assistants, etc., is also given to (male) members of the network though exclusive preference for them can rarely remain in the long term when distances are very great. Goods circulate also within a given trading network, but the specific patterns of circulation can vary greatly, according to the kind of business engaged in. One major difference is between those networks which include both wholesalers and retailers and those which are specialized in only one of these operations. In the latter case, an institutionalized relationship with one or several other trading networks is a necessity. Only those networks spanning the whole spectrum of trading operations can afford to be self-contained.

In the Indian case, a specific trading network is generally congruent with either a specific 'caste' or 'subcaste' (including Muslim 'quasi-castes') or with a cluster of castes, or with a localized section of a given caste or subcaste. I present here a table of the major international trading networks operating from India in the nineteenth and twentieth centuries which I have identified. It will be seen that the majority of these networks originated from a few regions, particularly Kutch,

Kathiawar, Sind, Kerala, and Tamil Nadu. The place occupied by the small Indian state of Kutch is particularly remarkable. Traders from that region, both Muslim (Memons who were Sunni and Khojas who were Shia, divided since the 1840s between Ismaili and Itna'ashari) and Hindu (Lohana and Bhatia) have been exceptionally active in the Indian Ocean since the end of the eighteenth century. Kutchi Bhatias played a crucial role in Oman from the 1820s onwards when they supplanted the Sindhi Bhatias who had been dominant in the trade of Muscat for many centuries.[31] Kutchi Bhatias were the major financiers of the slave trading network centred on Zanzibar and, as such, a prime target of British onslaughts against the trade, although they did not themselves trade in slaves. Thanks to their status as subjects of a native state, they managed for a while to resist British attempts to prevent them from continuing their activities, but in 1869 the ruler of Kutch was eventually persuaded to issue a proclamation to the effect that his subjects in Zanzibar would be considered British subjects and therefore forbidden to take part in the slave trade.[32] In spite of this blow, Kutchi Bhatias remained prominent in the trade of the western Indian Ocean till far into the twentieth century. Another group of Hindus from Kutch, the Kutchi Lohanas, became dominant in East African trade, particularly in Uganda,[33] during the first half of the twentieth century. Muslims from Kutch were also extremely active: the Khojas, particularly the Ismaili section, played almost as great a role in East Africa as the Lohanas. As for the Kutchi Memons, who, unlike the Khojas, were Sunni Muslims, they established a powerful trading network extending from Burma to the interior of Central Africa.

Thus the small native state of Kutch, with barely half a million people in 1931, provided a disproportionate share of the total number of commercial migrants from India in the nineteenth and the first half of the twentieth centuries. As for an explanation, apart from its geographical location close to the major maritime routes between western India and the western Indian Ocean, one is often referred to a terrible famine which took place in 1817, which seems to have been a local equivalent of the Irish potato famine. However, it remains to be understood why the different merchant communities from Kutch

TABLE 3

Major International Trading Networks Operating from India

| Caste | Region of origin | Areas of operation |
|---|---|---|
| Patidar | Central Gujarat | East and Central Africa |
| Lohana | Kutch | East and Central Africa |
| Bhatia | Kutch | Oman, East Africa |
| Memon | Kutch | East Africa, Burma, Ceylon, Mauritius |
| Khoja Ismaili | Kutch | East Africa |
| Khoja Itna'ashari | Kutch | East Africa |
| Bohra | Surat | Maldives, Ceylon, Yemen, Reunion, Malagasy |
| Halai Memon | Kathiawar | South and East Africa |
| Vania | Kathiawar | Horn of Africa |
| Marwari | Rajasthan | Burma, Japan |
| Arora | Punjab | Central Asia, Malaya |
| Khatri | Punjab | Central Asia |
| Mappillai | Kerala | Ceylon, Burma |
| Chettiar | Tamil Nadu | SE Asia, Burma, Ceylon, South Africa, Mauritius |
| Marakkayar | Tamil Nadu | Burma, SE Asia |
| Bhaiband | Hyderabad (Sind) | The whole world |
| Bhaiband | Shikarpur (Sind) | Central Asia, Burma |
| Bhatia | Thatta (Sind) | Persian Gulf |
| Khoja | Hyderabad (Sind) | Oman |
| Parsi | Bombay | Far East, Aden, UK |

were so uniformly successful in their commercial and financial ventures abroad. A possible line of explanation lies in the attitude of the rulers who maintained a large degree of independence from British interference in their domestic affairs and seem to have systematically given their support to the traders. However, further enquiries into the 'Kutchi miracle' are obviously needed.

Merchants from Kathiawar, both Muslim and Hindu, also figure prominently in the history of the Indian merchant diasporas. Traders from Porbandar, Memons as well as Vanias, seem to have been particularly active in Mauritius and South Africa, and it is through that network that Gandhi entered South Africa. The area was divided into many petty states, but they also seemed to have succeeded, in spite of their small size, to preserve some degree of independence from the

British, which was probably a help to their traders. The Kathiawar ports were the only ports outside British India which maintained a significant overseas maritime trade, mainly with the Persian Gulf, the Horn of Africa, and East Africa.

Central Gujarat, the home of some of India's most powerful merchant families, figures less prominently in the saga of the Indian merchant diasporas. However, traders from Surat and Broach, particularly Muslims belonging to the Daudi (Shia) Bohra community, played an important role from Thailand to Malagasy. The Patidars (Patels) are a special case: this community of relatively well-off peasants started acquiring a more urban and commercial orientation in its home ground of Kheda district in the first decades of the twentieth century. The Patidars have also been very successful in trade in East Africa, where they did not originally go as traders.

North of Gujarat, the province of Sind made a considerable, if often unrecognized, contribution to the Indian merchant diaspora. Several merchant networks originated from that region. The oldest one appears to have been that of the Bhatias of Thatta (not to be confused with the Kutchi Bhatias). They formed, from the late fifteenth to the early nineteenth centuries, the bulk of the large Indian trading community in Muscat. Some then moved to Zanzibar while the majority appear to have made their way to the Persian Gulf where they played a major role in the pearling trade of Bahrain, Kuwait, and Dubai till the middle of the twentieth century.[34] From the late eighteenth century onwards, Sindhi Khojas established in the recently founded capital of Hyderabad started making their way to Muscat where they were known as Luwatiyya and played a fairly important role in the trade of that emporium of the western Indian Ocean.[35] However, the two most important networks from Sind were Hindu networks centred around the two major inland trading cities of the province, Shikarpur and Hyderabad. The Shikarpuri *shroffs*, belonging to the Bhaiband sub-caste of the great Lohana merchant caste, established a powerful international banking network extending from Astrakhan on the Caspian Sea to the Straits of Malacca. Their hundis were the major currency all along the caravan routes of Central Asia and in India, where they were known, outside Sind, as Multanis, as well as in Burma, they specialized in the rediscount of hundis.[36] Another group of Bhaiband, based in Hyderabad, the capital of pre-British Sind, established the most extensive of all Indian merchant networks abroad, which around 1905 stretched from Kobe in Japan to Panama, with several firms having branches in all the major ports along the two main sea-routes, Bombay–Kobe (via Colombo, Singapore, Surabaya, Saigon, Canton, Shanghai, Manila) and Bombay–Panama (via Port-Sudan, Port Said, Alexandria, Valletta, Gibraltar, Teneriffe, or alternatively via Lourenco–Marques, Capetown, Freetown). By 1907, it was estimated that there were 5,000 of these Sindworkies, who specialized in the sale of silk and curios, scattered across the world.[37]

Punjab was also home to some adventurous merchant communities, whose members did not hesitate to cross deserts and high mountain passes to pursue trade in Central Asia. Thus Hindu Khatri merchants from the town of Hoshiarpur were active in the trade between India and Chinese Turkestan at the time when Macartney was the British Consul in Kashgar.[38] Others followed the maritime routes east of Calcutta: Sikh merchants from Rawalpindi, Lahore, Ludhiana, Jullundur and Amritsar were found in Malaya in the 1920s, some having moved directly from India, others having first spent time in Rangoon or Bangkok.[39]

However adventurous and far-ranging the merchants from western and northern India were, the majority of commercial migrants appear to have been south Indians. Merchants from present-day Kerala and Tamil Nadu formed the bulk of the Indian trading diaspora in Burma, Ceylon, and Malaya. Three communities have been particularly prominent. Of greatest economic importance has been the community of the Nattukottai Chettiars, who, from the end of the nineteenth century onwards, emerged as the main providers of rural credit to the peasants of Burma, Ceylon and Malaya. Their network extended also to French Indochina, Northern Sumatra, and probably Thailand in Southeast Asia, while they also operated, apparently on a smaller scale, in Mauritius and South Africa. These Shaivite Hindus, who used their temples as clearing houses, played a major role in financing commercial agriculture in Southeast Asia, particularly in the rice deltas of the Irrawaddy and the Mekong.[40] Of lesser importance in economic terms than these powerful bankers, but fairly ubiquitous, were two Muslim groups, the so-called 'Chulia', who were Tamil-speaking Muslims of whom the Marakkayar were a branch. Both communities were prominent in retail trade in the three territories. In Burma, the Chulias 'owned shops even in remote villages, in addition to those located in towns and cities'.[41] The Marakkayar, who numbered over 40,000 in Malaya in 1939, mostly settled in the Straits Settlements, were general merchants as well as shopkeepers.[42] There were also Mappillai (Moplah) merchants from Kerala in Ceylon as well as in Burma. In Ceylon, the 'Indian Tamil' traders constituted a broad category which, besides Chettiars, must have included merchants, mostly small scale, from diverse Tamil Hindu castes.

This rapid survey of the major Indian trading networks has no other purpose than to underline how diverse and how deeply segmented the Indian merchant diaspora was. This segmentation, at an institutional level, manifested itself in the mushrooming of commercial associations, generally community-based. Practically in no country was there only one Indian merchant association in which traders belonging to different communities were represented. There were Nattukottai Chettiars Associations, Sindhi Associations, Malabar Merchants Associations, and efforts at creating umbrella organizations were rarely very successful. This seems to confirm that Indian merchants abroad tended to think of themselves as Chettiars, Memons, Khojas, or Sindworkies rather than 'Indian'. This segmentation prevented the emergence of powerful Indian business lobbies, even in countries where Indian capital played a major economic role. However, it need not be seen as a failure: Indian merchants had no compelling reason to unite in defence of economic interests which were extremely diverse. Most networks occupied specific economic niches (the rice trade for the Kutchi Memons, the silk and curios trade for the Sindworkkies, rural credit for the Chettiars, etc.) and had no overall picture of a global 'Indian' interest.

## Patterns of Merchant Migration

The networks, once established, after the pioneering phase was over (it was generally over for all but a few destinations by the early twentieth century), offered the basic structure through which the movements of merchants and commercial employees were organized. It was not really possible for a merchant, except if he was exceptionally rich, to move alone. At every stage he needed the help that could only be provided by an existing network. Most merchants did not live in any of the big seaports from which they had to sail. Just to survive for a short period in Bombay, Calcutta, or Madras, while waiting for their passage, they used the lodging and boarding facilities often provided by their communities, which were the equivalent (though probably more comfortable) of the emigrants' hostels maintained by the government for the departing indentured labourers. Thus Nattukottai Chettiar financial houses maintained 'lodges' at all the major seaports in Tamil Nadu from where passengers departed for Burma, Ceylon, and the Straits Settlements, and South Indian Muslim communities had similar facilities, while in Calcutta, the main port of embarkation for North Indian merchants going to the Straits, Sikhs and Sindhis had *gurudwaras* and dharamshalas catering to the needs of the travellers.[43] Once they landed, the merchants also needed help to get going: cheap accommodation, cheap loans, which they could only get through an existing network. Of course the extended family was the basic structure of the merchant community, but its resources were not sufficient, except in the cases of very wealthy families, to cater to all the needs of the commercial migrant.

Although the migrants generally came through a network, the modalities varied. Most Indian commercial migrants were probably self-employed small-scale traders who had little capital and were therefore very dependent on credit to start in business in a new location. Having little or no collateral, they could not get it from European banks and had therefore to rely on informal, community-based credit networks. So, presumably, most commercial migration was 'chain migration'; a small merchant went to a place where merchants from his area in India were already settled (once again, leaving aside the case of the first pioneers), about which he had heard through oral or written channels; he went with some accumulated savings, but they were not enough to launch him into the business and he had to borrow from fellow merchants from his area at rates which were probably preferential but could nevertheless be high.

There were, however, other possibilities. Part of the commercial migration from India occurred through the expansion of firms which opened branches in foreign localities. There were thus many Indian firms which became 'international' in the nineteenth and twentieth centuries, while remaining family firms. The process sometimes entailed the physical migration of some family members. Thus the Parsi firm of Dadabhai & Co., founded by Dorabji Maneckji Vacha, had in 1917 two overseas branches in London and Tulear (Malagasy) which were respectively managed by two sons of the founder.[44] However, the most common arrangement was for the principals of a firm to entrust the creation of a branch to a manager, who could be either an employee or a partner of the firm. Shop assistants were also recruited in India and sent abroad on contracts which were generally for a duration of two and a half years. These could be very close to indenture contracts, although the state was not involved in them. Once firms had established a network, smaller operators belonging to the same community could then move on their own. This is very much the mechanism through which the Sindworkie community expanded from Hyderabad (Sind) into many countries. The migration of shop assistants on short-term contracts, which were sometimes renewed, not always for the same destination, represented an important, although rarely mentioned, component of the commercial migration from India. Commercial employees accounted for a significant share of the Indian trading population in the few territories for which detailed statistical data are available: in Malaya, for more than 25 per cent,[45] in Kenya for a little over 50 per cent.[46] Some Indian shop assistants were probably recruited by British firms in India, but the vast majority went abroad with Indian firms. They were generally recruited in the town where the firm had its headquarters or its immediate surroundings and belonged to the same community as the owners of the firm. This was a form of semi-skilled labour migration entirely organized by private firms, without any state intervention.

Some Indian commercial firms had a widespread network of branches abroad. This was the case in particular of the major Sindworkie firms, with their headquarters at Hyderabad (Sind), such as Pohoomull Bros, D. Chellaram, J.T. Chanrai & Co., K.A.J. Chotirmall and Co., M. Dialdas & Sons, K. Chellaram & Sons. The major Nattukottai Chettiar financial houses often had more than a hundred branches, situated in many localities in Burma, Ceylon, Malaya, and French Indochina. These firms were controlled from their headquarters in India, although local managers had a large autonomy in the day-to-day running of the business. In the Sindworkie firms, the accounting of all the branches was done yearly at Hyderabad, and most profits remitted to India on a regular basis. In such a system, tension between centralizing and centrifugal tendencies was inevitable. If the telegraph became the major channel of communication between the headquarters and the different branches, the physical presence of the principals was nevertheless felt to be necessary at fairly regular intervals. In the big Sindworkie firms, the principals made regular 'inspection tours' of the branches, which took them many months to complete.

A third possibility was the pure and simple relocation abroad of an Indian firm. Thus, in the years prior to the First World War, a big Tamil merchant, V.M. Pillay, came with capital from South India to Fiji and established a chain of general stores in the islands.[47] A Sindhi firm from Karachi, Kirpalani & Sons, relocated itself in Trinidad in 1927. Cases of migration of big capitalists from India nevertheless appear to have been rare before 1947. Even when most of their profits came from foreign operations, as was the case for the principals of the big Sindworkie firms or of the major Nattukottai Chettiar financial houses, capitalists preferred to reside in India. Cultural factors probably have a lot to do with it: it was difficult, especially for Hindus, to live the 'right life' outside India. But this kind of arrangement was also facilitated by the existence of certain loopholes in the Indian taxation law, which in effect permitted avoidance of taxation on profits earned outside India.[48]

However, most of the Indian immigrants who succeeded in business outside India had not left India with capital. They generally started as small-scale traders and gradually enlarged the scale of their operations. East Africa, where Indian businessmen were particularly successful, is a good case in point. None of the business families which made it big there had a previous history of business success in India, be it the Madhvanis or Mehtas in Uganda, Karimji Jivanji in Zanzibar and Tanganyika, or A.M. Jeevanjee in Kenya. The most successful Indian businessmen in East Africa tended gradually to diversify from trade into manufacturing (or rather processing of agricultural products) and transport, and some acquired land. On the whole, however, Indian businessmen abroad, prior to the 1950s, remained a trading class and the big shift towards industry occurred at a later stage.

On the basis of the evidence available, it can be safely assumed that the outmigration of traders was not sustained by a large-scale outflow of capital from India. Some capital was undoubtedly exported from India, especially by banking communities such as the Nattukottai Chettiars or the Shikarpuris, because the countries where they operated did not have a developed banking system and they could not therefore have borrowed the initial capital for their operations from banks. However, once the system had got started, given the high rates of interest obtained on loans, it was largely self-sustaining and did not need a regular injection of funds from India. The major problem for the Indian moneylenders was, as much as in India, to obtain the actual repayment of their loans. In normal conditions they seem to have managed it, but when the great depression of the early 1930s depressed peasant incomes, the Chettiars in particular had no option but to foreclose: they found themselves in possession of large tracts of land which were worth very little, and that was their undoing. However, for decades they had been able to transfer large amounts to India and it is doubtful that in the end they really lost out. No estimate of the economic balance sheet of the outside ventures of Indian capitalists in the pre-1947 period is even remotely computable, but there is reason to think that, even if one was able to take it into account, it would not make a big difference to the existing estimates of India's balance of payments. It is only at a micro level that such analysis could bring rewarding results. It would thus be interesting to be able to evaluate the impact on the regional economy of Gujarat, Sind, or Tamil Nadu, of the outside ventures of some of the local business communities.

## Indian Trading Migrations: The Wider Context

To come back to a macro perspective, some questions of a fairly general nature have to be asked, even if one cannot provide really satisfactory answers. The first one concerns the causes of these migrations. Is it possible to reason in terms of 'push' and 'pull' factors, as is still often done in migration studies? More precisely, can one identify, at a regional or micro-regional level, sets of socio-economic variables which would favour or hamper trading migrations? It seems fairly difficult. In the course of my own research on the Sindworkies, I tried to identify socio-economic transformations which could explain the sudden surge in outward ventures by Hyderabad firms which took place from 1860 onwards, and which led in less than fifty years to the setting up of a worldwide trading network centred on this inland city, situated in one of India's poorest provinces. One hopeful line of enquiry was in the direction of changes in the agrarian economy. Some years ago, David Washbrook argued that, in the late nineteenth century, the British failed to provide the legal and institutional framework necessary for proper 'capitalist' development in agriculture, and he related the growing tendency by mercantile capitalists to seek opportunities outside India to this state of affairs.[49] In the case of Sind, respondents to the Indian Banking Enquiry of 1929–30 tended to ascribe the outmigration of bankers from the province to the operation of the Sind Encumbered Estates Acts, the first of which was passed in 1877, which sought to protect big landholders in the province from seeing their estates dismembered.[50] However, this sounds like a fairly dubious ex-post-facto rationalization. Moneylending remained a profitable activity in Sind even after the passing of these Acts,[51] and the development of irrigated agriculture in the twentieth century opened new avenues of opportunity to enterprising banias: they came from Gujarat in fairly large numbers to Karachi and other localities of Sind to capitalize on that mini-boom. Therefore it is difficult to pinpoint a precise set of circumstances pushing Hyderabad merchants out of Sind to try their luck in the wide world. 'Pull' factors appear to have been more decisive, as the craft productions of Hyderabad and neighbouring towns found a ready-made market among Europeans in Bombay, which inspired some merchants to try and sell them to European tourists in Egypt and elsewhere. But there remains the question as to why some communities were better than others at exploiting opportunities of that kind abroad: the answer probably has partly to do with the way in which information on foreign markets circulated in India, a subject on which very little is known.

Attempts at identifying specific 'causes' for the migration abroad of given business communities are bound to run into great difficulties. Except in the case of economic disasters like the famines in Gujarat in the early nineteenth century, correlations between economic conjunctures at a micro-regional level and movements of traders are practically impossible to establish. An alternative and plausible hypothesis is that some groups developed a rather exclusive 'outward orientation' which led them gradually to insulate themselves from local conditions. I offer this as a tentative explanation, on the basis of my research on the Sindworkies. Among some trading groups, which could not be called 'marginal' in any significant sense, there seems to have developed a kind of 'migratory habitus', in some cases bred by centuries of participation in overseas or overland trade, but in other cases developed in a short period (undoubtedly the most puzzling case). Similar phenomena have been observed in the case of Lebanese, Jewish, and Chinese merchant groups, and it seems that we have there a trend which cannot be explained in a purely South Asian context but needs a broader comparative perspective.

Turning now to the obverse of the coin, that is, to the functions fulfilled by Indian traders in their places of business outside India, we are faced with a similar kind of questioning. It has somewhat become part of received wisdom that Indian traders abroad were typical 'middlemen' doing 'most of the spadework' for British capital in newly colonized territories.[52] Chettiars in Burma and Indians in general in East Africa have been considered among the most characteristic examples of middleman minorities. But not all Indian traders conformed to this model, which in any case appears too functionalist, leading to a complete obliteration of the agency of the merchants. The 'fit' between British imperial aims and the operations of the Indian traders and moneylenders assumed by most authors is a bit too neat to be entirely convincing. How can we be sure, for instance, that Chettiars were really the most economic agency for advancing money to the rice-growing peasants of Lower Burma?[53] And of what crucial importance to British interests in any case was the development of rice cultivation in Burma? Most of its rice found its way to India, Ceylon, or Mauritius, but it could have been bought elsewhere as well. Some British trading houses benefited by this development, but the Burma rice trade was increasingly dominated by Indian traders, in particular Kutchi Memons. So actually there was some 'fit' between Chettiars and Memons, but the British did not derive much benefit from the development of rice cultivation in Burma. Similarly the development of cotton cultivation in Uganda was of greater interest to Indian than to British millowners, and the ginneries established in Uganda by the Patidars and the Lohanas sold an increasing share of their production to the big Bombay cotton trading firms. British capital was not very much involved either.

Does it mean that the operations of Indian traders abroad are best understood within a separate Indian 'imperialist' or 'sub-imperialist' paradigm? One argument in favour of that view is that profits made outside India were sometimes reinvested in business ventures in India. Thus Chettiars, who had been practically inactive in the regional economy of Tamil Nadu for decades, came back as investors in the 1930s and 1940s on the strength of gains repatriated from Burma and elsewhere. As a general proposition, however, it appears doubtful, because it implies the existence of identifiable 'Indian' interests operating as such in some kind of unified manner, which was never the case, as already mentioned.

Looking at whatever little reliable statistical evidence on the activities of Indian traders abroad is available, one is struck by the lack of an obvious pattern. Burma is an interesting case in point. In the Burma Census of 1931, over 40 per cent of all Indians engaged in trade and finance are described as engaged in 'other trade in foodstuffs', a largely residual category which includes big rice merchants as well as small shopkeepers. The second-largest category, with some 20 per cent of all earners and working dependants, is 'hotels, cafes, restaurants'. Trade in textiles, which one associates typically with Indians in Southeast Asia, mobilizes 7 to 8 per cent of the total active Indian trading population, the same proportion as 'bank and credit' (in which are included both Chettiar bankers and Indian employees of British and other European-type banks).[54] It is obvious that nothing of significance can be derived from such figures. The search for an overall logic in the activities of Indian traders in Burma is bound to end up in failure. There are only network logics and they can be reconstructed only from sources internal to the various networks: Chettiar, Chulia, Mappillai, Kutchi Memon, Marwari, Sindworkie, Shikarpuri, etc. Not that the various networks did not intersect at some point: thus Shikarpuri bankers were mainly engaged in discounting bills from Chettiar firms which they rediscounted with bankers in Bombay;[55] Kutchi Memons exported rice grown by Burmese farmers with advances from Chettiar moneylenders, etc., but all this does not form a system of 'Indian' domination of the Burmese economy, in spite of the perceptions to the contrary by both British administrators and Burmese nationalists.

Therefore I can conclude this chapter only by calling attention to the need for more in-depth analysis of the various and diverse merchant networks which originated from India and linked the subcontinent with many countries of the world. It is only by shifting the focus of enquiry away from such abstract entities as 'India' and 'Indians' on the one hand, or 'the British imperial system' on the other hand, towards actually operational networks through which flowed capital, goods and human beings, that we can hope for a meaningful reconstruction of the rich history of the multifarious Indian trading diaspora.

## Notes

1. For a recent synthesis, see C. Clarke, C. Peach, and S. Vertovec (eds), *South Asians Overseas: Migration and Ethnicity* (Cambridge, 1990).
2. Calculated from *Fiji Census*.
3. K.S. Sandhu, *Indians in Malaya: Some Aspects of their Immigration and Settlement* (1786–1957) (Cambridge, 1969), Table 14, p. 247. In the Straits Settlements colony, where the Indian population was almost entirely urban, the proportion in commercial occupations reached 14.3 per cent (15.3 per cent for males). In the Malay States, where most Indians worked in rubber estates, it was much lower.
4. 18.1 per cent. Calculated from *Census of India, 1931*, vol. Xl, part II.
5. 3,305 out of 6,395, *Uganda Census Returns, 1931*.
6. Calculated from *Uganda Census Returns*, Table XXX, p. 39.
7. Calculated from *Kenya, Report on the Non-native Census Enumeration*, Table XII, p. 53.
8. There were 10,491 'Indian Tamil' (as distinct from 'Ceylon Tamil') male earners in trade and finance, presumably Chettiars and other Hindus from the Madras Presidency, as against 10,417 'Indian Moors' (as distinct from 'Ceylon Moors'), mostly Tamil-speaking Muslim immigrants from India. As for the 2,796 'other' male earners in trade and finance, there are no precise indications as to their religion. From *Census Publications, Ceylon, 1921*.
9. There were 38,371 'Non-Burmese Mahomedans' employed in trade, finance, and insurance, who can safely be assumed to have been Indian Muslims, and 30,973 Hindus, Sikhs and others (there were very few Sikh, Jain, and Parsi traders in Burma). *Census of India, 1921*, vol. X, *Burma*, part II, Tables, by S.G. Grantham (Rangoon, 1923), Imperial Table XX, pp. 440–1.
10. For testimonies of the presence of Hindu merchants in Muscat at the end of the fifteenth century, see C.H. Allen, 'The Indian Merchant Community of Masqat', *Bulletin of the School of Oriental and African Studies*, vol. 44 (1981), p. 39.
11. C.A. Bayly, *Rulers, Townsmen and Bazaars: North Indian Society in the Age of British Expansion, 1770–1870* (Cambridge, 1983), p. 386.
12. According to the British traveller Valentia, there were in Mocha around 1810 some 250 resident 'Banyans' (Hindu merchants). Quoted in R. Pankhurst, 'Indian Trade with Ethiopia, the Gulf of Aden and the Horn of Africa in the Nineteenth and Early Twentieth Centuries', *Cahiers d'Eludes Africaines*, 55: XIV/3 (1974), p. 455.
13. In a petition addressed to the Viceroy, Lord Curzon, dated 2 November 1903, ten prominent British Indian merchants of Bahrain wrote: 'May it

be known to Your Lordship that we came up the Persian Gulf about two hundred years ago. . .'. Enclosed in India Office Records (IOR), Politics and Secret Department Records L/P& S/7/134.

14. Allen, 'The Indian Merchant Community of Masqat', p. 45.

15. R.G. Gregory, *India and East Africa. A History of Race Relations within the British Empire 1890–1939* (Oxford, 1971), p. 18.

16. B. Benedict, *Indians in a Plural Society: A Report on Mauritius* (London, 1961), p. 26.

17. N.R. Chakravarti, *The Indian Minority in Burma* (London, 1971), p. 56.

18. J.S. Mangat, A *History of the Asians in East Africa c.1886 to 1945* (Oxford, 1969), p. 7.

19. *Gazetteer of the Province of Sind*, compiled by E.H. Aitken (Karachi, 1907), p. 395.

20. R.A. Huttenback, *Gandhi in South Africa: British Imperialism and the Indian Question, 1860–1914* (London, 1971), p. 41.

21. In the first half of the 1880s, yearly non-labour migration was on average 2,000–3,000. In the second half of the decade, it rose to an average of 5,000–6,000 and in the 1890s reached 7,000–8,000. Sandhu, *Indians in Malaya*, Appendix 3, pp. 312–13.

22. It rose from 129,566 in 1881 to 282,908 in 1891, according to the revised estimates of Chakravarti, *Indian Minority* in *Burma*, Table 2.6, p. 22.

23. G. Prunier, *l'Ouganda et la question indienne (1896–1972)* (Paris, 1990), p. 25.

24. Sandhu, *Indians in Malaya*.

25. Calculated from Sandhu, *Indians in Malaya*.

26. See A. Lemon, 'The Political Position of Indians in South Africa', in Clarke, Peach, and Vertovec (eds), *South Asians Overseas*, p. 131.

27. K. Davis, *The Population of India and Pakistan* (Princeton, 1951), Table 35, p. 99.

28. Where, in 1921, there were 5,065 'Indo-Mauritians' (Indians born in Mauritius) in commerce and finance, as against 882 'Indians' (Indians born in India). *Census of 1921*.

29. Calculated from *Census of India, 1931*, vol. XI.

30. The term seems to have been first used by Abner Cohen in his 'Cultural Strategies in the Organization of Trading Diasporas', in C. Meillassoux (ed.), *The Development of Indigenous Trade and Markets in West Africa* (London, 1971), p. 267. For a discussion, see Philip D. Curtin, *Cross-Cultural Trade in World History* (Cambridge, 1984), pp. 1–14.

31. See Allen, 'The Indian Merchant Community of Masqat'.

32. M. Rheda Bhacker, *Trade and Empire in Muscat and Zanzibar: Roots of British Domination* (London, 1992), p. 172. However, Kutchis continued to be involved in the slave trade in Portuguese territory. A memorandum

dated 3 January 1876 concluded that the Government of India had no jurisdiction over Kutchis in Mozambique and referred the question to the Foreign Office. IOR, Political & Secret Memorials *c.* 1840–1947 L/P& S/ 18, Memorandum B 12.

33. According to a survey of holders of trading licences in Uganda done in 1954, there were 1,300 Lohana amongst the 5,809 Indian licence holders. Although they were a little less numerous than the Patidars, they were economically the most powerful community in Uganda. See H.S. Morris, *The Indians in Uganda* (London, 1966), Table 6, pp. 184–5.

34. See Allen, 'The Indian Merchant Community of Masqat'.

35. See ibid.

36. L.C. Jain, *Indigenous Banking in India* (London, 1929), p. 83. For the Shikarpuris, I have drawn on my personal research on the history of Sindhi merchant networks, based on a variety of primary sources.

37. *Gazetteer of the Province of Sind.* I am preparing a history of the Sindworkies.

38. See Macartney's diary for November 1913, enclosed in Macartney to Deputy Secretary, Government of India in the Foreign Department, dated 9 December 1913, in which he reports having registered at Yarkand '20 Hoshiarpuri Hindus'. IOR, Political & Secret Separate (or Subject) Files 1902–1931 L/P& S/10/330.

39. Sandhu, *Indians in Malaya,* p. 119.

40. There is a vast literature on the Chettiars, to which I shall not refer in detail. However, mention should be made of D.W. Rudner, *Caste and Capitalism in Colonial India: The Nattukottai Chettiars* (Berkeley, 1994), the most recent and most complete work on the question.

41. Chakravarti, *Indian Minority in Burma,* p. 79. See also M. Yegar, *The Muslims of Burma* (Wiesbaden, 1972).

42. U. Mahajani, *The Role of Indian Minorities in Burma and Malaya* (Bombay, 1960), p. 98.

43. Sandhu, *Indians in Malaya,* pp. 119–20.

44. Mentioned in letter dated 26 May 1917 from J.E.C. Jakes, Deputy Secretary to the Government of Bombay, to Foreign Secretary, Government of India, in the Foreign and Political Department. The letter was enclosed in a file concerning demands by Indian merchants for the opening of a British Consulate in Tulear, a port in Southwest Malagasy, where there were hundreds of British Indians engaged in trade. IOR, India Foreign Proceedings (External), 1917.

45. Calculated from *British Malaya, a Report on the 1931 Census.*

46. Calculated from *Report on the Non-native Enumeration . . . in . . . Kenya, 1926.*

47. Mentioned in K.A. Gillion, *Fiji's Indian Migrants* (Melbourne, 1964), p. 134.

48. '. . . profits and gains of a business accruing or arising without British India were not chargeable, even if received or brought within British India, provided they were not received or brought in within three years of the end of the year in which they accrued or arose.' *Report of the Indian Taxation Enquiry Committee of 1924–1925*, vol. I (Madras, 1926), p. 191. The same report candidly acknowledged that 'administrative difficulties are experienced in ascertaining whether income has actually been received in British India' and that 'much fraud occurs'.

49. He wrote: 'mercantile capitalists, such as the Nattukottai Chetties of South India, began to vote on the issue with their feet and to take their capital out of India in protest at legal insecurities and frustrations.' D.A. Washbrook, 'Law, State and Agrarian Society in Colonial India', in C. Baker, G. Johnson, and A. Seal (eds), *Power, Profit and Politics: Essays on Imperialism, Nationalism and Change in Twentieth-Century India* (Cambridge, 1981), p. 676.

50. *Report of the Bombay Provincial Banking Enquiry Committee 1929–30, vol. 4* (Bombay, 1930), Evidence of the Shikarpuri Shroffs' Association, p. 351.

51. See David Cheesman, ' "The Omnipresent Bania": Rural Moneylenders in Nineteenth-Century Sind', *Modern Asian Studies*, 16: 3 (1982), pp. 445–62.

52. See E. Bonacich, 'A Theory of Middleman Minorities', *American Sociological Review*, 38 (October 1973), pp. 583–94.

53. Rudner, in *Caste and Capitalism*, pp. 80–1, quotes figures for 1935–42 tending to show that Chettiars in Burma could charge lower rates of interest than their Burmese and Chinese competitors, but admits that no figures are available to him that 'allow for a precise reconstruction of the Burmese credit market between 1870 and 1930'.

54. All figures calculated from *Census of India, 1931, Vol. XI*, pp. 192–3.

55. Mahajani, *The Role of Indian Minorities*, p. 17.

10

EPILOGUE

## Returning the Merchant to
## South Asian History?

IN THE LAST DECADE, A CURIOUS DISJUNCTION HAS APPEARED between the dominant media discourse on South Asia and historical scholarship. While on the one hand, newspapers and magazines, in India and abroad, have celebrated the entry of India into the select club of emergent economic powers in the company of China, and have laid particular stress on the role of the Indian business class as a powerful agent of economic change in the subcontinent, on the other hand the most recent historical scholarship has paid only scant attention to the role of merchant communities and individual businessmen in the modern history of South Asia. In this piece, I intend to interrogate this disjunction and discuss possible ways of returning the merchant to South Asian history. The reason I am engaging in this kind of exercise is not only that as a historian who has devoted a lot of time and energy to researching the merchant world of South Asia, I feel somewhat marginalized and estranged from the dominant historiographical fashion, but also that I feel this disjunction is harmful in more ways than one, not only in clouding our view of the past, but even more our understanding of present-day India, a point to which I shall come back in my conclusion.

The history of the mercantile world of India has for long been a relatively neglected area of modern Indian history. One could argue that this neglect has its roots in a certain kind of construction of India's history which goes back to the beginnings of the colonial period. Granted that Indian history, as a modern literary genre, first developed under the auspices of a company of British merchants who had little reason to draw attention to the achievements of indigenous merchants, its subsequent failure to redress that bias, even after it had become from the 1920s onwards a proper academic discipline, could probably be explained by the durable impact of 'Orientalism', which, in its efforts at 'Othering' India, tended to emphasize all that was different from Europe, and to underplay all that could point to similarities between conqueror and conquered. Therefore, while Brahmins, Rajputs, and kings engaged the attention of the colonial historians of India, British or Indian, the merchant world hardly figured in their accounts, except when, as at the time of Palasi, merchants such as the Jagat Seths happened to have been prominent participants in crucial political events. Post-1947 historians, whether of an 'imperialist' or 'nationalist' hue, likewise had little time to spare for a section of society which appeared to have played a largely passive role in the unfolding saga of the Indian freedom struggle and seemed fated for slow extinction in the 'socialistic' framework of society that India claimed to be building up in the Nehruvian and immediate post-Nehruvian era. While the European commercial companies provided fodder to a thriving school of maritime and economic historians, represented, after its doyen Holden Furber, by such stalwarts as K.N. Chaudhuri, Tapan Raychaudhuri, Om Prakash, and Sinnapah Arasaratnam, Indian merchants and businessmen languished in an obscurity which many thought well deserved as they were guilty, in the eyes of both Liberals and Marxists, of having failed their historic mission of creating the bases of a bourgeois capitalist society in India. The strictures of colonial administrators railing against the greed of the banias resonated powerfully with anti-colonial historians who saw in them auxiliaries of the colonial semi-feudal exploitation of the peasantry, and were unaware of or indifferent to the fact that the anti-bania discourse of the administrators largely reflected the anti-semitic prejudices of the squirearchy[1] transplanted into an Indian context. As to those historians and social scientists who were more inclined towards praising private enterprise, they saw little in the activities of the Indian mercantile world to fit in with their normative ideas about what an entrepreneurial class should be.

The earliest serious scholarly literature on the history of Indian business was in the form of the two surveys produced by D.R. Gadgil in the 1950s.[2] They established some of the basic facts, in particular the existence of well-defined 'business communities', a notion which, in spite of its ambiguity, has remained a basic tool of analysis of the Indian business world. While a few authors in the 1950s emphasized the existence of 'creative response' in certain sectors of the Indian economy and in certain regions,[3] it was mostly in the new Indian Institutes of Management that a small group of scholars developed, from the 1960s onwards, a genuine interest in the antecedents of an Indian corporate world which, in spite of dire predictions to the contrary, was flourishing in the interstices of the post-Nehruvian state-dominated 'socialist' economy. Dwijendra Tripathi and Thomas Timberg are the two names which come to mind when one thinks of the work produced there. The former oversaw the production of a number of collective volumes which established new standards in the field of Indian business history[4] and also wrote the first biography of an Indian entrepreneur, Kasturbhai Lalbhai of Ahmedabad,[5] which conformed to the scholarly canons of the genre rather than being a sheer piece of hagiography. The latter produced a history of the Marwaris, India's premier business community, which has remained a classic.[6] Business history, however, remained a separate subfield of history and 'mainstream' historians paid little attention to it. The reasons for this compartmentalization of the discipline of history, which is of course not unique to India, are complex, and it is not my intention here to go into them in any detail.

In the late 1970s and early 1980s, the merchant world was, however, to attract the attention of two prominent 'mainstream' historians, and a new era in Indian historiography seemed to be dawning. Merchants came for the first time to occupy a place in South Asian history outside the relatively narrow confines of 'maritime history' and 'business history'. Briefly revisiting the literature of this period, I shall bring out both its strengths and some of its limitations, which may have contributed to the subsequent eclipse suffered by the merchant on the South Asian historiographical scene. I must state at the outset that I shall limit myself to a consideration of post-1700 Indian history, as I am not qualified enough to comment even cursorily on earlier periods.

It is only fair to start this survey with Ashin Das Gupta, for his work on Indian merchants was truly pioneering, in the sense that he entered largely uncharted territory in looking at the indigenous merchant world of India in the still relatively neglected eighteenth century from a non-teleological perspective, that is, not with the intention of explaining the advent of British rule by the inability of an Indian bourgeoisie to set up a capitalist revolution of its own, as some nationalist or Marxist authors were then prone to do, but with an interest in the role of merchants *per se.* Coming from maritime history, he managed to break away from its confines and carve a place for merchants in mainstream historiography. While his *Malabar in Asian Trade*[7] was still somewhat steeped in the genre of maritime history, albeit in an innovative manner, especially in the way it looked at the role of indigenous merchants, in his magnum opus *Indian Merchants and the Decline of Surat*,[8] as well as in numerous subsequent articles, he definitely overstepped its boundaries and brought in fresh insights and new vistas which helped make merchants full-time actors in the economic, social, and political history of late pre-colonial India. His classic picture of Surat in the first half of the eighteenth century remains a model of an approach to the history of trade which considered merchants in all their dimensions, and not purely at the economic level. Not that he idealized Indian merchants. About the Kapol bania merchants from Diu who dominated the trade of Yemen in the early eighteenth century, he thus wrote in an article, 'they were not ideal men',[9] and certainly they were not. But this lucid judgement did not preclude on his part a certain amount of empathy, which is always an asset to the historian. Although he relied mostly on European sources, he also brought in Persian and vernacular materials, which gave more depth to his picture of a varied trading world coping with the challenge thrown up by a delicate transition in the overall pattern of the Indian economy.

While Das Gupta's work focused primarily on the merchants of maritime India, mostly those of the west coast of the subcontinent, Christopher Bayly took in the little-known merchant world of Gangetic northern India and gave it central place, in his brilliant revisionist work, *Rulers, Townsmen and Bazaars*,[10] in sustaining the dynamics of regional economies in the transition between the late Mughal and early colonial periods. Merchants were crucial to Bayly's analysis inasmuch as they were an essential link between the agrarian economy in the late eighteenth and early nineteenth centuries in northern India and its post-Mughal polities, including Company Bahadur in its pre-1830 phase, which Bayly saw fundamentally (and this was one of the most controversial aspects of his book) as an Indian power. It was largely through their agency that agrarian surplus was recycled into luxury consumption and military expenditure, which, according to Bayly, were the twin pillars of the prosperity of eighteenth-century Gangetic northern India. Although they were only one of the intermediate groups which played a major role in the post-Mughal transition as depicted by Bayly (others being the small Muslim nobility of the *qasbas* and the scribal communities of the Kayastha and Khatris), they emerged in his work in a clearer light than other groups. The important place given to merchants in his overall scheme even led Bayly to devote two chapters of his book to an in-depth examination of their organizational structure and of their 'moral economy', conceived of in Chayanovian terms, an analysis which has established itself as a kind of classic, although I personally think it is in need of some amount of revision.

One could end this brief review of the literature with a mention of Rajat Ray's contribution, mostly three lengthy articles, the last one published in 1995,[11] in which he covered a broad span of the history of the Indian merchant communities during the colonial period, both within India and in a broader geographical context. Ray focused mostly on the complex relationship between Indian merchant communities and British colonialism, and produced a nuanced view of it, in which he balanced evidence of 'collaboration' with manifestations of independence, even of active resistance. His most important contribution was the notion of the 'bazaar' as a separate economic sector, dominated by indigenous operators, not directly subject to the domination of British colonial capitalists. This notion had its advantages, insofar as it reintroduced an element of Indian agency in an economic history which was then heavily influenced by the dependency school and other variants of that paradigm, but also its drawbacks inasmuch as it assumed a fairly dualistic shape and tended to artificially separate domains which were to a large extent intertwined. The cognate question of the relationship between the business communities and Indian nationalism also attracted at the time a measure of interest, and I, amongst others, contributed to it with a book written in 1985,[12] which, in its attempt at debunking exaggerated claims about the contribution of businessmen to the freedom struggle and simplistic explanations for their mobilization in terms of the old pseudo-Marxist notion of a 'national bourgeoisie'—claims which were recently reiterated by Aditya Mukherjee in a book[13] in which he followed the lead of his old teacher Bipan Chandra—probably underplayed, or at least this is how I feel now, certain aspects of a relationship which was not without importance in steering the course of independent India.

By the late 1980s, it could be said that there existed a body of work focusing on the role of merchants and businessmen in the story of India's transition to colonial and post-colonial modernity, and that some of its wisdom had become mainstream, as shown for instance in the importance given to the subject in such a popular textbook as Sumit Sarkar's *Modern India*.[14] One could remark that this body of work was often biased in favour of big business, with a tendency to neglect the lower echelons of the merchant world, and was also uneven in its regional coverage, with too much weight given to the great centres such as Bombay, Calcutta, and Ahmedabad, and insufficient attention paid to other important foci of commercial and industrial activity. It represented, however, a marked improvement on the generalizations about Indian capitalism which had previously prevailed and which were based on very flimsy empirical foundations.

In the 1990s, however, and particularly in the late 1990s and early 2000s, merchants and businessmen suffered an almost complete eclipse on the Indian historiographical scene. Even authors who had taken an interest in them appeared to have largely lost it. Thus Bayly, in his *Empire and Information*,[15] which examined the same area as his previous book during roughly the same period in a different perspective, paid only scant attention to the role of merchant communities in the emergence of a new 'informational order' during the phase of transition to colonialism in northern India.

That this eclipse was partly an effect of the so-called 'linguistic turn' in Indian history, linked to the advent of post-modernism and post-colonial studies, is fairly self-evident. Merchants not being themselves great producers of 'discourse' nor of central interest to the field of colonial knowledge, it is not surprising that they practically disappeared from the sights of historians, including those belonging to the Subaltern Studies collective, who were increasingly preoccupied with colonial textuality. That studies of merchants and businessmen suffered from the increasing discredit attaching to all that could smack of 'economicism', de facto equated with any kind of causal explanation, even non-deterministic, grounded on a consideration of economic factors, is also certainly true, but an added twist is that focusing on people who continued to make money under colonial rule is now denounced by some 'post-colonial' theorists as complicity with colonialism. I cannot resist quoting from Nicholas Dirks's recent book, *Castes of Mind,* more specifically from the coda 'The Burden of the Past: Colonialism and the Writing of History', a piece of rather exaggerated polemics against the so-called Cambridge school (a particularly durable Aunt Sally): 'The salience of the historical structures of colonial rule cannot be trivialized by pointing to a handful of Indian "capitalists" who managed to secure wealth for themselves during colonial times',[16] a transparent allusion to some of David Washbrook's writings, in particular an article of the late 1980s in which he had attributed an important role to Indian capitalists in the transition to colonialism.[17] This passage raises a certain number of interesting questions, including firstly that of whether really only a 'handful' of capitalists managed to secure wealth for themselves during colonial times, which seems open to question, as very little is known about the history of wealth in India, and secondly that of whether focusing on even a 'handful' would necessarily mean 'trivializing' the reality of colonial oppression, which seems also a disputable proposition. But I have quoted Dirks, not because I want to engage in a polemics with him, but because he seems here to embody the presently dominant view about the illegitimacy of any inquiry into aspects of the history of colonial India which do not fit within the prevailing postcolonial doxa centred around the power–knowledge paradigm. In the face of such strictures, one possible strategy is adaptive, and it was chosen by historians who wanted to continue looking at social and economic realities while situating themselves somewhat within the new paradigm. A few attempts were thus made in the 1990s at reading merchants in the light of the new historiography. I will focus briefly on two of them.

The first one, by one of the founder-members of the Subaltern Studies collective, David Hardiman, probably the one who has remained most faithful to the original Subalternist project, *Feeding the Baniya*,[18] turns out to be rather quixotic. In that book, banias are certainly given a central role, but as the 'bad guys'. Focusing on the relationship between peasants and 'usurers'(the term itself being colonial) in colonial western India, the book takes a unilaterally negative view of that relationship as purely exploitative, without taking into account the macro context of an economy in which there was no alternative to the advances of the banias as a source of capital for agriculture. Although it is fairly innovative in looking at the way in which the relationship went beyond economics to include important and often overlooked cultural aspects, one of its drawbacks is its largely uncritical reliance on colonial sources regarding the banias. In spite of his own guru Ranajit Guha's call to always read such sources 'against the grain', Hardiman tends to take them quite literally in their railings against the greed of the banias. Often there is a simple falling back on an old Marxist discourse regarding 'forced commercialization'.

Different problems bedevil another attempt, Anand Yang's *Bazaar India*,[19] although Yang took a much more subtle line regarding the role of merchants in the agrarian economy of colonial Bihar. What Yang tried to do was to read merchants, or rather markets, in the new historiographical mode, by substituting spatiality for textuality. Given the fact that there is very little textual evidence coming from the merchants themselves and that Yang was more aware than Hardiman of the pitfalls of relying too exclusively on the testimony of colonial administrators, he attempted to analyse the spatial structure of markets as a kind of text to produce a 'cultural history' of markets as connecting local communities to larger networks of commerce, culture, and political power. He thus tried to cobble together two printed narratives of the bazaar in Gangetic Bihar, one written in Persian by the historian Ghulam Hussain Tabatabai in the famous *Siyar-ul-Mutakharein*, in the late eighteenth century, and the other, a travel narrative penned in Telugu by Veeraswamy around 1830, with an analysis of the functioning of the same bazaar in the early 1920s at the time of the non-cooperation movement, and its link with nationalism. The idea was to 'textualize' the bazaar, read it as a hybrid place, where non-cooperation could confront the state at the lower level of the marketing hierarchy. Although the book was imaginative and well crafted, the approach it took appeared contrived and somehow failed to really convince, and I am afraid Yang did not succeed in his avowed aim of rescuing merchants and markets from their new-found marginality.

On the other hand, historians such as Lakshmi Subramanian in her book *Indigenous Capital and Imperial Expansion*,[20] a study of the transition to colonialism in western India at the turn of the eighteenth century and Kumkum Chatterjee in her *Merchants, Politics and Society in Early Modern India*,[21] a study of the Patna bankers at the time of the colonial transition in eastern India, remained faithful to more classical modes of history-writing. Subramanian, a pupil of Das Gupta, followed chronologically in his trail, focusing on Surat in the second half of the eighteenth century, and put forward the thesis of the emergence in that period of an 'Anglo-Bania' order in Western India, mainly on the evidence of large-scale transfers of Company funds from Bengal to Bombay through the agency of the shroffs, and of the role played by the banias in the Castle Revolution of 1759 in Surat. Her thesis about the 'Anglo-Bania' order, its sudden emergence and its even more sudden disappearance, which is based on a de facto equation between finance and politics (akin to saying that because the Rothschilds financed the British victory at Waterloo, there emerged in Europe after 1815 an 'Anglo-Jewish order'), basically failed to convince, although some of the analysis of the commercial and financial scene she produced was very worthwhile. Chatterjee's book, a fine study which combined painstaking research in the archives with contemporary textual evidence in the vernacular, was less forthright in putting forward a thesis on collaboration between the Indian bankers and Company Bahadur, and emphasized the existence of many 'grey areas' in the complex relationship between Indian merchants and a rising colonialism. Taking a new look at the Palasi conspiracy, she showed that it was not the intention of the Jagat Seths to install the Company in power, and she therefore carefully avoided talking about an Anglo-Bania conspiracy. These two monographs seem to have been the latest and may be the last examples of a certain genre of writing about the relationship between trade and politics, a topic which seems to have somewhat exhausted its fecundity. In spite of their evident qualities (in particular Chatterjee's book), they failed to attract much attention, and if one looks at the spate of general histories of India which were published between 1998 and 2002, by Burton Stein,[22] Peter Robb,[23] David Ludden,[24] and Barbara and Tom Metcalf,[25] one will not fail to notice that they generally pay little attention (with the partial exception of David Ludden's) to the role of Indian merchants in the transition to colonialism, and more generally in the history of modern and contemporary India (while Stein has an interesting passage on the role of merchant guilds in medieval India). In the last few years, no significant new work seems to have been produced that made a contribution to that field,[26] with one exception that I shall mention a bit later.

Basically, beyond one's subjective feelings, the question one has to answer is the following: has something important been lost with the general eclipse suffered by the study of merchants on the Indian historiographical scene and what is it? I would answer tentatively that there has been a loss in regard to connectivity, and therefore to intelligibility. It could be argued that markets in colonial India were the main thread connecting society, much more than the apparatus of an alien colonial State or a so-called Brahmanical hegemony, which has been shown to be largely a colonial construct, both literally and figuratively. In a society characterized by low literacy and great linguistic diversity, in which labour rarely circulated across very long distances, the circulation of goods organized through a hierarchy of markets, and often accompanied by a circulation of merchants, was a crucial connective mechanism. Although markets were penetrated by the State and kept under its overall control, they nevertheless had a dynamics of their own which could at least partly escape the disciplinary grid of the alien masters. Thus Yang was right to correlate non-cooperation with local markets in northern Bihar, and Shahid Amin has shown in his *Event, Metaphor, Memory*,[27] how the local market at Chauri-Chaura (which was not a locality, but a *hat*) was the real playing field for the drama of February 1922. However, whatever economists may say, markets are not impersonal institutions; they are animated by actors, and, amongst the foremost actors in markets (although of course not the only ones) are merchants, not necessarily individual merchants, but rather merchant networks. The connectivity of markets in colonial India partly coincided with the connectivity of pan-Indian merchant networks, such as those of Marwari or Gujarati banias,[28] and it is at this level that the agency of merchants is most visible. In that case, connectivity ties up directly with intelligibility. Without bringing in the powerful agency of pan-Indian merchant networks, including their role in the growth of 'print capitalism', to use Benedict Andersons' now trivialized expression, it becomes difficult to understand the spread of Indian nationalism. Discursive formations, such as nationalist discourse, whether derivative or not (which is not a problem which interests me here) gained added potency from being connected with a cash and hundi nexus. Gandhi's charisma, to take only one instance, was partly underwritten by the financial weight and connective pull of powerful all-India merchant communities, mostly Gujarati and Marwari, and it is difficult to explain his success as a nationalist leader without bringing in this aspect.[29]

The erasure from the historical record of a group which basically represented indigenous agency in the economic field results, as I see it, in the return to a strangely 'Orientalist' reading of the trajectory of Indian society under colonial rule. Focusing, in a binary mode, on forms of 'resistance' to colonialism, postcolonial historians tend to locate them almost exclusively in the realm of 'culture', in particular in the attempt to preserve a space for family, caste, and religion protected from the encroachments of a colonial power with hegemonic pretensions. Work is not considered a field worth investigating any more, as if most Indians had belonged to a leisurely elite. Thus, amongst others, the immensely varied world of the market largely escapes scrutiny, and some of its principal actors, such as the merchants, have all but disappeared from the scholarly horizon. What makes this elision particularly problematic is that, in present-day India, the market has staged a rather spectacular comeback. But it is a market without history, willed into existence, so to say, out of nothingness in 1991, from the dual nights of colonialism and Nehruvian and post-Nehruvian socialism. If we are to believe some of the apologists of the new liberal economic order, *Homo economicus Indicus* would have suddenly come into his own in 1991, leaving behind four decades of 'Hindu rate of growth' and two centuries of colonial stagnation. Although I am aware that I tend to caricature the dominant discourse of today, I feel nevertheless that there is a grain of truth in my description. Since we all know that Indian capitalism was not born in 1991, and that many of its actors of today actually go back a long time, more precisely to the colonial period, or even earlier epochs, there has to be some way to re-establish a minimum of continuity between the past and the present. What I am targeting here is the de facto complicity between the elision of the market in postcolonial history and the elision of history in the present-day discourse on the market.

I shall then discuss, in a programmatic fashion, some of the possible ways in which the merchant could be returned to South Asian history, thus contributing to a less Orientalist reading of colonial society. I am convinced that it is not mostly through a return to a straightforward kind of economic history—although such a move may have merits of its own, and Tirthankar Roy made a forceful plea for it in his recent

*Rethinking Economic Change in India,*[30] in which he argued in particular for a greater focus on problems of labour use in colonial India—that the merchant can be most effectively returned to the South Asian historiographical scene. One of the reasons is the lack of reliable quantitative data, and the reluctance of merchant firms, with a few exceptions, to open up their archives to researchers. A more promising strategy, at least in the short and medium terms, appears to be one of focusing on the various ways in which merchants interacted with the state and society at large, by stressing their role in the emerging informational order as well as their participation in wider cultural processes, such as vernacularization.

Regarding the role of the merchants in pre-colonial Indian state formations, an interesting recent contribution is Madhu Tandon Sethia's book, *Rajput Polity: Warriors, Peasants and Merchants,*[31] which makes use of the rich Kotah archives in Bikaner, to show the extent and depth of the involvement of bankers and merchants in agrarian management and taxation in that Rajput state in the eighteenth century. It partly covers the same ground as Norbert Peabody's book on Kotah, *Hindu Kingship and Polity in Pre-Colonial India,*[32] which is much more focused on the symbolic aspects of royal power. The two books should obviously be seen as complementing each other, but it is already apparent that Peabody's will generate more interest, not only for its intrinsic qualities, but also because it fits better with dominant fashions (although Peabody himself is certainly no 'post-modernist'). Sethia's book addresses the important question of the circulation of skills between the world of trade and the world of statecraft, which in the Indian tradition were considered very close to each other. Accounting skills immediately come to mind and they were certainly the ones which circulated most between those two spheres. But this only opens up the more general question of the place of merchants in what Bayly, in his above-quoted book, has called the 'informational order', in which he rightly included questions relating to skills and knowledge production.

I am aware that this is a little-explored area in Indian historiography and that I am venturing into largely uncharted territory. I just want to make a few very general remarks, with the aim of opening up a field for further investigation and debate. As an opening statement, I would offer the following: merchant networks represented an apparatus for gathering and disseminating information which in India was largely independent from the State and often was more efficient than the apparatus of the State, whether pre-colonial or colonial. The information which circulated through merchant networks was of course primarily information about markets, about supply and demand, about prices, about currency rates (prior to currency uniformization which was achieved, albeit imperfectly, by the 1830s), but it had also a strong political content, and it went much beyond India. Merchants had their own system of couriers for the transmission of that information, and it was particularly efficient: thus, to take only one instance, the Pune bankers knew about the Panipat disaster of 1761 before the Pune darbar, and it helped them limit their losses to a certain extent. The particularly strong position occupied by merchants on the market for that essential commodity, information, has partly to do with the fact that, in India, prior to the late nineteenth century, when the telegraph and the press really became developed, information was not really a public good, because there was no 'public sphere' in the Habermasian sense. Information circulated largely through networks which were 'private', through family, kinship, etc., and the only networks which covered large areas of the subcontinent were those of pan-Indian merchant communities such as the Gujaratis or the Marwaris. Merchants thus occupied a very strong position in the overall 'informational order' and, by the late nineteenth century, when a public sphere, in the modern sense of the term, started developing, they were able to translate it into a partial domination of the new domain opened up by the development of 'print capitalism' in the various linguistic areas. This is an aspect which has been little studied, but deserves serious research. A long time ago, historians of the original Cambridge school had drawn attention to the link between 'publicists' and their patrons and its importance to the emergence of nationalism in the Indian hinterlands, and this kind of material could be revisited in a more global perspective.

Information is obviously linked to knowledge and one of the strong points in Bayly's book was precisely this linkage. Here also I feel there has been a general underestimation of the role of merchants. History of knowledge in India has focused too much on 'high' forms of knowledge, in which evidently merchants played no role, and neglected more mundane or everyday forms of knowledge, which, at the level of society, might actually be of greater consequence. My hunch, for which I must admit I do not have much empirical evidence at the moment, is that merchant communities were important sites for the production of everyday forms of knowledge, not only those which were of direct use to merchants, such as knowledge concerning accounting or measures, but also some which had wider social currency. By focusing on vernacular tracts about various forms of practical knowledge rather than on English-language books about 'high science', one could write a completely different history of knowledge practices in pre-colonial and colonial India, in which the role of merchants as writers and promoters of various knowledge-oriented ventures would, I am convinced, appear in a much brighter light than it does in the present dispensation.

This leads me to the question of 'vernacularization', a theme which has been recently taken up by Sheldon Pollock. The growth of vernacular literatures in India had a lot to do with merchants as patrons, as customers, and as inspiration for writers. After all it is no pure coincidence if the first Hindi novel, the *Pariksaguru* of Srinivasdas of 1882, is directly based on the story of the decline and fall of the Mathura Seths,[33] the greatest banking and merchant firm of northern India in the nineteenth century. The father of Hindi literature, Bharatendu Harischandra,[34] came from a merchant background, as, by the way, did the father of modern Gujarati prose who is none else of course than Mahatma Gandhi. This is not unknown, and is often mentioned in passing by the specialists of literature, but it needs to be formalized and systematized in some way by scholars with a deep knowledge of both the literary and the historical field.

Returning the merchant to the historiographical scene would also help in redirecting the focus of attention towards the lower levels of the business world which, in the last decade, have been eclipsed by an exaggerated attention paid to the software billionaires and other heroes of the recent liberalization. If one holds true the late Burton Stein's insight about India being basically a petty bourgeois country,[35] as I personally tend to do, then it remains necessary to have a better grasp of the genesis of India's still-dominant petty capitalism, including its impact on the political and cultural spheres, which may also lead to a more grounded appreciation of present-day realities.

To close, it must be admitted that the question mark in the title of this lecture is likely to remain. Although I personally find a return of the merchant to South Asian history desirable for the reasons I have briefly enunciated, there is no knowing whether it will happen in the near future. While there are pointers to a certain exhaustion of the post-colonial paradigm, and rumblings of a renewed interest in economic history, the emergence of a more balanced view of India's past, and particularly of its colonial past, remains a doubtful proposition.

## Notes


1. For a general view of the problem, see C. Holmes, *Anti-Semitism in British Society 1876–1939* (London, 1979).

2. D.R. Gadgil, *Business Communities in India* (New York, 1951) (mimeographed) and *Origins of the Modern Indian Business Class: An Interim Report* (New York, 1959) (mimeographed).

3. D.P. Pandit, 'Creative Response in the Indian Economy: A Regional Analysis', *The Economic Weekly* IX (1957), pp. 283–86 and H. Acharya, 'Creative Response in the Indian Economy: A Comment', *The Economic Weekly* IX (1957), pp. 547–9.

4. D. Tripathi (ed.), *Business Communities of India: A Historical Perspective* (Delhi, 1984), and (ed.), *The State and Business in India: A Historical Perspective* (Delhi, 1987).

5. D. Tripathi, *The Dynamics of a Tradition: Kasturbhai Lalbhai and His Entrepreneurship* (Delhi, 1981).

6. T.A. Timberg, *The Marwaris: From Traders to Industrialists* (Delhi, 1978).

7. A. Das Gupta, *Malabar in Asian Trade 1740–1800* (Cambridge, 1967).

8. A. Das Gupta, *Indian Merchants and the Decline of Surat c. 1700–1750* (Wiesbaden, 1979, reprint Delhi, 1994).

9. A. Das Gupta, 'Gujarati Merchants and the Red Sea Trade 1700–1725', in

B.B. Kling and M.N. Pearson (eds), *The Age of Partnership: The Europeans in Asia before Dominion* (Honolulu, 1979), pp. 123–58.

10. C.A. Bayly, *Rulers, Townsmen and Bazaars: North Indian Society in the Age of British Expansion 1770–1870* (Cambridge, 1983).

11. R.K. Ray, 'Asian Capital in the Age of European Domination: The Rise of the Bazaar, 1800–1914', *Modern Asian Studies*, 29: 3 (1995), pp. 449–554.

12. C. Markovits, *Indian Business and Nationalist Politics 1931–39: The Indigenous Capitalist Class and the Rise of the Congress Party* (Cambridge, 1985; reprint, 2002).

13. A. Mukherjee, *Imperialism, Nationalism and the Making of the Indian Capitalist Class, 1920–1947* (Delhi, 2002).

14. S. Sarkar, *Modern India, 1885–1947* (Delhi, 1982).

15. C.A. Bayly, *Empire and Information: Intelligence Gathering and Social Communication in India, 1780–1870* (Cambridge, 1996).

16. N.B. Dirks, *Castes of Mind: Colonialism and the Making of Modern India* (Princeton, Oxford, 2001), p. 313.

17. D.A. Washbrook, 'Progress and Problems: South Asian Economic and Social History *c.* 1720–1860', *Modern Asian Studies*, 22: 1 (1988), pp. 57–96.

18. D. Hardiman, *Feeding the Baniya: Peasants and Usurers in Western India* (Delhi, 1996).

19. A.A. Yang, *Bazaar India: Markets, Society, and the Colonial State in Bihar* (Berkeley, Los Angeles, London, 1998).

20. L. Subramanian, *Indigenous Capital and Imperial Expansion: Bombay, Surat and the West Coast* (Delhi, 1996).

21. K. Chatterjee, *Merchants, Politics and Society in Early Modern India: Bihar 1733–1820* (Leiden, Koln, 1997).

22. B. Stein, *A History of India* (Oxford, 1998).

23. P. Robb, *A History of India* (London, 2002).

24. D. Ludden, *India and South Asia: A Short History* (Oxford, 2002).

25. B.D. Metcalf and T. Metcalf, *A Concise History of India* (Cambridge, 2002).

26. I deliberately leave aside the work produced on Indian merchants outside India, which raises different kinds of problems.

27. S. Amin, *Event, Metaphor, Memory: Chauri-Chaura 1922–1992* (Delhi, 1995).

28. See my 'Merchant Circulation in India (Eigtheenth to Twentieth Centuries): The Rise of Pan-Indian Merchant Networks', in C. Markovits, J. Pouchepadass, S. Subrahmanyam (eds), *Society and Circulation: Mobile People and Itinerant Cultures in South Asia 1750–1950* (Delhi, 2003), pp. 131–62. [Chapter 8 in this volume.]

29. See my *The Un-Gandhian Gandhi: The Life and After-Life of the Mahatma* (Delhi, 2004).

30. T. Roy, *Rethinking Economic Change in India: Labour and Livelihood* (Delhi, 2005).

31. M.T. Sethia, *Rajput Polity: Warriors, Peasants and Merchants (1700–1800)* (Delhi, 2003).

32. N. Peabody, *Hindu Kingship and Polity in Precolonial India* (Cambridge, 2003).

33. See A.S. Kalsi, 'Pariksaguru (1882): The First Hindi Novel and the Hindu Elite', *Modern Asian Studies*, 26: 4 (1992), pp. 763–90.

34. See V. Dalmia, *The Nationalization of Hindu Tradition: Bharatendu Harischandra and Nineteenth-Century Banaras* (Delhi, 1997).

35. B. Stein, 'Towards an Indian Petty Bourgoisie: Outline of an Approach', *Economic and Political Weekly*, XXVI.4, 26 January 1991, pp. PE9–PE 18.

# INDEX